NATIONAL GEOGRAPHIC LEARNING
CENGAGE Learning

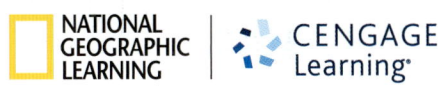

Life

PRE-INTERMEDIATE STUDENT'S BOOK

John Hughes
Helen Stephenson
Paul Dummett

Contents Split Edition A

Unit	Grammar	Vocabulary	Real life (functions)	Pronunciation
1 **Health** pages 9–20	present simple adverbs and expressions of frequency present simple and present continuous	leisure activities *do*, *go* or *play* wordbuilding: verb + noun collocations word focus: *feel* medical problems	talking about illness	/s/, /z/ or /ɪz/ sound and spelling
VIDEO: Slow food **page 18** ▶ REVIEW **page 20**			
2 **Competitions** pages 21–32	verb + *-ing* forms *like -ing* / *'d like to* modal verbs for rules	wordbuilding: word forms sport venues and equipment competition words word focus: *like*	talking about interests	/ŋ/ silent letters
VIDEO: Cheese rolling **page 30** ▶ REVIEW **page 32**			
3 **Transport** pages 33–44	comparatives and superlatives *as … as*	modes of transport transport (1): nouns wordbuilding: compound nouns transport (2): verbs transport words	going on a journey	*than* sentence stress intonation
VIDEO: Indian railways **page 42** ▶ REVIEW **page 44**			
4 **Adventure** pages 45–56	past simple past continuous	personal qualities wordbuilding: negative prefixes geographical features *in*, *on* or *at* for time expressions	telling a story	/d/, /t/ or /ɪd/ *was* intonation for responding
VIDEO: Alaskan ice climbing **page 54** ▶ REVIEW **page 56**			
5 **The environment** pages 57–68	countable and uncountable nouns quantifiers definite article (*the*) or no article	materials household items wordbuilding: hyphenated words results and figures word focus: *take*	phoning about an order	/ðə/ or /ði:/ sounding friendly
VIDEO: Coastal clean-up **page 66** ▶ REVIEW **page 68**			
6 **Stages in life** pages 69–80	verb patterns with *to* + infinitive future forms: *going to*, *will* and present continuous	life events stages in life celebrations word focus: *get* wordbuilding: synonyms	inviting, accepting and declining	/tə/ contracted forms emphasising words
VIDEO: Steel drums **page 78** ▶ REVIEW **page 80**			

COMMUNICATION ACTIVITIES **page 81** ▶ GRAMMAR SUMMARY **page 83** ▶ AUDIOSCRIPTS **page 91**

Listening	Reading	Critical thinking	Speaking	Writing
someone talking about two elderly ballroom dancers a health expert analyses sleep a radio interview about long life	a quiz about how well you sleep an article about centenarians an article about measuring health and happiness	the main argument	a quiz your current life measuring happiness	text type: online advice writing skill: conjunctions (*and, or, so, because, but*)
someone describing an Ironman competition three people talking about sport a reporter describing the rules of a competition	quotes by famous sports people an article about crazy competitions an article about female wrestlers in Bolivia	reading between the lines	guess the ambition explaining the rules of a competition your opinions about sport	text type: an advert or notice writing skill: checking your writing
someone describing a photo of a girl travelling by train in India two people discussing the pros and cons of electric cars two documentaries about using animals for transporting	an article about transport in the future an article about dog sledging an article about the fate of the rickshaw in Kolkata	reading between the lines	transport you use attitudes to using animals for transporting arguing for and against keeping rickshaws in Kolkata	a report about how people travel around town text type: notes and messages writing skill: writing in note form
a caver describing Rumbling Falls Cave an interview with a survival expert	an article about adventurers an article about a climbing accident	identifying opinion	asking about your past qualities needed for an expedition events you remember retelling a story	text type: a true story writing skill: using *-ly* adverbs in stories
extract from a documentary about the artist George Sabra a radio phone-in show about recycling	an article about e-rubbish an article about the Greendex an article about a boat made of plastic bottles, the *Plastiki* an online order	close reading	opinions on recycling presenting a report an interview with an environmentalist	a report of a survey text type: emails writing skill: formal language
an explanation to a riddle three people talking about their plans and intentions a news item about Mardis Gras	an article about how a couple changed their life an article about how Mardis Gras is celebrated around the world an article about a Masai rite of passage	identifying the key information	life-changing decisions your favourite festival describing annual events	text type: a description writing skill: descriptive adjectives

WORKBOOK
UNIT 1 page 96 ▶ UNIT 2 page 104 ▶ UNIT 3 page 112 ▶ UNIT 4 page 120 ▶ UNIT 5 page 128
UNIT 6 page 136 ▶ AUDIOSCRIPTS page 144 ▶ ANSWER KEY page 149

Contents Split Edition B

Unit	Grammar	Vocabulary	Real life (functions)	Pronunciation
7 Work	prepositions of place and movement present perfect simple	jobs wordbuilding: suffixes office equipment *for* or *since* job satisfaction word focus: *make* or *do* job adverts	a job interview	intrusive /w/ irregular past participles
VIDEO: Butler school ▶ REVIEW				
8 Technology	defining relative clauses zero and first conditional	the internet wordbuilding: verb prefixes expedition equipment word focus: *have* technology verbs	asking how something works	intonation in conditional sentences linking
VIDEO: Wind power ▶ REVIEW				
9 Language and learning	present simple passive *by* + agent past simple passive	education phrasal verbs wordbuilding: phrasal verbs	describing a process	stress in two-syllable words stress in phrasal verbs
VIDEO: Disappearing voices ▶ REVIEW				
10 Travel and holidays	past perfect simple subject and object questions *-ing* / *-ed* adjectives	holiday words (types of holiday, accommodation, activities, travel items) holiday adjectives wordbuilding: dependent prepositions places in a city	direct and indirect questions	*'d* number of syllables /dʒə/
VIDEO: Living in Venice ▶ REVIEW				
11 History	*used to* reported speech	archaeology wordbuilding: word roots *say* or *tell* word focus: *set*	giving a short presentation	/s/ or /z/ pausing
VIDEO: The lost city of Machu Picchu ▶ REVIEW				
12 Nature	*any-, every-, no-, some-* and *-thing, -where, -one, -body* second conditional *will* / *might*	classification of animals extreme weather society and economics wordbuilding: adjective + noun collocations	finding a solution	*would* / *'d* word stress
VIDEO: Cambodia Animal Rescue ▶ REVIEW				

Listening	Reading	Critical thinking	Speaking	Writing
someone talking about triplet police officers a documentary about working as a photographer an interview with an engineer	workplace messages with instructions an article about the cost of new jobs to an area an article about modern-day cowboys	the author's opinion	giving directions describing past experiences your opinion of a job	text type: a CV writing skill: action verbs for CVs
a documentary about the importance of technology a science programme about a new invention	an explorer's blog an article about biomimetics	supporting the main argument	problems that inventions solved inventing a new robot planning an expedition using nature to improve designs	text type: a paragraph writing skills: connecting words; topic and supporting sentences
an English teacher talking about working in Japan a radio documentary about learning Kung Fu in China	an article about the history of writing an article about saving languages	fact or opinion	adult education a general knowledge quiz the author's opinion	a general knowledge quiz text type: forms writing skill: providing the correct information
an interview with a herpetologist two conversations about problems whilst on holiday an interview with a *National Geographic* tour guide	an article about tipping in other countries an article about the tunnels in Paris	reading between the lines	a holiday or journey you remember planning the holiday of a lifetime a tourist website	a tourist webpage text type: a formal letter writing skill: formal expressions
an historian talking about Scott's hut at the Antarctic an interview with an archaeologist	an article about moments in space history a biography of Jane Goodall	relevance	items for a time capsule how we used to live moments in history reporting an interview an interview for a biography	text type: a biography writing skill: punctuation in direct speech
a nature expert talking about how animals camouflage themselves a documentary about a photographer	an article about storm chasers a profile on Greenland	close reading	promoting your region planning for every possibility predicting your country's future	text type: a press release writing skill: using bullet points

Video in Split Editions A and B

Life around the world

Unit 4 Alaskan ice climbing

How to climb a wall of ice.

Unit 5 Coastal clean-up

A global effort to clean up the world's beaches.

Unit 8 Wind power

How the wind turbines of Spirit Lake save the schools energy and money.

Unit 6 Steel drums

Steelband music, or pan, is an important part of this Caribbean island's culture.

Unit 2 Cheese rolling

The ancient tradition of cheese rolling in a village in England.

Unit 7 Butler school

Find out how to become a butler.

Unit 11 The lost city of Machu Picchu

The impact of tourism on the Inca city of Machu Picchu.

Unit 1 Slow food

A city that is enjoying itself – taking life slowly.

Unit 10 Living in Venice

Learn what it's like to live in Venice.

Unit 3 Indian railways

Learn more about the Indian railway system.

India

Cambodia

Unit 12 Cambodia Animal Rescue

Rescuing victims of illegal animal poaching in Cambodia.

Australia

Unit 9 Disappearing voices

A project to record the last speakers of disappearing languages.

Split Editions A and B

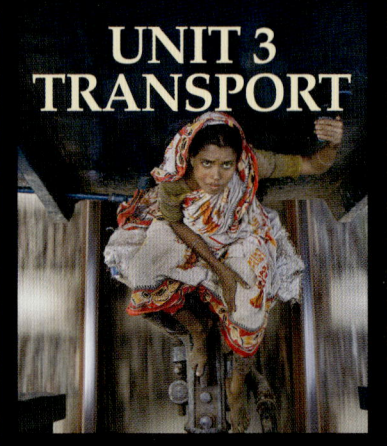

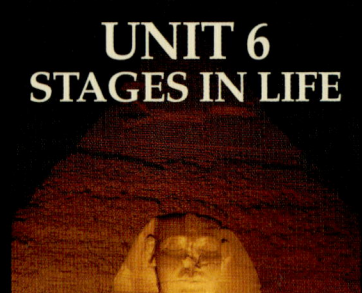

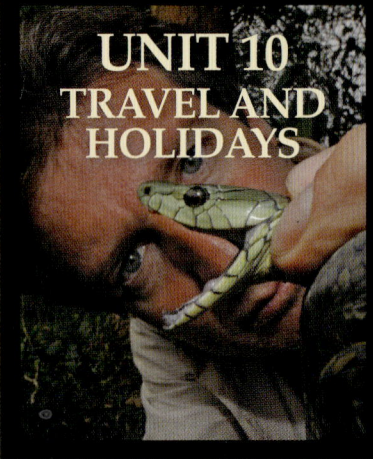
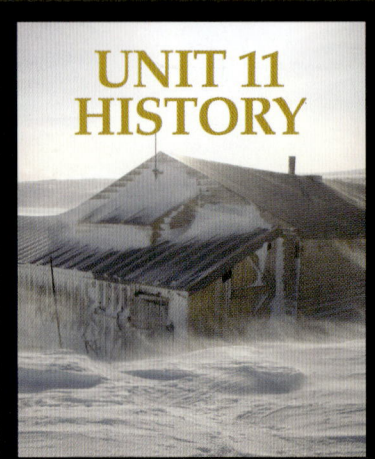

Unit 1 Health

Dance practice, Australia
Photo by Brendan McCarthy

FEATURES

10 How well do you sleep?
Take a quiz and find out about how well you sleep

12 The secrets of long life
How can you live to be one hundred?

14 Health and happiness
Measure the level of happiness where you live

18 Slow food
A video about a healthier way of life in an Italian town

1 Look at the two people in the photo. Why do you think they are happy?

2 1.1 Listen to someone talking about the people in the photo. Answer the questions.
1. Who are they?
2. How often do they practise dancing?
3. Why do they think dancing is good for their physical and mental health?

3 Work in pairs. Look at these activities. Tell your partner which activities you often do. Why do you do them?

> cycle through the countryside   do crosswords
> go for a long walk   work long hours   read a book
> play computer games   run marathons   watch TV

> I often cycle through the countryside because it's good for my health.

4 Think about other activities you do in your free time that are good for your physical or mental health. Tell your partner.

TALK ABOUT • ▶ A QUIZ   ▶ YOUR CURRENT LIFE   ▶ MEASURING HAPPINESS   ▶ ILLNESS   WRITE   ▶ ADVICE

9

reading and speaking the secrets of sleep • listening analysis of your answers •
grammar present simple and adverbs of frequency • pronunciation /s/, /z/ or /ɪz/ • speaking and writing a quiz

1a How well do you sleep?

Reading and speaking

1 Do you feel tired today? Why? / Why not?

2 Do the quiz below about sleep. Make a note of your answers.

Listening

3 1.2 Listen to a health expert talking about the quiz. Tick the characteristics which are true for each answer.

People with mostly A answers:
1 You have regular routines.
2 You are hardly ever tired.

People with mostly B answers:
3 You wake up once or twice a night.
4 You need more sleep than other people.

People with mostly C answers:
5 You regularly work in the evening.
6 You don't like sport.

4 Work in pairs. Compare your answers in the quiz. Which type of person are you? Do you need to change your lifestyle?

Grammar present simple and adverbs of frequency

5 Match the sentences from the quiz (1–2) with the uses of the present simple tense (a–b).

1 Before bedtime, I often do some work.
2 I'm never tired at work.

a to talk about things that are always true
b to talk about habits and routines

> **PRESENT SIMPLE**
>
> I/you/we/they sleep
> he/she/it sleeps
>
> I/you/we/they don't sleep
> he/she/it doesn't sleep
>
> Do you sleep ...?
> Does he sleep ...?
>
> For further information and practice, see page 84.

How well do you sleep?

Question: **1** 2 3 4 5 6

Q: Do you often feel tired?

A No, I don't often feel tired.
B I sometimes feel tired after a long day at work.
C All the time! I'm always ready for bed.

Question: 1 **2** 3 4 5 6

Q: How many hours a night do you sleep?

A Between seven and eight hours.
B More than nine. I rarely stay up late.
C Fewer than six.

Question: 1 2 **3** 4 5 6

Q: Before bedtime, I often ...
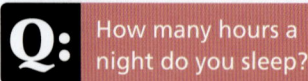

A watch TV or read a book.
B do some exercise.
C do some work.

Question: 1 2 3 **4** 5 6

Q: At the weekend, I ...

A usually sleep the same amount as any other day.
B sometimes sleep for an hour or two extra.
C always sleep until midday! I never get up early.

Question: 1 2 3 4 **5** 6

Q: How often do you wake up in the middle of the night?

A I never wake up before morning.
B I rarely wake up more than once, and I usually fall asleep again quite quickly.
C Two or three times a night.

Question: 1 2 3 4 5 **6**

Q: Are you often sleepy during the day?
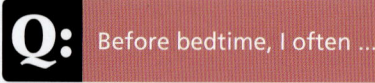

A No, I'm never tired at work.
B Sometimes, so I take a nap after lunch. After that I'm ready for work again.
C Always! That's because I work long hours and get home late.

fall asleep /fɔːl əˈsliːp/ start sleeping
take a nap /teɪk ə næp/ a short sleep that you have during the day

Unit 1 Health

6 Look at the grammar box. Then complete the article about sleep with the present simple form of the verbs.

Why ¹ *do we sleep* (we / sleep)?
From birth, we ² _____ (spend) a third of our lives asleep but scientists still ³ _____ (not / know) exactly why.

Why ⁴ _____ (humans / have) problems sleeping?
In modern society, many people ⁵ _____ (not / get) the recommended seven or eight hours a night. We ⁶ _____ (work) long hours and we rarely ⁷ _____ (go) to bed at sunset.

Why ⁸ _____ (we / sleep) differently?
It ⁹ _____ (depend) on the time of year and also our age. Teenagers always ¹⁰ _____ (need) more sleep than adults. Lots of elderly people ¹¹ _____ (not / sleep) longer than four or five hours, but they often ¹² _____ (take) naps during the day.

7 Pronunciation /s/, /z/ or /ɪz/

🔊 1.3 Listen to the ending of these verbs. Write /s/, /z/ or /ɪz/. Then listen again and repeat.

1 feels /z/   5 goes
2 needs   6 dances
3 watches   7 does
4 sleeps   8 works

8 Discuss the questions.

1 What time do people normally get up in your country? How late do they stay up? Do they ever take a nap in the afternoon?
2 How does this change during the year? Do people sleep longer in the summer or in the winter?

9 Complete this table with adverbs of frequency from the quiz in Exercise 2.

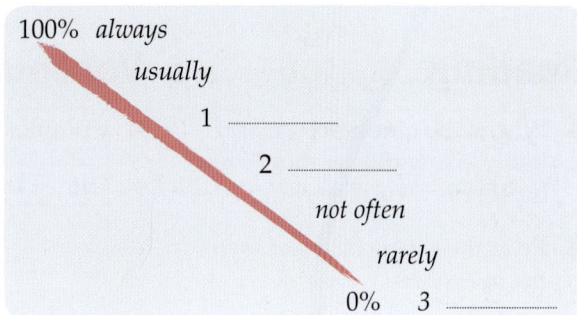

100% always
    usually
      1 _____
        2 _____
          not often
            rarely
0%   3 _____

10 Look at the position of the adverbs and expressions of frequency in the example sentences in the grammar box. Then choose the correct options to complete the rules (1–2).

> ▶ ADVERBS and EXPRESSIONS OF FREQUENCY
>
> She's **usually** late for work.
> I **often** wake up at seven.
> How **often** do you wake up in the night?
> She wakes up **two or three times a night**.
> **In the winter**, we sleep longer.
>
> For further information and practice, see page 84.

1 An adverb of frequency goes *after / before* the verb *to be* but it normally goes *after / before* the main verb.
2 An expression of frequency usually goes *at the beginning / in the middle* or at the end of a sentence.

11 Work in pairs. Ask and answer questions about these things. Use an adverb or expression of frequency in your answers.

do exercise	be late for work
take public transport	read a novel in the bath
eat out in restaurants	be in a bad mood
do gardening	go on holiday
play board games	be busy at weekends
check your emails	be stressed at work

How often do you do exercise?

Two or three times a week.

Speaking and writing

12 Work in groups. Prepare a *How healthy are you?* quiz for another group. Start each question with *How often …? Are you often …?* or *Do you ever …?* and offer three choices of answer (A, B or C).

13 When you are ready, join another group and ask the questions in your quiz. Afterwards, tell the class about their answers. Do you think the other group is very healthy?

TALK ABOUT ▶ A QUIZ ▶ YOUR CURRENT LIFE ▶ MEASURING HAPPINESS ▶ ILLNESS WRITE ▶ ADVICE

11

reading the island of Okinawa • vocabulary *do, go* or *play* • listening in search of a long life • grammar present simple and present continuous • speaking your current life

1b The secrets of long life

Reading

1 Who is the oldest person you know? How old are they? How healthy is their lifestyle?

2 Read the article below. Answer the questions.
   1 Why are the people of Okinawa famous?
   2 What are the reasons for their good health?

3 Which of the reasons for good health in the article are true for your life? Tell your partner.

Vocabulary *do, go* or *play*

4 Complete the table with activities from the article in Exercise 2.

do	go	play
	fishing	

5 Add these activities to the table in Exercise 4. Use your dictionary to help you, if necessary. Then think of one more activity for each verb.

cards   hiking   homework   nothing   running   shopping
tennis   the piano   yoga   football   karate   surfing

▶ WORDBUILDING verb + noun collocations
We can only use certain nouns with certain verbs. These are called collocations. For example, *go fishing* but not *do fishing* or *play fishing*.

For further information and practice, see Workbook page 103.

The Secrets of Long Life

The island of Okinawa in Japan has some of the oldest people in the world. It's famous for its high number of centenarians – men and women who live beyond 100 years of age. There have been many scientific studies of their lifestyle and you can even buy cookery books based on their diets. Some of the reasons for their good health are that they …

- go fishing and eat what they catch.
- regularly do gardening and grow their own fruit and vegetables.
- go cycling and never drive when they can walk.
- often spend time with friends. They meet at people's houses and play games.
- rarely buy food from a supermarket.
- do regular exercise, go swimming and lead active lives.

Listening

6 🔊 **1.4** Listen to a radio interview with David McLain, an explorer and journalist. Answer the questions.

1 What does David want to know?
2 Why is he in Sardinia?

7 🔊 **1.4** Listen again. Are the sentences true (T) or false (F)?

1 David McLain is travelling to different countries.
2 He's talking to the radio presenter in the studio.
3 Men don't live the same number of years as women on Sardinia.
4 Sardinian families often eat together.
5 David thinks Sardinia is less stressful than other countries.
6 Younger people are eating more unhealthy food and they aren't getting much exercise.

Grammar present simple and present continuous

8 Look at the five sentences from the interview in Exercise 6. Which two sentences use the present simple tense? Why?

1 He's currently travelling to places and regions.
2 He's speaking to us right now on the phone.
3 Men live the same amount of time as women.
4 Every Sunday the whole family meets and they eat a huge meal together.
5 Young people are moving to the city so they are doing less exercise because of their lifestyle.

9 The three other sentences in Exercise 8 use the present continuous tense. How do you form the tense? Match the three sentences to the uses (a–c).

a to talk about things happening at the moment of speaking
b to talk about things happening around now but not necessarily at the moment of speaking
c to talk about current trends and changing situations

> ▶ **PRESENT CONTINUOUS**
>
> I am speaking
> you/we/they are speaking
> he/she/it is speaking
>
> I'm not travelling
> you/we/they aren't travelling
> he/she/it isn't travelling
>
> Am I moving?
> Are you/we/they moving?
> Is he/she/it moving?
>
> For further information and practice, see page 84.

10 Complete the sentences with the present simple or present continuous form of these verbs.

check	not / do	not / eat	go	~~learn~~	play
read	spend				

1 We _'re learning_ a new language at the moment.
2 My friends and I often _____ time at each other's houses.
3 One moment! I _____ my emails and then I'm ready to go.
4 How often _____ you _____ to the gym?
5 I _____ a really interesting book at the moment.
6 Currently, a friend of mine _____ any sweets and he says he feels healthier.
7 I'm nearly eighty but I _____ any exercise!
8 Which computer game _____ you _____? It looks fun.

Speaking

11 Work in pairs. Take turns to ask and answer the questions. Use the present simple and present continuous tense in your answers.

1 What's your typical working day? Are you working on anything new at the moment?
2 How do you spend your free time? Are you getting much exercise?
3 Do you often read novels? Are you reading anything interesting at the moment?
4 Where do you normally go on holiday? Are you planning your holidays for this year?
5 Do you speak any other languages? Are you learning any new languages?

TALK ABOUT ▶ A QUIZ ▶ YOUR CURRENT LIFE ▶ MEASURING HAPPINESS ▶ ILLNESS WRITE ▶ ADVICE

speaking feeling happy • critical thinking the main argument • reading happy and healthy • word focus *feel* • speaking measuring happiness

1c Health and happiness

Speaking

1 Which of these things make you feel happy? Order them from 1 to 5 (1 = most happy). Compare with your partner.

- Sleeping for a long time
- Having money 2
- Relaxing on holiday 1
- Going out with friends
- Doing exercise

Critical thinking the main argument

2 Read the article on page 15. Which of the sentences (1–3) is the best summary of the main argument?

1 Happiness improves our health.
2 Denmark is the happiest country in the world.
3 There are different ways to measure happiness.

Reading

3 Choose the correct answer (a–c) for the questions, according to the information in the article.

1 How did the King of Bhutan measure the country's development?
 a by money   b by health
 c by happiness

2 Which is easier to measure?
 a happiness   b health
 c sickness and ill health

3 Why was Iceland number one in a survey?
 a for its money   b for its health
 c for its happiness

4 How did researchers measure happiness in 155 countries?
 a with answers to questions
 b by looking at people's faces
 c by measuring the number of sick people

5 What do visitors to Krikortz's website click on?
 a questions   b faces   c numbers

6 How many categories does Krikortz have for measuring happiness?
 a three   b five   c seven

7 What colour are the lights on the building when Stockholm is happy?
 a red   b green   c purple

Word focus *feel*

4 Look at the sentences (1–4) from the article. Match *feel* in each sentence with the uses (a–d).

1 It's also easy to measure how many people **feel** ill or unhealthy in a country.
2 Denmark **feels** happier than other countries.
3 Krikortz **feels** that there are other ways of measuring happiness.
4 The coloured lights are also useful if you **feel like** visiting the city.

a to give an opinion
b to talk about an emotion
c to talk about physical illness
d to talk about wanting something or wanting to do something

5 Match the questions (1–3) to the responses (a–c).

1 How do you feel today?
2 What do you feel about Krikortz's project?
3 Do you feel like going for a coffee after the class?

a Fine, thanks. How about you?
b Yes, I'd like to.
c I'm not sure. It's quite interesting I suppose.

6 Work in pairs. Take turns to ask the questions in Exercise 5. Answer with your own words.

Speaking

7 Work in groups. Discuss the questions.

1 In paragraph 1, the King of Bhutan talks about 'Gross National Happiness'. How happy do you think your country is? Give reasons for your answer.
2 In paragraph 2, a doctor said, 'Happy people generally don't get sick.' How much do you agree with this opinion?
3 In paragraph 3 and 4, there are different questions and categories for measuring happiness. Which do you think are useful for measuring happiness? Which are not very useful?

8 Work in the same group. Make a list of five categories for measuring happiness (e.g. money, sleep). Then everyone in the group gives a score for each of the categories (1 = very happy, 2 = happy, 3 = OK, 4 = not very happy). How happy is your group? Present your categories and result to the class.

14

measuring HEALTH AND HAPPINESS

Unit 1 Health

The small country of Bhutan in the Himalayan mountains is over one thousand years old. In the past it was a poor country and not many people visited it. But nowadays, it is becoming more and more popular with tourists. Medicine and health is improving and its economy is growing. King Jigme Singye Wangchuck, the king of Bhutan until 2006, talked about his country's 'Gross National Happiness'. In other words, he thought happiness is the way to measure the country's development.

But how do you measure happiness? Perhaps health is the best way because a famous doctor once said, 'Happy people generally don't get sick.' It's also easy to measure how many people feel ill or unhealthy in a country. For example, one survey says Iceland is the 'healthiest country in the world' because men and women live a long time there, the air is very clean and there are more doctors available per person than anywhere else in the world.

However, there was another survey of the happiest countries in the world and Iceland was not near the top. The questions on this survey included: How much do you earn? How healthy are you? How safe do you feel? After visiting 155 different countries, the researchers decided that Denmark feels happier than other countries.

So does happiness equal money and good health? Not according to the artist Erik Krikortz. He feels that there are other ways of measuring happiness. Krikortz has a website and visitors click on different happy or sad faces to comment on how well they sleep, their family and friends, their level of stress, their inspiration and their physical activity. When you finish, his website adds the results for each area and it gives you a final result for your happiness.

In his home city of Stockholm, Krikortz also shows the results of his survey as different coloured lights on the side of a large building in the city. For example, red means the people of Stockholm are very happy, green is OK and purple means many people are sad. 'A lot of people look at the building every day and see how "we" are,' Krikortz says. The coloured lights are also useful if you feel like visiting the city. For example, if the lights are red, you know the locals are feeling happy!

inspiration (n) /ˌɪnspəˈreɪʃn/ a feeling that makes you want to do something or gives you exciting new ideas

TALK ABOUT ▶ A QUIZ ▶ YOUR CURRENT LIFE ▶ MEASURING HAPPINESS ▶ ILLNESS ▶ WRITE ▶ ADVICE

vocabulary medical problems • pronunciation sound and spelling • real life talking about illness

1d At the doctor's

Vocabulary medical problems

1 Look at the pictures. Match the people (1–8) with the medical problems (a–h).

a I've got a headache.
b I've got back ache.
c I've got a runny nose.
d I've got earache.
e I've got stomach ache.
f I've got a temperature.
g I've got a sore throat.
h I've got a bad cough.

2 Pronunciation sound and spelling

a Many English words have the same vowel sounds but different spellings. Match the words with the same vowel sounds.

1 head	wake
2 sore	saw
3 throat	off
4 cough	note
5 ache	here
6 ear	bed

b 🔊 1.5 Listen and check your answers. Then listen again and repeat.

3 What do you do when you have the medical problems in Exercise 1? Categorise them into the three groups. Then compare with your partner.

1 I go to bed.
2 I take medicine or pills.
3 I go to the pharmacy or see my doctor.

Real life talking about illness

4 🔊 1.6 Listen to two conversations, one at a pharmacy and the other at a doctor's. Write the number of the conversation (*1* or *2*) next to the person's medical problems and medical advice they receive.

Medical problem	Medical advice
sore throat *1*	take this medicine twice a day *1*
bad cough	go to bed
runny nose	drink hot water with honey
earache	and lemon
feel sick	take one pill twice a day
temperature	buy a box of tissues
	drink lots of water

5 🔊 1.6 Listen again and complete the sentences. Then match them with the correct section in the box.

1 I _____ _____ a sore throat.
2 You _____ take this medicine.
3 It's _____ _____ a sore throat.
4 You _____ a box of tissues.
5 If you still feel ill in a few days, see a _____.
6 Let me have a _____.
7 Do you _____ sick?
8 Let me check your _____.

▶ **TALKING ABOUT ILLNESS**

Asking and talking about illness
I don't feel very well.
I feel sick / ill.
Have you got a temperature?
How do you feel?

Giving advice
Try drinking hot water with lemon.
You need to take one of these.
Drink lots of water.

6 Work in pairs. Practise this conversation. Then change roles and repeat the conversation.

Student A: You have a medical problem. (Choose one from Exercise 1.)

Student B: You are a pharmacist. Ask how Student A feels and give advice.

Writing online advice • Writing skill conjunctions (*and, or, so, because, but*)   Unit 1 Health

1e Medical advice online

Writing online advice

1 Many people look for medical advice on the internet before they visit their doctor. Do you think this is a good idea? Why? / Why not?

2 Look at the advice forum on a website. Answer the questions.
1 What medical problem has each person got?
2 Do you think the doctor gives them good advice?
3 Can you think of any more advice for each person?

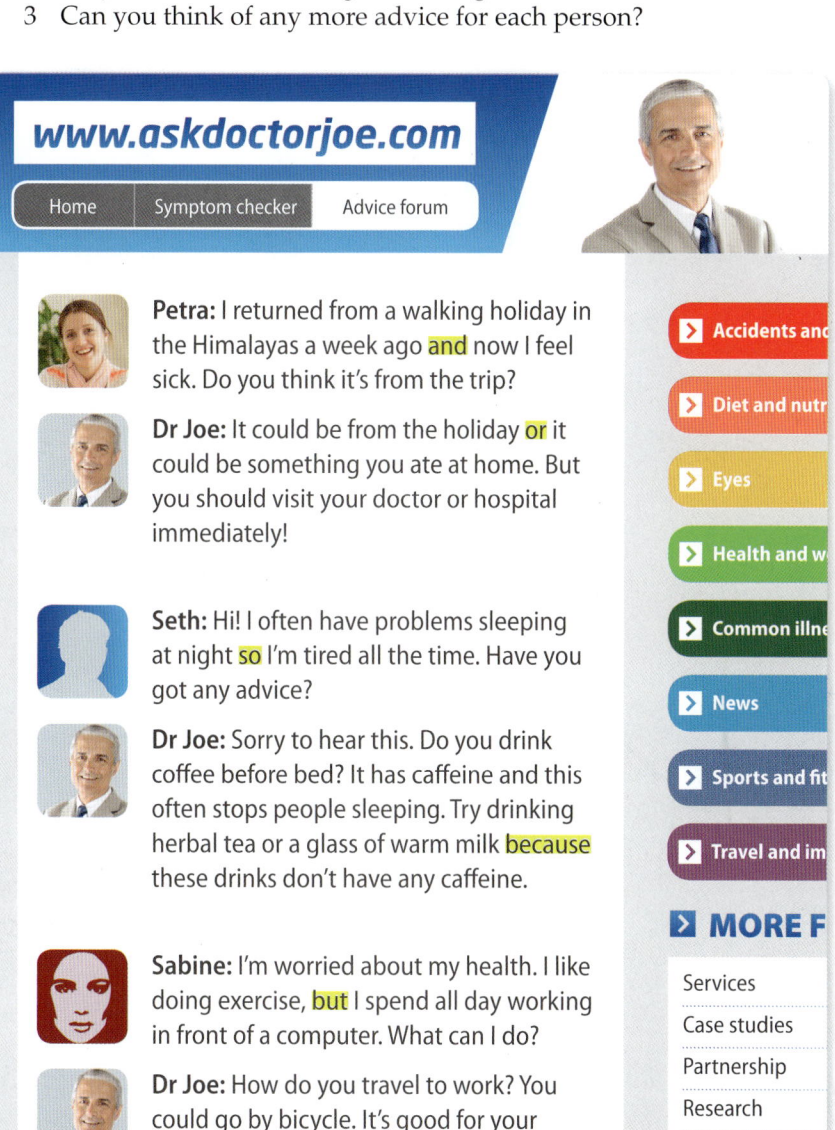

3 Writing skill conjunctions (*and, or, so, because, but*)

a Look at the highlighted conjunctions in the forum in Exercise 2. Then complete the rules with those words.

1 We use *and* to connect two words or parts of a sentence.
2 We use _____ to introduce an idea that is different.
3 We use _____ to say 'with the result that.'
4 We use _____ to explain the reason.
5 We use _____ to connect an alternative word or idea.

b Complete the sentences with the conjunctions in Exercise 3a.

1 You need to do more exercise _____ eat healthy food.
2 Jogging is healthy, _____ eating chocolate is nicer!
3 You could try cycling _____ go walking if you don't have a bicycle.
4 Fruit and vegetables are good for you _____ they are full of vitamins.
5 Fruit and vegetables are full of vitamins, _____ they are good for you.

4 Imagine you want advice from the forum. Choose a medical problem. Then write a message to Doctor Joe and ask for advice.

5 Exchange your message with your partner. Imagine you are Doctor Joe. Write a reply with two or three pieces of good advice. Remember to use conjunctions.

1f Slow food

A place where time is slower.

Unit 1 Health

Before you watch

1 Work in groups. Look at the title of the video and the photo. Discuss the questions.

1. What do you think 'slow food' is?
2. How do you think the people in the photo feel?
3. What do you think the photo caption means?
4. What do you think the video is about?

2 Tick the things you think will be in this video.

> countryside
> farmers and people making food
> fast food restaurants
> lots of cars
> a modern city
> relaxed people enjoying food

While you watch

3 Watch the video and check your ideas from Exercise 2.

4 Watch the video again. Are these sentences true (T) or false (F)?

1. Chianti is a region in Spain.
2. Four thousand people live in Greve.
3. Greve is part of the Slow Cities League.
4. Salvatore Toscano runs an American-style restaurant.
5. His restaurant is in Greve.
6. Farmers make pecorino cheese from cows' milk.
7. Pecorino cheese is not very popular nowadays.
8. Greve wants to escape from the modern world.

5 Watch the video again. Answer these questions.

1. What is Greve famous for?
2. How many cities are in the Slow Cities League?
3. What is the purpose of the Slow Cities League?
4. How many members does the slow food movement have?
5. Why is pecorino cheese popular again?
6. What can you find everywhere in the world?

After you watch

6 Match the people (1–4) with what they say (a–d).

1. the narrator
2. Salvatore Toscano
3. Greve's mayor
4. the cheese maker

a. Our aim is to keep Greve the same. We want to keep Greve and all the other slow cities special.
b. It's about taking more time so you are more calm and relaxed.
c. In the mountains of Pistoia, in northern Tuscany, farmers produce pecorino cheese.
d. Not everyone knows about our product. But now the slow food movement means people know about us.

7 Roleplay a conversation with Salvatore Toscano

Work in pairs.

Student A: You are Salvatore Toscano. Read the questions below and make notes about yourself. Then ask your customer about his life.

- Why do you like Greve?
- What is it like living in Greve?
- Do you enjoy your job?

Student B: You are a customer in Salvatore Toscano's restaurant. You come from a large busy city. Read the questions below and make notes about yourself. Then ask Salvatore about his life in Greve.

- What's your name?
- What's your job?
- Do you like visiting Greve? Why?
- Do you want to live somewhere like Greve?

Act out the conversation. Compare your lives. Then change roles and repeat the conversation.

8 Read what the man says at the end of the video. Answer the questions.

From Singapore to Macao, in New York, in Rome, you always find the same pizza, the same hamburgers. Slow food doesn't want this.

1. Do you agree?
2. Do you think slow food is a good idea?

9 Work in pairs. Discuss these questions.

1. Would you like to live in Greve? Why? / Why not?
2. Do you live a quiet life or do you live in the fast lane? In what ways?

---

die out (v) /daɪ ˈaʊt/ disappear
mayor (n) /ˈmeɪə/ the head of the administration of a town
vineyard (n) /ˈvɪnjɑːd/ a place where grapes grow
worldwide (adv) /ˈwɜːldwaɪd/ all over the world

19

UNIT 1 REVIEW

Grammar

1 Work in pairs. Look at the photo. Where are the man and the elephant? What are they doing?

2 Choose the correct forms to complete the text about the man in Exercise 1.

Every day, Nazroo ¹ *drives / is driving* elephants for a living, but, as you can see here, ² *he takes / he's taking* his favourite elephant, Rajan, for a swim. In this photo ³ *they swim / they're swimming* in the sea around Andaman Island. Sometimes they ⁴ *like / are liking* to relax this way after a hard day. I was surprised because Rajan ⁵ *doesn't seem / isn't seeming* worried about being under the water. I guess it feels good after a long, hot day at work.

3 Work in pairs. How often do Nazroo and Rajan go swimming? How often do you go swimming? How do you like to relax?

I CAN
talk about regular actions and events using the present simple
describe actions in progress (now or around now) using the present continuous
ask and answer questions with *How often …?*

Vocabulary

4 Which words can follow the verb in CAPITAL letters? Delete the incorrect word.

1 FEEL   tired, happy, ache, sick
2 DO   exercise, housework, relaxing, yoga
3 PLAY   golf, swimming, games, tennis
4 GO   marathon, racing, hiking, driving

5 Work in pairs. How do you feel about your new English course? Do you feel worried about anything? (Tell your teacher if you are.)

I CAN
talk about leisure activities
say how I feel

Real life

6 Choose the correct words to complete the conversation between two friends.

A: ¹ *How do / Do* you feel?
B: Not very ² *well / ill*. I've got a ³ *pain / sore* throat.
A: ⁴ *Do you feel / Have you got* a high temperature?
B: I don't know. I feel a bit hot.
A: ⁵ *Try / You need* drinking some honey and lemon in hot water.
B: Good idea.
A: But ⁶ *you should / it's a good idea* also see your doctor.

7 Work in pairs. Practise two similar conversations.

Conversation 1:
Student A has got a headache. Student B gives advice.

Conversation 2:
Student B has got stomach ache. Student A gives advice.

I CAN
talk about feeling ill
give advice

Speaking

8 Complete these questions to ask someone about their everyday habits and interests.

1 Do you often play …?
2 How often do you go …?
3 Do you ever …?
4 What are you *-ing* …?
5 Why do you …?

9 Work in pairs. Ask and answer your questions from Exercise 8.

Unit 2 Competitions

Ironman competition
Photo by Patrick McFeeley

FEATURES

22 Competitive sports
What it takes to be a real winner

24 Crazy competitions!
When people from all over the USA make new rules

26 Bolivian wrestlers
Women competing in a national sport

30 Cheese rolling
A video about a crazy and dangerous competition in England

1 Look at the photo. What kind of competition is it? Do you like this kind of sport?

2 🔊 **1.7** Listen to someone talking about the photo. Answer the questions.

1 What are the three different types of sport in an Ironman competition?
2 Where is the annual championship?
3 Why do thousands of spectators watch the championship?

3 Work in groups. Discuss the questions.

1 Are you normally a competitor or a spectator? Which do you prefer?
2 Are you competitive? What kinds of competition do you compete in?

▶ **WORDBUILDING word forms**

When you learn a new word, try to learn its other forms.
For example:
compete (verb) – *competitive* (adjective) – *competition* (noun) – *competitor* (noun/person)

For further information and practice, see Workbook page 111.

TALK ABOUT ▶ AMBITIONS ▶ COMPETITION RULES ▶ SPORTS ▶ INTERESTS   WRITE ▶ AN ADVERT

21

reading and speaking popular sports • grammar verb + -ing forms • pronunciation /ŋ/ •
vocabulary and listening talking about sports • grammar like + -ing / 'd like to • speaking guess the ambition

2a Competitive sports

Reading and speaking

1 Read the quotes by famous sports people (1–6). Then discuss the questions.

1. How are the six quotes similar?
2. Are all these sports popular in your country? What other sports are popular?

1 'Winning isn't everything, but wanting it is.'
Arnold Palmer, winner of 92 golf tournaments

2 'I never thought of losing.'
Muhammad Ali, three times boxing World Heavyweight Champion

3 'I just love winning.'
Ayrton Senna, racing driver and three times Formula One World Champion

4 'Swimming isn't everything, winning is.'
Mark Spitz, swimmer and winner of seven gold medals at the 1972 Munich Olympics

5 'A champion is afraid of losing. Everyone else is afraid of winning.'
Billie Jean King, tennis player, won 129 major tournaments

6 'I hate losing.'
Sachin Tendulkar, often called the greatest batsman in the history of cricket

Muhammad Ali taunting Sonny Liston

Grammar verb + -ing forms

2 Underline the verb + -ing forms in the quotes in Exercise 1. Which of the underlined forms are:

1. the subject of the sentence?
2. after verbs (e.g. like, dislike) as an object?
3. after a preposition?

▶ VERB + -ING FORMS
- Subject of the sentence: **Swimming** is good for you.
- After verbs (often like, love, enjoy, prefer, don't like, hate, can't stand) as an object: I like **playing** tennis.
- After a preposition: I'm good **at learning** languages.

For further information and practice, see page 85.

3 Look at the grammar box. Then correct the conversation between two friends. Change eight verbs into the -ing form.

A: The *Tour de France* is on TV tonight! I love ~~watch~~ it. *watching*

B: Oh no! Cycle is so boring.

A: I really enjoy see the cyclists on the mountains.

B: But it lasts for days! I hate wait for the end.

A: Today is the final day. It's exciting.

B: Sit in front of the TV is not exciting. I prefer do something. Hey! Are you good at play tennis? We could play this afternoon.

A: But I want to watch this.

B: I see. Are you afraid of lose against me or something?

4 Pronunciation /ŋ/

a 🎵 1.8 Listen to the words and underline the part of the word with the /ŋ/ sound. What is the most common spelling with the /ŋ/ sound? Listen again and repeat.

1	watching	6	losing
2	language	7	winning
3	waiting	8	English
4	thinks	9	competing
5	cycling	10	thanks

b Read the conversation in Exercise 3 aloud. Pay attention to the /ŋ/ sound in the verb + -ing forms.

Unit 2 Competitions

5 Work in pairs. Ask questions to complete the sentences for both of you with the names of any sports or leisure activities.

1 I love watching _____ but my partner doesn't.
2 My partner likes _____ but I prefer _____.
3 I think _____ is boring but my partner loves it!
4 We both enjoy _____ but we can't stand _____.
5 I'm good at _____ but my partner isn't.

Do you like -ing?   *What do you like -ing?*
Are you good at …?

Vocabulary and listening
talking about sports

6 Write about the six sports in Exercise 1. Use these words to say where you play each sport and what you need. Then think of two other sports you like and describe them in a similar way.

where you play	what you need
court course pitch pool ring track	ball bat car club gloves goggles net racquet

Example:
You play golf on a golf course. You need a golf club and a ball.

7 Work in pairs. Take turns to describe a sport for your partner to guess.

The two teams play on a pitch. They use a bat and a ball.   *Cricket.*
Correct!

8 🔊 **1.9** Listen to three people talking about sport. Make notes in the table.

	Which sport are they talking about?	Do they like or dislike doing the sport?	Why do they do the sport?
Meg			
Paul			
Kirsty			

coach (n) /kəʊtʃ/ a person who trains sports people

Grammar *like + -ing / 'd like to*

9 🔊 **1.10** Listen to Kirsty again and complete the sentences (a–b). Then answer the questions (1–2).

a I _____ _____ tennis so much that currently I'm working with a tennis coach.
b One day I _____ to become a professional player.

1 Which sentence describes a future ambition?
2 Which sentence is true now and talks about a general feeling?

> ▶ **'D LIKE TO**
>
> would ('d) like + to + infinitive
> She'd like to play tennis later.
> He'd love to become a boxer one day.
> They wouldn't like to judge the competition.
>
> For further information and practice, see page 85.

10 Make sentences about each pair of pictures using these words. Use *like + -ing* and *'d like to*.

1 love / drive / formula one cars

2 like / play golf

3 not like / lose

Speaking

11 Write down three ambitions for the future, one true and two false. Take turns to read them to your partner. Can he/she guess which of your ambitions are false?

I'd like to become a rock star.   *No, you wouldn't.*

I'd like to jump from an aeroplane with a parachute.   *Yes, you would.*

TALK ABOUT ▶ AMBITIONS ▶ COMPETITION RULES ▶ SPORTS ▶ INTERESTS   WRITE ▶ AN ADVERT

reading crazy competitions • grammar modal verbs for rules • listening rules of the competition • vocabulary competitions • speaking rules for a competition

2b Crazy competitions!

Reading

1 Look at the photos of competitions (A–C) in the article. Which do you think is a fight, a match and a race?

2 Read about the competitions. Check your predictions in Exercise 1.

3 Read the article again. Match the sentences (1–8) with the competitions (A–C).
1 Competitors run from one place to another. ___
2 You can win money. ___
3 It's for individual competitors. ___
4 The competition is once a year. ___, ___
5 You use a type of transport. ___, ___
6 The rules are the same as another real sport. ___
7 It's for teams. ___, ___
8 There is a time limit. ___

4 Which of these sports would you like to play or watch? Do you have any similar competitions in your country?

Crazy competitions!

Ross McDermott and Andrew Owen travel round the United States going to different festivals and write about their experiences on the blog *The American Festivals Project*. Many of these festivals are also competitions.

A The Idiotarod

The Idiotarod is an annual race in New York City. Each team must have five people and a shopping cart. They can decorate their carts but they can't change the wheels. All the teams have to start and finish at the same place but they don't have to run on the same roads. The teams can choose their route but the members of each team must arrive at the finish line together. And they mustn't finish without the cart!

B Mud Bowl Championship

Mud Bowl football is similar to normal American football. The match is shorter but there are two teams and a referee. The winner is the team with the most goals at the end of sixty minutes. The only real difference is that the players have to play in half a metre of mud!

C Combine Harvester Fight

Combine harvesters are normally on farms but, for one day every summer, in the small town of Hillsdale in Michigan, farmers compete against each other for a prize of $1,500. For three hours, the giant machines have to fight until only one combine harvester is still moving.

Grammar modal verbs for rules

5 Look at the sentence from the article about the Idiotarod. What does the highlighted modal verb mean? Choose the correct answer (1–4).

*Each team **must** have five people and a shopping cart.*

1 It is necessary and an obligation.
2 It is allowed according to the rules.
3 It is not necessary (but allowed).
4 It is not allowed.

6 Find five more modal verbs in the article about the Idiotarod. Match them to the meanings (1–4) in Exercise 5.

> ▶ **MODAL VERBS FOR RULES**
>
> • Necessary and an obligation: *must, have to*
> • Allowed: *can*
> • Not necessary (but allowed): *don't have to*
> • Not allowed: *mustn't, can't*
>
> For further information and practice, see page 85.

7 Choose the correct options to complete the sentences about different sports.

1 You *have to / don't have to* play cricket with a bat and a ball.
2 Competitors *don't have to / mustn't* argue with the judge's decision.
3 Rugby players *can / can't* throw the ball forwards. It must always go backwards.
4 Competitors *can't / must* run 42 kilometres in a marathon.
5 A referee *can / mustn't* send a player off the pitch.
6 The goalkeeper in football *has to / doesn't have to* stay in the penalty area.
7 A tennis player *has to / doesn't have to* hit the ball inside the white lines.
8 The players *mustn't / don't have to* win every point to win a match.

Listening

8 🔊 **1.11** Listen to a description of another race: The Woolly Worm Race. What does the speaker describe? Choose the correct answer (1–3).

1 why people like racing woolly worms
2 the rules of the competition
3 the history of the competition

9 🔊 **1.11** Listen again. Answer the questions.

1 How often is the competition?
2 How old do you have to be to enter?
3 Do you have to bring your own woolly worm?
4 Can you touch your worm during the race?
5 What is the prize for the winner?

Vocabulary competitions

10 Complete the pairs of sentences with the correct words. Use a dictionary to help you.

1 (win / beat)
   My woolly worm _____ yours!
   Did you _____ the race?
2 (score / win)
   How many matches did you _____?
   How many goals did you _____?
3 (fans / spectators)
   We're your biggest _____! We come to every match.
   There were about 50,000 _____ at the match.
4 (referee / judge)
   The _____ sent the player off.
   One _____ gave the ice skater 10/10.
5 (trophy / prize)
   The President gave the winning team the silver _____.
   The _____ for the winner is $500.

Speaking

11 Work in groups. Imagine that you want to have a new annual competition for your town. Follow these steps.

1 Decide on a crazy competition.
2 Discuss the rules and write a list. Also discuss any other details.
3 Present your new competition to the class and explain the rules.

Unit 2 Competitions

TALK ABOUT ▶ AMBITIONS ▶ COMPETITION RULES ▶ SPORTS ▶ INTERESTS   WRITE ▶ AN ADVERT

reading an unusual sport • critical thinking reading between the lines • word focus *like* • speaking opinions about sport

2c Bolivian wrestlers

Reading

1 Look at the photos on pages 26 and 27. Before you read, do you think the statements (1–3) will be true (T) or false (F)? Read the article and check your predictions.

   1 Wrestling is popular in Bolivia.
   2 Only men can wrestle in public.
   3 People earn a lot of money from wrestling.

2 Read the article again. Which paragraph (1–6) describes:

   a the two wrestlers before the fight? 2
   b the popularity of male and female wrestling in Bolivia?
   c the moments before the wrestlers enter?
   d Yolanda's family life?
   e the reason why a fan watches it?
   f the fight between the two women wrestlers?

3 Find words in the first three paragraphs of the article to match these definitions.

   1 three words meaning a large group of people at a performance or sporting event: a_____, s_____, c_____
   2 two verbs meaning to speak loudly and make a lot of noise: s_____, s_____
   3 to clap your hands together: a_____
   4 people who support someone famous: f_____
   5 to get away from someone or something: e_____
   6 three verbs to describe fast movements: j_____, s_____, t_____
   7 the bad person (usually in a story, film or book): b_____
   8 the good person (usually in a story, film or book): g_____

Critical thinking reading between the lines

4 An article doesn't always tell us everything about how the people feel, but we can often guess. Match these people from the article (1–3) with the sentences (a–c).

   1 Yolanda
   2 One of Yolanda's daughters
   3 Esperanza

   a I don't like the days when the wrestling is happening.
   b I get a wonderful feeling every time I go out there.
   c Life is very hard for people like me.

Word focus *like*

5 Look at the sentences from the article. Match *like* in each sentence (1–4) with the uses (a–d).

   1 Would they **like** to become wrestlers one day?
   2 Yolanda and Claudina walk through the crowds **like** pop stars.
   3 Esperanza explains why she **likes** watching the wrestling.
   4 She also has two daughters who both look **like** her.

   a enjoys in general
   b wants to do in the future
   c similar behaviour to
   d similar appearance to

Speaking

6 Discuss the questions.

   1 Do you like watching sports with women in your country? Would you like to watch the type of wrestling in the article?
   2 How important are sport and sports people in your country? Do any of them look like or behave like pop or film stars?
   3 Do you think most people like watching sport because they want to 'forget their problems' for a few hours? Are there any other reasons?

26

Unit 2 **Competitions**

Bolivian wrestlers

In El Alto in Bolivia, an audience is sitting around a huge wrestling ring. The spectators are getting impatient and so they start to scream: 'Bring them on! Bring them on!' Suddenly, an announcer speaks into the microphone: 'Ladies and Gentlemen. It's time for Yolanda and Claudina!' The crowd shouts and applauds with excitement.

Two women enter. Yolanda and Claudina walk through the crowd like pop stars. They smile and greet their fans until suddenly the music stops. Both women jump into the wrestling ring and within seconds, Claudina hits Yolanda. Yolanda grabs Claudina. Claudina tries to escape, but Yolanda doesn't let her go. She spins Claudina round and throws her down on the floor. The audience goes crazy!

As Claudina lies on the floor, Yolanda is smiling and waving to the crowd. She doesn't see Claudina get up behind her. Then Claudina pushes Yolanda onto the ropes. The crowd shouts at her. Claudina is the baddie in this competition so when Yolanda – the goodie – gets up and throws Claudina out of the ring, the crowd cheers with happiness. One minute Yolanda is winning. The next minute, Claudina is winning.

Wrestling in Bolivia is incredibly popular and after a hard day's work many people love watching this mixture of sport, drama and entertainment. Usually, the wrestling matches are between men wearing masks and special costumes. But in El Alto, where it's especially popular, you can also see women wrestling.

The women wrestlers fight here and we laugh and forget our problems for three or four hours.

Yolanda is one of the top women wrestlers. Her father was also a wrestler so it's a family tradition. During the day she makes clothes. She also has two daughters who both look like her. Would they like to become wrestlers one day? Yolanda doesn't think so. 'My daughters ask me why I do this. It's dangerous and they complain that wrestling doesn't bring any money into the house.' But Yolanda loves wrestling because of her fans, and she has lots of them!

One fan called Esperanza Cancina pays $1.50 (a large part of her salary) to sit near the ring. She explains why she likes watching the wrestling: 'It's a distraction. The women wrestlers fight here and we laugh and forget our problems for three or four hours. At home, we're sad.'

TALK ABOUT ▸ AMBITIONS ▸ COMPETITION RULES ▸ SPORTS ▸ INTERESTS   WRITE ▸ AN ADVERT

27

speaking clubs and membership • real life talking about interests • pronunciation silent letters

2d Joining a club

Speaking

1 Who is a member of a club or local group in your class? Ask them these questions.

1 Does the club have regular meetings? How often?
2 Do you pay a membership fee? How much is it?
3 What are the benefits of being a member?
4 Does it ever have competitions?

2 Look at the adverts (A–C). Which of the questions in Exercise 1 do they each answer?

A

Would you like to **get fit** and **make new friends?**

Our running group meets at 7 p.m. every Wednesday.
There are two groups:
• Beginner's group (for anyone)
• Experienced (you must be able to run twenty or more kilometres)
It's non-competitive and a fun way to get fit!
Call Mike Burgess on 0776 58945.

B

Join us and **WIN** *a new camera!*

The Barton Photography Club welcomes new members. We are a busy club with regular speakers at our club meetings. Join before 1st March and you can also enter our summer photography competition. Three prizes including a brand new camera. The entry fee is 15 euros (including club membership for a year). Visit www.bartonphotoclub.com to download an entry form and for membership details.

C

Theatre group

A local theatre group is looking for actors and actresses to be in a musical comedy this summer. You must be available twice a week starting 2nd April. Enthusiasm is more important than talent!
Contact Mandy Giles on mandy76@dmail.com

Real life talking about interests

3 🎧 1.12 Two people are looking at the adverts in their local newspaper. Listen to their conversation and number the adverts in the order they discuss them.

4 🎧 1.12 Listen again and complete the sentences from the conversation.

1 You're really _____ _____ doing that.
2 Well, _____ _____ joining something else?
3 Are you _____ acting?
4 I _____ standing up in front of people.
5 I'm _____ good at singing.
6 Go _____. I think you'd _____ it.
7 I think I'd _____ join this on Wednesday evenings.
8 It _____ fun. _____ you come too?

5 Match the sentences in Exercise 4 with the three categories in the box.

▶ **TALKING ABOUT INTERESTS**

Asking about interests
Do you like taking photographs?

Talking about interests (and likes/dislikes)
I'd like/prefer to join a running club.
I'm good at acting.
I wouldn't like to do it.
I'm (not) interested in photography.

Recommending and encouraging
It looks interesting.
I think you'd enjoy it.
You should do it with me.

6 Pronunciation silent letters

🎧 1.13 Some letters are not pronounced in English words. Listen to these words from the conversation in Exercise 3 and cross out the silent letters. Then listen again and repeat.

1 interested   4 evenings
2 should   5 something
3 friends   6 what

7 Work in pairs. Imagine you are interested in joining a club. Talk about each advert in Exercise 2 and each other's interests. Then choose one of the clubs to both join.

28 | TALK ABOUT ▶ AMBITIONS ▶ COMPETITION RULES ▶ SPORTS ▶ INTERESTS WRITE ▶ AN ADVERT

writing an advert and notice • writing skill checking your writing   Unit 2 Competitions

2e Advertising for members

Writing an advert or notice

1 Read the advice about how to write effective adverts and notices. Then look back at the three adverts on page 28. Answer the questions.

1. Which advert follows most of the advice?
2. How could you improve the other adverts?

> *How to* **WRITE EFFECTIVE ADVERTS AND NOTICES**
>
> - Start with a good headline. You could ask a question or solve a problem.
> - The advert should explain the benefits.
> - If possible, offer something for free or a prize.
> - Include any other important information (dates, times, location, etc.).
> - Photos, pictures or images always help.

2 Work in pairs. You are going to plan a new club. Discuss the questions.

1. What type of club is it (e.g. a chess club, a tennis club, a walking group)?
2. Who is the club for?
3. Are there any rules for members?
4. Is there a membership fee? How much is it?
5. How often will it meet?

3 Plan and write an advert for your new club.

4 Writing skill checking your writing

a It's always important to check your writing for mistakes, especially when a lot of people will read it (e.g. in an advert). Read the sentences (1–8) from different adverts and find the mistake in each. Match the sentences with the types of mistake (a–h). Then correct the mistakes.

1. Would you like to learn a musical instrument ? *c*
2. *Enter our exciteing competition!*
3. **Are you good at play tennis?**
4. *We meet at Tuesdays and Thursdays.*
5. **It's fun way to get fit.**
6. Join this club new!
7. Get healthy and play yoga.
8. **Call peter on 077 237 5980.**

a spelling   e grammar
b missing word   f word order
c punctuation   g capital letter
d preposition   h wrong word

b Read your advert in Exercise 3 again. Are there any mistakes? Correct them.

5 Display your adverts around the classroom. Walk around and read about each other's new clubs. Consider these questions.

- Which clubs would you like to join?
- Which adverts are effective? Why?

TALK ABOUT ▶ AMBITIONS ▶ COMPETITION RULES ▶ SPORTS ▶ INTERESTS   WRITE ▶ AN ADVERT   29

2f Cheese rolling

Cheese rolling has been a tradition in the town of Brockworth since the early 1800s.

Unit 2 Competitions

Before you watch

1 Work in groups. Look at the photo and discuss the questions. Use the words in the glossary to help you.

1 What are the people doing?
2 Why do you think they are doing this?
3 Do you think they enjoy doing this?

2 Complete the summary with words from the glossary.

Most towns have their own ¹t_____. However, one town in England has a very unusual one: the annual cheese-rolling ²r_____. At the start, the ³c_____ wait at the ⁴t_____ of Cooper's Hill. Then someone pushes a wheel of cheese down the ⁵s_____ slope. The competitors run after the cheese. The winner is the first person who gets to the ⁶b_____ of the hill. The ⁷p_____ is the wheel of cheese. The race can be dangerous, for the competitors and the ⁸s_____. One year a wheel of cheese went into the crowd and thirty people were ⁹i_____. Nowadays there are ¹⁰c_____ to protect the crowd.

While you watch

3 Watch the video and check your answers from Exercise 2.

4 Watch the video again. Put these people and events in the order you see them.

a Doctors helping an injured person.
b People clapping to encourage the competitors.
c Someone carrying a British flag.
d A Japanese man with blond hair talking.
e Craig Brown holding up the cheese.
f The view from the top of Cooper's Hill.

5 Watch the video again. Are these sentences true (T) or false (F)?

1 The race is more than 200 years old.
2 The cheese travels at more than forty miles an hour.
3 Competitors have to catch the cheese before it reaches the bottom of the hill.
4 Craig Brown works in a pub.
5 There is no protection for spectators.
6 The race is dangerous for competitors when the weather is cold.
7 You can only compete once a day.

After you watch

6 Roleplay an interview with Craig Brown

Work in pairs.

Student A: You are a journalist for *National Geographic*. Use the ideas below to prepare questions to ask Craig Brown.

Student B: You are Craig Brown. Look at the ideas below. Think about what you are going to say to the journalist.

- age
- interests
- why you take part in the race
- how many times you have taken part
- if you have ever been injured

Act out the interview. Then change roles and repeat the interview.

7 At the end of the video, the narrator says: 'It's more than just cheese that makes people want to win.' What does she mean?

8 Work in pairs. Discuss these questions.

1 What kind of people do you think take part in the race?
2 Would you like to take part in the race? Why? / Why not?
3 Would you go to watch the race? Why? / Why not?
4 Do you have any unusual traditional races in your country? What are they and why are they popular?

---

accident (n) /ˈæksɪdənt/ an event where a person is hurt unintentionally
balance (n) /ˈbæləns/ a position in which your body stays in an upright position
bottom (n) /ˈbɒtəm/ the lowest part of a thing or place
competitor (n) /kəmˈpetɪtə/ a person who takes part in a sporting event
crash barrier (n) /ˈkræʃ bæriə/ an obstacle that stops people being hurt
crazy (adj) /ˈkreɪzi/ mad
crowd (n) /kraʊd/ a large group of people
fail (v) /feɪl/ be unsuccessful
ground (n) /graʊnd/ what is under your feet when you are outside
injured (adj) /ˈɪndʒəd/ hurt
protect (v) /prəˈtekt/ keep someone or something safe
prize (n) /praɪz/ something given to a person who is successful in a competition
race (n) /reɪs/ an event to see who can go the fastest
slope (n) /sləʊp/ the side of a mountain or hill
spectator (n) /spekˈteɪtə/ a person who watches a sporting event
steep (adj) /stiːp/ going up or down at a sharp angle
top (n) /tɒp/ the highest part of a thing or place
traditions (n pl) /trəˈdɪʃənz/ things that people have done for a long time
wheel (of cheese) (n) /wiːl/ a round object

UNIT 2 REVIEW

Grammar

1 Put the words in order to make sentences and questions.

1 than / losing / winning / is / fun / more
2 I'm / new / good / learning / at / games
3 learning / languages? / you / do / like
4 like / a musical instrument? / learn / would / to / you
5 you / like / who / look / do / in your family?

2 Complete the description of a competition with these verbs.

| can | don't have to | have to | mustn't |

There's a competition in Alaska where you ¹_____ arrive without facial hair! That's because it's the world's moustache and beard competition. The judges ²_____ choose the winners from the beards and moustaches of over 300 contestants from all over the world. But you ³_____ have the longest moustache or biggest beard because there are many different categories. For example, you ⁴_____ win the prize for 'Best English moustache' and 'Best natural moustache'.

3 Work in pairs. Which sport on TV do you like watching most? Explain the rules to your partner.

I CAN
talk about likes, dislikes and ambitions
describe the rules of a competition or sport using modal verbs

Vocabulary

4 Choose the correct options.

1 My favourite football team *scored / beat* another goal!
2 In ice-skating, the *judges / spectators* gives points to the competitors.
3 My grandmother won a *trophy / prize* of a thousand dollars in a competition.
4 My team always loses. We never *win / beat* any matches.
5 Hit the tennis ball with your *racquet / net*!
6 During the fight, the two boxers must not leave the *court / ring*.
7 Wear these *gloves / goggles* over your eyes when you ski.
8 The *track / pitch* is 100 metres long. The fastest runners can complete it in less than ten seconds.

5 Work in pairs. Which sports person would you like to meet one day? Why do you admire this person?

I CAN
talk about different kinds of sports
talk about future ambitions

Real life

6 Complete the conversation. Write one word in each gap.

A: Are you interested ¹_____ painting? There's a new evening course at my college.
B: I'm afraid I'm not very good ²_____ art.
A: I'm not either but I'd like ³_____ learn. Go ⁴_____. You should do it with me.
B: Sorry.
A: ⁵_____ you like taking photos? There's also a course for that.
B: Actually, it looks interesting.

7 Complete these sentences with your own interests.

1 I'm good at …
2 I wouldn't like to …
3 I'm also interested in …
4 I think I'd enjoy learning …

I CAN
talk about interests
recommend and encourage people to do things

Speaking

8 Work in pairs. Take turns to tell each other about your interests in Exercise 7. Then recommend one of your interests to your partner and encourage them to do it in the future.

Unit 3 Transport

Taking the train
Photo by Amy Helene Johansson

FEATURES

34 Transport in the future

Is electricity the fuel of the future?

36 Animal transport

Where animals are still better for transporting

38 The last days of the rickshaw

How much longer can the rickshaw survive?

42 Indian railways

A video about one of the world's largest transport networks

1 Look at the photo. Where is the woman? Why do you think she is travelling like this?

2 🔊 **1.14** Listen to someone talking about the photo. Why isn't the woman inside the train?

3 Work in pairs. Which of these modes of transport would you use for the activities (1–10)? Explain your reasons why.

by bicycle	by bus	in my car	on a ferry	on foot
by lorry	on a motorbike	on a plane	on a ship
in a taxi	by train

1 visit relatives
2 move house and furniture
3 get to the airport
4 see the countryside for pleasure
5 cross a river
6 get to the railway station
7 go out in the evening to a party or restaurant
8 take children to school
9 cross the sea
10 go shopping

4 What is your favourite way to travel? Why? Tell your partner.

TALK ABOUT ▸ TRANSPORT IN THE CITY ▸ ATTITUDES TO ANIMALS ▸ ARGUMENTS FOR AND AGAINST ▸ GOING ON A JOURNEY
WRITE ▸ NOTES AND MESSAGES

reading daily travel and commuting • vocabulary transport (1): nouns • listening electric cars •
grammar comparatives and superlatives • pronunciation *than* • speaking and writing transport in the city

3a Transport in the future

Reading

1 Do you travel and use transport every day? How do you commute to work? Are there many travel problems early in the morning?

2 Read the texts in the diagram below about transport in the future. What kind of transport does it describe? How is it different from transport today?

3 Read the texts again. Answer the questions.

Who …
1 commutes to work every morning?
2 knows in advance when there is a problem on the road?
3 don't use electric cars?
4 can't drive a long distance without recharging?
5 always needs to plug in the car before bedtime?
6 has a car which stops you from driving too quickly?
7 doesn't need to commute to his work.
8 works in an office?

Vocabulary transport (1): nouns

4 Find the words in the texts in Exercise 2 for these definitions.
1 machines with engine for transporting people, e.g. car or bus v_____
2 people who travel to work every day c_____
3 period in a day when lots of people travel to and from work r_____ h_____
4 long line of vehicles on the road t_____ j_____
5 construction or maintenance on part of a road r_____ w_____
6 place to fill your car with petrol p_____ s_____
7 the maximum speed you can legally drive s_____ l_____
8 people on foot in a town or city p_____

> ▶ WORDBUILDING compound nouns
> You can join two nouns to make a new noun:
> *rush* + *hour* = *rush hour*, *traffic* + *jam* = *traffic jam*,
> *speed* + *limit* = *speed limit*
>
> For further information and practice, see Workbook page 119.

5 Do you think the predictions in the texts are true? Are any of the predictions true now? Would you prefer an electric car to a petrol one? Why? / Why not?

T R A N S P O R T   I N   T H E   F U T U R E

Meet the Watts. They are a three-car family in the near future which uses electric vehicles.

Bob is similar to most commuters. He charges his car at home overnight so it's ready for the morning rush hour. If he needs more electricity, there's a 'charging station' in the office car park.

Sonia's car travels about 30 kilometres on a full battery so it's good for short trips such as going to the shops or visiting friends nearby. The car also has its own computer which tells her if there are traffic jams or road works on the road ahead.

Justin works from home but enjoys going on a long journey in his sports car at the weekend. Instead of going to a petrol station for petrol, he can change his battery on the motorway or plug into a high-voltage charger. Another device in the car's engine stops him from going over the speed limit.

Their neighbours still use a car with a petrol engine but most cars have electric engines. The roads are quieter and there is less pollution so life is also better for pedestrians and cyclists!

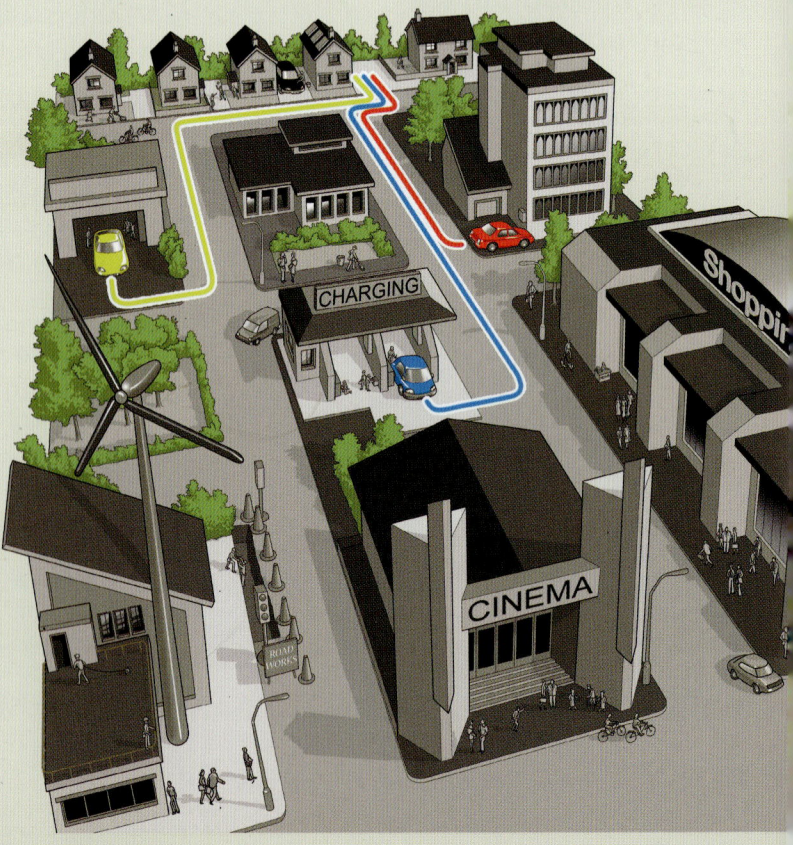

Listening

6 🔊 **1.15** Listen to two people discussing electric cars. What reasons do they give for and against this kind of transport?

7 🔊 **1.15** Listen again. Choose the correct options.
1. Electric cars are much *cleaner / louder* than petrol cars.
2. Electric cars have the *more efficient / most efficient* type of engine.
3. Electric cars are much *cheaper / more expensive* than petrol cars.
4. Eight o'clock in the morning is the *best / worst* time of the day for commuting.
5. The town needs *better / faster* public transport.

Grammar comparatives and superlatives

8 Look at the comparative and superlative adjectives in Exercise 7. Answer the questions.
1. What letters do you add to regular short adjectives to form comparative and superlative adjectives? How do you form the comparative and superlative forms with longer adjectives?
2. Which are examples of irregular comparative and superlative adjectives?
3. Which word usually comes after a comparative adjective? Which word usually comes before a superlative adjective?
4. What word adds emphasis to a comparative adjective?

▶ **COMPARATIVES and SUPERLATIVES**

Regular adjectives

clean	clean**er**	clean**est**
big	big**ger**	big**gest**
happy	happ**ier**	happ**iest**
expensive	**more** expensive	**most** expensive

Irregular adjectives

| good | better | best |
| bad | worse | worst |

For further information and practice, see page 86.

9 Pronunciation *than*

🔊 **1.16** Listen to the pronunciation of *than* in sentences 1 and 3 in Exercise 7. Notice how we say /ðən/ not /ðæn/. Practise saying the two sentences.

10 A local town council asked residents for their views on transport. Look at the grammar box in Exercise 8. Then complete this extract from the report with the comparative or superlative form of the adjectives.

◀◀◀ **REPORT BACK**

Your views on transport

For commuting and daytime travel, the ¹ _____ (popular) form of public transport is the bus. ² _____ (large) number of people in the survey use buses every day to get to work or school. However, taking the bus isn't ³ _____ (fast) form of transport. Everyone said that parking in the town centre is still the ⁴ _____ (big) problem so they don't often drive their car. The situation is much ⁵ _____ (good) in the evenings than during the day. As a result, taxis are ⁶ _____ (popular) than private cars. However, taxis are the ⁷ _____ (expensive) form of transport so many people want buses to run ⁸ _____ (late) in the evenings.

Speaking and writing

11 Look at the questionnaire for the survey in Exercise 10. Use these questions to interview other students about transport where they live. Make a note of their answers.

QUESTIONNAIRE ▶▶▶

Resident views on transport

- How do you usually commute to and from work/college? Why?
- How often do you use public transport?
- What types of public transport do you use?
- How do you rate car parking in the town?
  Excellent ___ Good ___ Poor ___
- How often do you take taxis?
- Do you have any suggestions to improve travel and transport in the town?

12 Work in pairs. Compare your notes and answers from the questionnaire. Then write a short report, similar to the one in Exercise 10.

TALK ABOUT ▶ TRANSPORT IN THE CITY ▶ ATTITUDES TO ANIMALS ▶ ARGUMENTS FOR AND AGAINST ▶ GOING ON A JOURNEY
WRITE ▶ NOTES AND MESSAGES

listening using animals for transporting • grammar as ... as • pronunciation sentence stress • reading dog sledging • speaking attitudes to animals

3b Animal transport

Listening

1 Look at the photos. What is each animal transporting? Do people use animals for transporting in your country?

2 🔊 1.17 Listen to an extract from two documentaries. What kind of modern transport does the speaker compare each animal to?

3 🔊 1.17 Listen again. Answer the questions.

Documentary 1
1 What special event is happening?
2 What jobs did the Asian elephant do in the past?
3 What kind of people do they transport nowadays?

Documentary 2
4 Lester Courtney is a 'logger'. What do loggers do?
5 Why does Lester prefer to use horses?

Grammar as ... as

4 Look at the sentence from the documentary. Answer the questions (1–2).

Elephants are as heavy as cars but they aren't as fast – and most people also think elephants aren't as comfortable as cars.

1 Are elephants and cars the same weight?
2 Do they travel at the same speed?

> ▶ AS ... AS
>
> Use *as* + adjective + *as* to compare something and say they are the same or equal.
> Use *not as* + adjective + *as* to compare two things and say they are different or not equal.
>
> For further information and practice, see page 87.

5 Look at the grammar box. Then complete the second sentence so that it has the same meaning as the first sentence.

1 Most people think cars are more comfortable than elephants.
  Most people think elephants aren't as _____ .
2 Elephants have the same importance now as they did in the past.
  Elephants are _____ as ever.
3 Lester believes horses are better than modern machines.
  Lester doesn't believe modern machines are as _____ horses.
4 Lorries and trucks are stronger than horses.
  Horses _____ as _____ as lorries and trucks.
5 Trucks are noisier than horses.
  Horses _____ as trucks.

6 Pronunciation sentence stress

🔊 1.18 Listen to these sentences. Notice the stressed words in each sentence. Then listen again and repeat.

1 **Lorries** are **heavier** than **horses**.
2 **Elephants** are as **heavy** as **trucks**.
3 They **aren't** as **fast** as **cars**.
4 **Horses** are the **fastest**.

36

Unit 3 Transport

7 Work in pairs. Make sentences using the adjective to compare these animals. Use comparative and superlative adjectives and (not) as + adjective + as.

1 strong: lion, mouse, horse
2 fast: snail, cheetah, elephant
3 comfortable: car, camel, plane
4 heavy: hippopotamus, blue whale, elephant
5 dangerous: shark, alligator, snake

8 Read out your sentences from Exercise 7, stressing the most important words.

Reading

9 Complete the article on the right with these words.

| as | best | fast | longest | more | much |
| than | the | | | | |

10 Read the article again. Then discuss the questions.

1 What are the advantages and disadvantages of the huskies in Alaska?
2 Why do you think some people say the *Iditarod* is cruel for the dogs?
3 What sports do you have in your country with animals? Do people think they are cruel for the animals?

Speaking

11 Work in groups. Read and discuss these comments from different people about using animals for transport and sport. What's your opinion? Do you agree or disagree?

It's more natural and cleaner to use animals for work and transportation than engines. We should use them more.

It's wrong to use animals like horses and dogs in sports.

Modern transport is much better. There's no reason to use animals.

We still need animals for certain kinds of work.

I think it's better because …

I don't think it's as bad as …

In my opinion, it's worse because …

I agree …

THE BEST WAY TO TRAVEL

In the most northern state of the USA you'll see every type of modern transport. But during the winter months the state of Alaska becomes one of [1] _____ coldest parts of the world. Temperatures fall as low [2] _____ – 50 °C. Car engines can freeze and even if your car starts, the snow and ice on the road can make travel impossible. When the weather is like this, the [3] _____ way to travel is with a team of huskies pulling you. That's according to people like Geoff Roland who prefer travelling by dog sledge. 'Huskies might not be as [4] _____ as a modern snowmobile but they are better for the environment. The journey is also much quieter [5] _____ by snowmobile. It's what makes travel through the wilderness so enjoyable.'

When Geoff was younger he took part in the *Iditarod*. The word *Iditarod* originally comes from an old native American word meaning 'a faraway place' but nowadays it's the name of the world's [6] _____ dog sledge race which takes place in Alaska each spring. The 1,600 kilometre route follows the old roads which the original Indians once used. As years passed, aeroplanes and snowmobiles became [7] _____ common and people started to forget about the old trails. But in 1973 a group of people started the race in order to maintain Alaska's history and its traditional form of transport. Some people criticise the *Iditarod* because they think it's cruel for the dogs but Geoff disagrees: 'Huskies are natural racers. I think they're [8] _____ happier when they're in front of the sledge.'

cruel (adj) /kruːəl/ causing pain to people or animals

TALK ABOUT ▸ TRANSPORT IN THE CITY ▸ ATTITUDES TO ANIMALS ▸ ARGUMENTS FOR AND AGAINST ▸ GOING ON A JOURNEY
WRITE ▸ NOTES AND MESSAGES

reading traditional transport • vocabulary transport (2): verbs • critical thinking reading between the lines • speaking arguments for and against

3c Last days of the rickshaw

Reading

1 Look at the photo of the rickshaw in the article on page 39. Why do you think people choose this kind of transport? Are there any advantages with a rickshaw compared with other types of transport?

2 Read the first paragraph of the article. Which of these words and expressions describe Kolkata?

| busy   highly-populated   noisy   polluted   quiet |
| safe for pedestrians |

3 Read the second and third paragraph of the article. Which of these arguments in favour of rickshaws does the article mention?

Rickshaws are useful because …

1 they are better in traffic jams.
2 they can travel down small streets.
3 they don't produce pollution.
4 they are good for shopping.
5 they are cheaper than other public transport.
6 they always travel during the monsoons.

4 Read the last paragraph. Why don't local officials and politicians ban rickshaws? Choose the correct reason (1–3).

1 There isn't much other employment for the drivers.
2 The tourists want them.
3 The drivers don't want to go back to the countryside.

Vocabulary transport (2): verbs

5 Find these verbs in the article Underline them and the noun which follows.

| catch   take   pick up   miss   drop off |
| get on / off   go by |

Example:
catch a train

6 Replace the verbs in bold in the sentences with a verb of similar meaning from Exercise 5.

1 Do you want me to **collect** the children from school?
   pick up
2 We need to **leave** the train at the next station.
3 I was late and I nearly didn't **get** my flight.
4 You'd better leave now. You don't want to **not catch** your flight.
5 I should **travel by** a taxi. It's much quicker.
6 Ask the driver to **leave** the children outside their school.

Critical thinking reading between the lines

7 Using the information in the article, which of these statements do you think people in Kolkata often say about the rickshaws in their city?

1 'Rickshaw drivers always blow their horns so loudly.'
2 'They represent our city!'
3 'They should not be on the roads!'
4 'They are very useful for day-to-day life.'
5 'You can never find a rickshaw when you need one.'
6 'Rickshaws are cruel.'

Speaking

8 Work in groups. Make a list of the reasons for and against keeping rickshaws in Kolkata. Use the information in the article and add your own ideas.

Example:
Rickshaws don't have engines so they are quiet and don't pollute the air.

9 You are going to have a debate to decide if Kolkata should ban rickshaws. Each person in the group has a role. Choose one of the roles below and think about if your person wants to ban rickshaws or to keep them in Kolkata. Choose arguments for or against from your list in Exercise 8 and plan your arguments for the debate. When you are all ready, discuss the topic and try to find a solution.

- a rickshaw driver in Kolkata
- a local politician who wants to modernise Kolkata
- a foreign tourist visiting the city
- a local person who uses rickshaws for shopping and sending the children to school
- a taxi driver in the city

In my opinion we should ban rickshaws because …

I think rickshaws are good for the city because …

Unit 3 Transport

Last days of the rickshaw

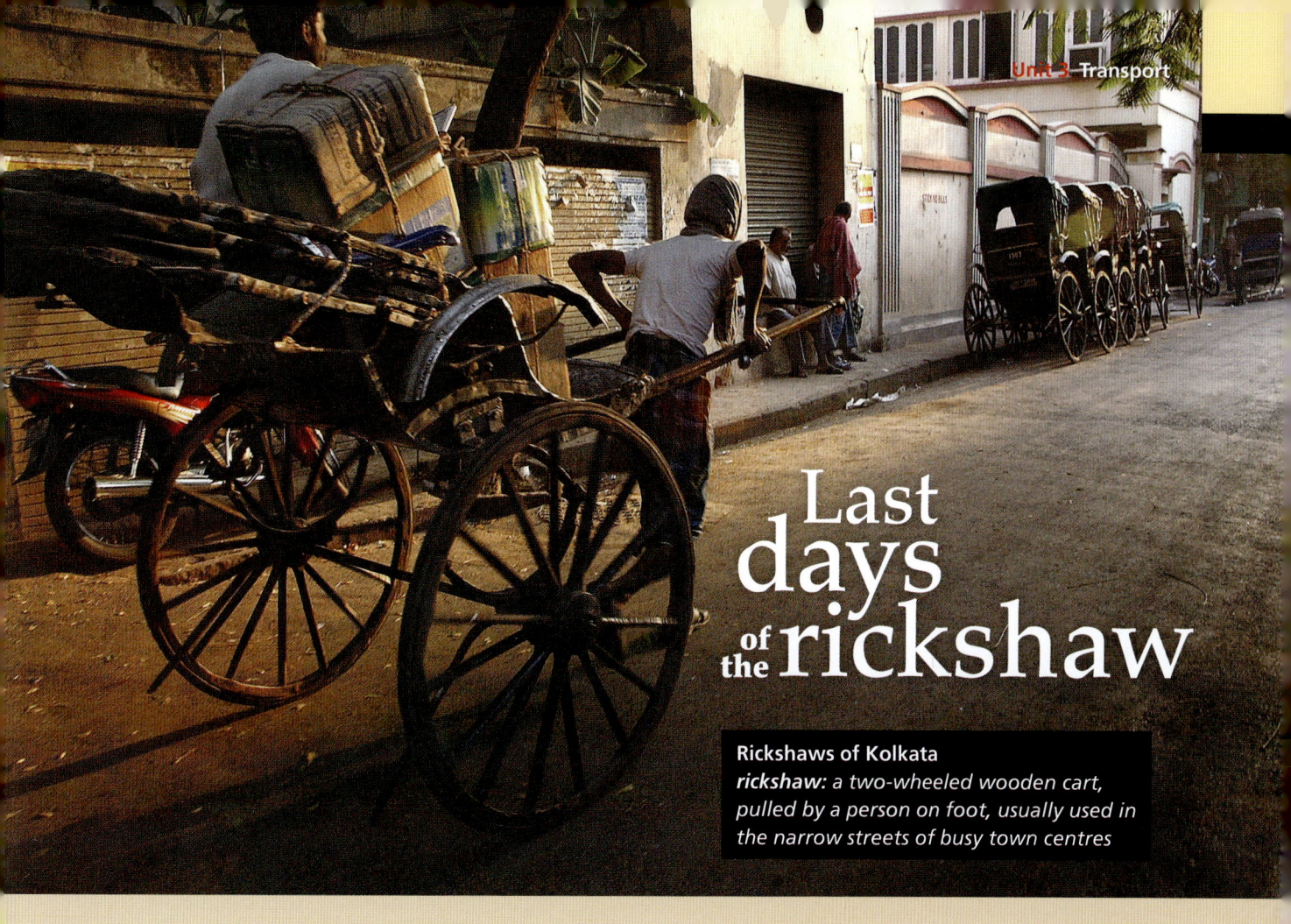

Rickshaws of Kolkata
rickshaw: a two-wheeled wooden cart, pulled by a person on foot, usually used in the narrow streets of busy town centres

Kolkata (previously known as Calcutta) is the famous capital of West Bengal in India and the home of nearly 15 million people. The traffic jams and engine fumes begin early in the morning with long lines of private cars, public buses, taxis, three-wheeled scooters and pedicabs. There aren't many alternatives. You can catch a train through the city or take the underground but sooner or later you have to go on foot and walking in Kolkata is a dangerous activity. As the drivers race towards pedestrians, they blow their horns. The sound never stops from morning to night.

So when I crossed a small road on my first day in the city, I was surprised because I heard a bell – not a horn. It was a tiny man pulling a rickshaw. He stopped and picked up two children from the front door of their house and then, with great strength, pulled them to school. For many people, the rickshaw is a symbol of Kolkata and they have many advantages. When the traffic is bad, rickshaws find a way through the traffic. If you miss your bus and there aren't any taxis, you can always find a rickshaw in Kolkata. Rickshaws are also very popular with local shoppers. The driver takes you from your house to the market and waits for you. Then he loads all your purchases, drops you off outside your home and helps you unload. No other type of public transport offers this kind of service.

You also see lots more people getting on and off rickshaws during the monsoon season. That's the period from June to September when Kolkata gets heavy rainfall. Sometimes it rains for 48 hours without a break. In the older parts of the city, the roads flood. The water can rise as high as people's waists in the worst part. When it's this bad, anything with an engine is useless. But the rickshaw drivers never stop working, even with water all around them.

But not everyone thinks rickshaws are a good thing. Some local officials and politicians want to ban rickshaws on 'humanitarian grounds'. They believe it is wrong for one man to pull another person when there is modern transport in the city. However, there is a problem with this plan. Many of the rickshaw drivers come from the countryside with no job and no qualifications. The only job they can find in Kolkata is pulling a rickshaw. If the city bans rickshaws, these men won't have a job or income. So for the moment, the people of Kolkata still go by rickshaw.

fumes (n) /fjuːmz/ smoke and gases from an engine
scooter (n) /ˈskuːtə(r)/ a small motorbike
pedicab (n) /ˈpedekæb/ a type of taxi with no engine. The driver cycles.
monsoon (n) /ˌmɒnˈsuːn/ period from June to September with lots of rain
flood (v) /flʌd/ when water covers an area (e.g. a floor, road, city)
ban (v) /bæn/ to stop or make illegal

TALK ABOUT ▶ TRANSPORT IN THE CITY ▶ ATTITUDES TO ANIMALS ▶ ARGUMENTS FOR AND AGAINST ▶ GOING ON A JOURNEY
WRITE ▶ NOTES AND MESSAGES

vocabulary and listening taking transport • real life going on a journey • pronunciation intonation

3d Getting around town

Vocabulary and listening
taking transport

1 Look at these pairs of words. Match them with the correct definition (a or b).
   1 stop / rank
     a where you can get a taxi
     b where you can get a bus
   2 fare / price
     a the money you pay for a journey by bus, train or taxi
     b the amount of money something costs
   3 change / receipt
     a the money you receive when you pay more than the price because you don't have the correct amount
     b the piece of paper you receive to show you paid for something
   4 gate / platform
     a where you get on a train
     b where you get on a plane
   5 book / check in
     a when you buy a ticket in advance
     b when you arrive at the airport and leave your bags

2 🔊 1.19 Shelley and Javier are going to the airport and they take different transport. Listen to their conversations and answer the questions.
   1 At the taxi rank: Where does Javier want to go?
   2 In the taxi: How much is the fare? Does Javier want a receipt?
   3 At the bus stop: Where does Shelley want to go? What type of ticket does she buy?
   4 At the train station: How much is the ticket? Which platform does the train leave from?
   5 At the airport: Where did Shelley book her plane ticket? Does she check in any bags?

Real life going on a journey

3 🔊 1.19 Look at the expressions for going on a journey. Then listen to the conversations again. Tick the sentences you hear.

▶ GOING ON A JOURNEY

In a taxi
I'd like to go to the station, please.
You can drop me off here.
How much is that?
Do you have change?
Do you want a receipt?

On a bus
Do you stop at the airport?
A single or return ticket?
Please stop at the next one.
That's two pounds.

At the train station
A return ticket to the airport, please.
First or second class?
Can I pay by credit card?
Which platform is it?

At the airport
Can I see your passport?
How many bags are you checking in?
I only have this carry on.
Window or aisle?
Can I have a seat next to my friend?

4 **Pronunciation** intonation

🔊 1.20 People often ask questions with incomplete sentences, e.g. *Single or return?* instead of *Do you want a single or return ticket?* Listen to these questions. Mark the intonation ↗ or ↘ down on the words. Then listen again and repeat.
   1 Single or return?
   2 Window or aisle?
   3 Credit card or cash?
   4 Bus or train?
   5 North or south?
   6 First or second?

5 Work in pairs. Student A is going to the airport. In each situation, Student B is the driver or the person at the ticket office or check-in desk. Practise the conversations, using the expressions for going on a journey to help you.

| In the taxi. A has a $50 note. The fare is $23.50. | On the bus. | At the train station. | At the airport. You have two bags. |

6 Change roles and repeat the four conversations in Exercise 5.

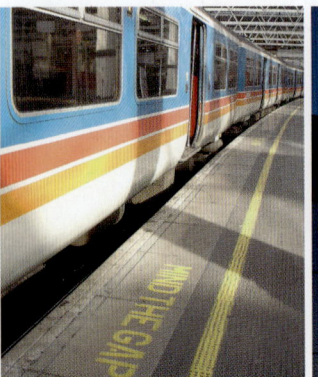

TALK ABOUT ▶ TRANSPORT IN THE CITY ▶ ATTITUDES TO ANIMALS ▶ ARGUMENTS FOR AND AGAINST ▶ GOING ON A JOURNEY
WRITE ▶ NOTES AND MESSAGES

writing **notes and messages** • writing skill **writing in note form**   Unit 3 Transport

3e Quick communication

Writing notes and messages

1 Read these notes and messages (1–8). Match them with the reasons for writing (a–e).

a thanking
b apologising
c giving travel information
d suggesting a time and place
e giving a message from someone else

2 Writing skill writing in note form

a People often miss out words in notes and messages. This is called elision. Find examples of these kinds of words missing in the notes and messages in Exercise 1.

- articles
- pronouns (e.g. *I, me*)
- auxiliary verbs
- polite forms (e.g. *Would you like to …? Can we …?*)

Example:
(Can we) Meet outside (the) airport at 2? (Is that) OK?

b Rewrite these transcripts from a telephone voicemail as shorter messages.

1 'I'm sorry but I'm stuck in a traffic jam. I'll see you in half an hour.'
   Sorry. Stuck in traffic. See you in 30 mins.
2 'Thank you for booking the train tickets. I'll pay you when we meet at the station.'
3 'Take the underground to Oxford Street and the Moon café is at the end of platform one.'
4 'Peter wants to come with us in the taxi. Can you call him and tell him where to meet us?'
5 'My flight is an hour late. Meet me at the arrivals terminal at five o'clock.'

3 Work in pairs. Write a short note or message for each situation.

1 You have to work late. Write a short text message to your friend. Say you will arrive at the bus station an hour later.
2 You are meeting tonight in the city centre. Suggest your friend takes a taxi from the taxi rank outside the train station.
3 You cannot travel with your friend on the underground to the airport. Explain you will travel by bus and meet him/her at the check-in desk.

4 Write a short message to your partner. Then, exchange messages. Can you understand your partner's message? Write a reply if necessary!

1 Meet outside airport at 2? OK?

2 Sorry. Bus late. Will be 15 minutes late.

3 Javier called. Call him back. 0770 657 655.

4 Train leaves platform 6.

5 Thanks for getting tickets. Here's the money.

6 Plane at gate 6. Boarding now.

7 Am in taxi. See you outside museum in 5?

8 Afraid I missed meeting. My apologies.

TALK ABOUT ▶ TRANSPORT IN THE CITY ▶ ATTITUDES TO ANIMALS ▶ ARGUMENTS FOR AND AGAINST ▶ GOING ON A JOURNEY
WRITE ▶ NOTES AND MESSAGES

41

3f Indian railways

In this country, the best way to travel is by train.

Unit 3 Transport

Before you watch

1 Work in groups. Look at the photo and the caption. Discuss the questions.

1. How important are trains in your country?
2. Do many people travel by train? Why? / Why not?

2 Work in pairs. Think about Indian railways and choose the option you think is correct.

1. Every day approximately *two hundred thousand / two million* passengers pass through Mumbai train station.
2. There are over *two billion / one billion* people in India.
3. The British built the railways in India in the *eighteenth / nineteenth* century.
4. There are over *38,000 / 3,800* miles of railway track in India.
5. The Grand Trunk Express has travelled through India since *1939 / 1929*.
6. India's railways carry *four billion / four million* passengers every year.
7. Indian Railways employs *one hundred thousand / one and half million* staff.

While you watch

3 Watch the video and check your answers from Exercise 2.

4 Watch the video again and answer the questions.

1. When did the first steam train run in India?
2. Is it easy for everybody in India to get to a railway station?
3. What is the key man's job?
4. Who tries to get travellers' attention and money at Indian railway stations?
5. What do passengers do on the train?

5 Complete the sentences with words from the glossary.

1. At the Victoria Terminus, Mumbai, it always seems to be _____ .
2. Many of the trains have _____ names.
3. India's railways are the world's largest _____ .
4. A huge _____ keeps this enormous system running.

After you watch

6 **Roleplay** a conversation between passengers

Work in pairs.

Student A: You are from the city. Use the questions below to make notes about yourself and your journey.

Student B: You are from a small village, a day's walk from the station. Use the questions below to make notes about yourself and your journey.

- What's your name?
- How old are you?
- Who do you live with?
- What's your job?
- What's your daily routine like?
- What's the best moment of your day? And what's the worst?

Act out the conversation. Describe your journey to the station today, your life at home and give your reason for travelling.

7 At the end of the video, the narrator says: 'The Indian railways are their own adventure.' What does she mean?

8 Work in pairs. Discuss these questions.

1. In what way are trains in your country similar to, or different from, trains in India?
2. Is travelling by train a good way to see a country? Why? / Why not?

---

employer (n) /ɪmˈplɔɪə/ a person or organisation that gives work to other people
impressive (adj) /ɪmˈpresɪv/ something that causes admiration
passenger (n) /ˈpæsɪndʒə/ a person who travels in a vehicle
rural (adj) /ˈrʊrəl/ of the countryside
rush hour (n) /ˈrʌʃ aʊə/ the busiest time of day, when a lot of people are going to or from work
staff (n) /stɑːf/ people who work for an organisation
track (n) /træk/ metal rails that a train runs on
villager (n) /ˈvɪlɪdʒə/ a person who lives in a very small town, often in the countryside
workforce (n) /ˈwɜːkfɔːs/ people who work for an organisation

UNIT 3 REVIEW

Grammar

1 Complete the article with the correct form of the adjectives.

The city of Guangzhou wins transport prize

China has the ¹ _____ (large) population in the world and its capital city, Beijing, has some of ² _____ (bad) traffic problems. A few decades ago, China's streets weren't as ³ _____ (polluted) as they are now because most people rode bicycles. But in modern China, cars are selling ⁴ _____ (fast) than in the USA.

However, one city in China recently received a prize for its transportation system from the Institute for Transportation and Development Policy (ITDP). The ITDP works with cities to make city life ⁵ _____ (good). This year it gave the city of Guangzhou a prize because it has one of the ⁶ _____ (good) public transport systems, not only in China, but worldwide. The system transports 800,000 people a day and runs on time. And bicycles are still as ⁷ _____ (popular) as ever because of the extensive network of bicycle paths. It all means the air in Guangzhou is much ⁸ _____ (clean) than in other cities.

2 Work in pairs. Compare your country to its nearest neighbours. Make five sentences using comparatives, superlatives or *as ... as* about these things:

- size (larger / smaller / as big as)
- population
- age
- other?

I CAN

compare differences between two or more things

talk about the similarities between things

Vocabulary

3 Complete the sentences with transport words.

1 I work from home so I don't have to c_____ to and from work every day.
2 You can avoid the r_____ hour if you leave home earlier in the morning and leave work earlier in the afternoon.
3 There's always a bad traffic j_____ on the roads through the centre of the city. You sit in your car and never move.
4 The speed l_____ on a motorway in the UK is 70 miles per hour.
5 Look out! There's a p_____ crossing the road.
6 You can either cross the river by driving south for 30 minutes to the bridge or wait for the f_____ to arrive.

4 Complete the sentences with a preposition.

1 Can you pick _____ my shopping on the way home?
2 Please drop me _____ outside the café on the corner.
3 We both fell asleep on the train and so we didn't get _____ at our station!
4 I think I'll go _____ foot today and save some money.
5 Did you come _____ your car or _____ your motorbike?

I CAN

talk about transport and travel in the city

Real life

5 Number the lines of a conversation in the correct order (1–8).

<u>1</u> Hi. I'd like a ticket to Moscow, please.
___ At ten thirty. Here's your ticket.
___ Single or return?
___ OK. A single ticket is 61 euros. Is that OK?
___ Thanks. Which platform does it go from?
___ Yes, that's fine. What time is the next one?
<u>8</u> Platform eight.
___ Single, please.

6 Work in pairs. Roleplay this situation.

Student A: You are a tourist in Kolkata, India. Ask a rickshaw driver to take you to your hotel.

Student B: You are rickshaw driver. Talk to the tourist and discuss your price.

I CAN

ask for and buy a ticket

go on a journey using different types of transport

Speaking

7 Work in pairs. What is your favourite way to travel (e.g. by plane, train, bus)? What is your least favourite way to travel? Why?

44

Unit 4 Adventure

The Rumble Room in Rumbling Falls Cave, Tennessee
Photo by Stephen Alvarez

FEATURES

46 Adventurers of the year
Profiles or some of the world's top adventurers

48 The survivors
What personal qualities do survivors need?

50 The right decision?
The real-life story of two climbers and how tough decisions saved their lives

54 Alaskan ice climbing
A video about adventure in the snow and ice of Alaska

1 Look at the photo. Where are the people? Do you think it looks exciting or dangerous?

2 🔊 **1.21** Listen to a caver whose favourite cave is the Rumbling Falls. Answer the questions.

1 Why do colleagues at work think Vic is 'a bit crazy'?
2 Why do cavers need to be physically fit?
3 What does Vic say 'The Rumble Room' is like?

3 Match these words from the caver's description (1–3) with the definitions (a–c).

1 risk   2 challenge   3 achievement

a something which is dangerous
b something after a lot of hard work and effort (e.g. passing an examination)
c something new and very difficult to do

4 Work in groups. Discuss the questions.

1 Do you think you are a person who takes risks or are you usually very careful?
2 What is your biggest achievement in life so far?
3 What is your biggest challenge in the future?
4 Is there any kind of adventurous or risky activity you would like to try in the future?

TALK ABOUT ▸ YOUR PAST ▸ EVENTS YOU REMEMBER ▸ THE MAIN EVENTS ▸ A HAPPY ENDING   WRITE ▸ A TRUE STORY

4a Adventurers of the year

Reading

1 Read the article. Complete the diagram with the phrases (1–6).

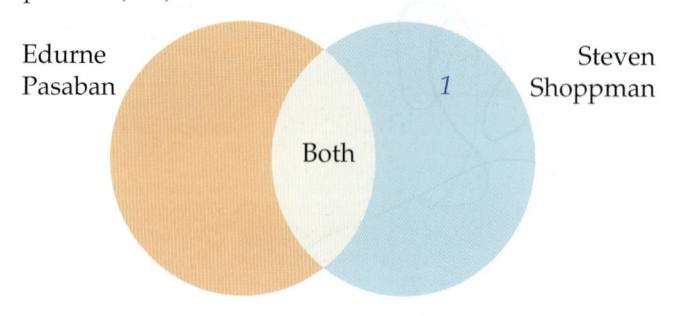

Edurne Pasaban — Both — Steven Shoppman

1

1 born in the USA
2 travelled round the world
3 qualified in engineering
4 is famous
5 finished the adventure
6 loves adventure

2 Read the article again. Answer the questions.
 1 What was Edurne's biggest challenge?
 2 Why is she famous?
 3 What was Steven and Stephen's ambition?
 4 What was their biggest risk?

Grammar past simple

3 Underline all the verbs in the past tense in *The mountaineer* section of the article. Answer the questions.
 1 What do you add to regular verbs in the past simple?
 2 What auxiliary verb do you use to make the verb negative?

ADVENTURERS of the YEAR

EVERY YEAR, READERS OF NATIONAL GEOGRAPHIC MAGAZINE VOTE FOR THEIR ADVENTURERS OF THE YEAR. HERE ARE TWO OF THEM.

THE MOUNTAINEER

As a child, Edurne Pasaban lived in the mountainous Basque region of Spain and she climbed her first mountain when she was fourteen. At university, she studied engineering but she didn't want a nine-to-five job. In May 2010 she finished her biggest challenge, to climb the world's fourteen tallest mountains. Nowadays she is famous for her many climbing achievements, However, she didn't climb in order to become famous. She says, 'For me, adventure is a way of life.'

THE ROAD TRIPPERS

Steven Shoppman and Stephen Bouey were old friends who grew up together in Denver. But they knew each other a lot better after their adventure. They both had an ambition to go on a road trip round the world. From 2007 to 2010, they drove through 69 different countries during their 122,000-kilometre journey and had many adventures. They took a big risk when they went across a minefield (see photo). They also got help from lots of people and they found that the world wasn't as dangerous as they thought!

road trip (n) /ˈrəʊdtrɪp/
a long journey by road

46

Unit 4 **Adventure**

4 Pronunciation /d/, /t/ or /ɪd/

1.22 Listen to the *-ed* ending of these regular verbs. Write /d/, /t/ or /ɪd/. Then listen again and repeat.

1 lived /d/
2 finished /t/
3 wanted /ɪd/
4 studied
5 waited
6 looked
7 decided
8 climbed

> **PAST SIMPLE**
>
> He climbed the mountain.
> He didn't climb a mountain.
> Did he climb a mountain?
>
> For further information and practice, see page 87.

5 Find the past tense form of these irregular verbs in *The road trippers* section of the article in Exercise 1.

1 be — *was / were*
2 drive
3 find
4 get
5 go
6 grow up
7 have
8 know
9 take
10 think

6 Complete the text about another adventurer with the past simple form of the verbs.

THE PHOTOGRAPHER

Reza ¹ *was born* (be born) in Tabriz, Iran, in 1952. He ² _____ (study) architecture at the university in Tehran but he ³ _____ (not / become) an architect. When he was a teenager, Reza ⁴ _____ (love) photography and, after university, he ⁵ _____ (get) a job with a local newspaper as a photographer. But he ⁶ _____ (not / want) to take photos of local news and in 1978 he ⁷ _____ (go) abroad and he ⁸ _____ (take) photos of wars. Nowadays he works for *National Geographic* magazine.

7 Read the text in Exercise 6. Answer the questions.

1 When was Reza born?
2 Where did he study architecture?
3 What did he love when he was a teenager?
4 What did he do after university?
5 Did he want to take photos of local news?
6 When did he go abroad?

> **PAST SIMPLE QUESTIONS**
>
> When were you born? In 1989.
> What did you study at university? Economics.
> Did you go abroad when you were young?
> Yes, I did. / No, I didn't.
>
> For further information and practice, see page 87.

8 **1.23** Work in pairs. Read the article in Exercise 1 again. Write questions for these answers (1–6). Then listen and compare your questions with the recording.

1 In the mountainous Basque region of Spain.
2 When she was fourteen.
3 Engineering.
4 From 2007 to 2010.
5 A minefield.
6 That the world wasn't as dangerous as they thought.

Speaking

9 Write eight to ten questions to ask your partner about their past. Use some of these prompts to help you.

> where / born?   where / live?
> what subjects / like / at school?
> go / university?   what job / want?
> what / do after that?

10 Take turns to interview each other. Make notes about your partner's answers.

11 Swap partners and describe your first partner's life.

> *Chan was born in Hong Kong in 1982 …*

TALK ABOUT ▶ YOUR PAST ▶ EVENTS YOU REMEMBER ▶ THE MAIN EVENTS ▶ A HAPPY ENDING   WRITE ▶ A TRUE STORY

vocabulary and speaking personal qualities • listening the survivors • grammar past continuous • pronunciation *was* • speaking events you remember

4b The survivors

Vocabulary and speaking
personal qualities

1 Look at the photo of an expedition. How dangerous is this situation? What kind of people do this, do you think?

2 Read the sentences and comments (1–8) about this kind of expedition. What kind of personal quality does each describe? Match these adjectives to the sentences.

| ambitious | careful | decisive | determined |
| experienced | intelligent | patient | reliable |

1 'The leader of our team has climbed in the Himalayas many times before in his thirty years as a mountaineer.'
2 'Whatever the risk, we always achieved our goal. Nothing stopped us.'
3 'Even as a child, I wanted to be the best at everything.'
4 'It's important to plan before any expedition.'
5 'When the weather is really bad, you have to wait. There's no point in taking stupid risks.'
6 'Everyone in the team always has to be there for each other. You won't survive without each other's help and support.'
7 'He has a quick brain and you need that for this kind of expedition.'
8 'The leader is the person who makes the final decision and everyone has to agree.'

▶ **WORDBUILDING negative prefixes**
You can make some adjectives for personal qualities negative by adding a prefix: *unambitious*, *indecisive*, *impatient*.

For further information and practice, see Workbook page 127.

3 What personal qualities do these people need? Make sentences with the adjectives in Exercise 2 and explain your reasons.

a teacher	a close friend	a language learner
a news photographer	a President
a sports competitor	a TV presenter

Example:
A teacher is patient because the students need time to learn.

Listening

4 🔊 1.24 Listen to part of a radio interview with survival expert Doctor Weisz. Match the survivors (1–3) to the situations (a–c).

1 Maria Garza
2 Bethany Hamilton
3 Mr and Mrs Carlson

a lost at sea for thirty-one days
b escaped from a burning aeroplane
c surfing when attacked by a shark

48

Unit 4 Adventure

5 🔊 **1.24** Listen again. Choose the correct option (a–c) to complete the sentences.

1 The main aim of the TV programme is to talk about _____.
  a recent survival stories
  b the best survival stories
  c the personal qualities of survivors

2 Doctor Weisz says all survivors _____.
  a are decisive
  b need determination
  c are decisive and need determination

3 The Carlsons' story is different to Bethany's because _____.
  a they were at sea for a long time
  b they were in the water
  c they didn't have experience

4 Most survivors _____.
  a don't take risks
  b often take risks
  c aren't very careful

6 Do you ever need the personal qualities of a survivor? For example, are there other situations when you need to be decisive, experienced or careful?

Grammar past continuous

7 Look at the highlighted verbs in the extract from the interview in Exercise 4. Answer the questions.

She was sitting on an aeroplane in Denver airport with her one-year-old child when she saw a fire from the window. While the other passengers were running to the exits, Maria climbed out of the window.

1 Do all the highlighted verbs talk about the past?
2 Which verbs describe a completed action?
3 Which verbs describe actions in progress at a particular time?
4 How do you form the past continuous tense? What is the auxiliary verb? What is the form of the main verbs?

▶ **PAST CONTINUOUS**

I/he/she/it was sitting	you/we/they were sitting
I/he/she/it wasn't sitting	you/we/they weren't sitting
Was I/he/she/it sitting?	Were you/we/they sitting?

We often join the past continuous tense with the past simple with the words *when* or *while* to talk about one action happening at the same time as another.
Maria was sitting on an aeroplane in Denver airport **when** she saw a fire from the window.
While the other passengers were running to the exits, she climbed out of the window.

For further information and practice, see page 88.

8 Look at the grammar box. Then choose the correct options to complete the true life survival stories.

TRUE life SURVIVAL STORIES!

The sun ¹ *shone / was shining* when Bethany Hamilton arrived at the beach on a beautiful morning in Hawaii. But hours later, the young teenager ² *surfed / was surfing* out at sea when a shark attacked her and she lost her left arm. Amazingly, Bethany ³ *swam / was swimming* back to the beach with one arm and, as she was swimming, she told other surfers to get out of the water.

While Steven and Rachel Carlson ⁴ *sailed / were sailing* around the Canary Islands, their boat sank. They ⁵ *didn't have / weren't having* much food and water but after 31 days at sea they still survived.

It was a normal afternoon at Denver airport but as Flight 455 was taking off, passengers ⁶ *saw / was seeing* a fire from the window. Immediately, the plane's captain realised that the engines ⁷ *didn't work / weren't working* and radioed for help. While passengers ⁸ *ran / were running* towards the front exits, Maria Garza pulled her daughter through the window exit next to the wing.

9 Which survival story do you think is the most amazing? Why?

10 Pronunciation *was*

🔊 **1.25** Listen to these sentences. Notice how the pronunciation of *was* changes. Then listen again and repeat.

/wəz/
1 She was surfing in Hawaii.

/wɒznt/
2 It wasn't snowing.

/wɒz/
3 Was it raining?

Speaking

11 Work in pairs. Tell your partner which of these events happened to you in the past. Explain:
1 when they happened
2 what you were doing at the time

| broke a bone | got your first job |
| first fell in love | fell off your bicycle |

I was climbing on a wall when I was eight. I fell and broke my arm.

12 Think of three more real or special events in your life. Tell your partner.

Examples:
While I was working in …, I met …
I was living abroad when I …

TALK ABOUT ▶ YOUR PAST ▶ EVENTS YOU REMEMBER ▶ THE MAIN EVENTS ▶ A HAPPY ENDING   WRITE ▶ A TRUE STORY

reading a mountaineering story • vocabulary geographical features • critical thinking identifying opinion • vocabulary *in*, *on* or *at* for time expressions • speaking the main events

4c The right decision?

Reading

1 Work in pairs. What was your best decision in life? What was your worst decision? What happened? Tell your partner.

2 Read the true story on page 51 about two climbers, Simpson and Yates. What decision did Yates make? What decision did Simpson make?

3 Read the story again. Are the sentences true (T) or false (F).

Joe Simpson

Simon Yates

1 The accident happened while Simpson and Yates were climbing up the mountain.
2 They didn't reach the top of Siula Grande.
3 Yates cut the rope because he wanted to survive.
4 Yates didn't look for Simpson afterwards.
5 Simpson managed to get to the base camp on his own.

Vocabulary geographical features

4 Match these words from the story to the picture.

| lake | north face | mountain | cave | summit | ridge |
| glacier | cliff | crevasse |

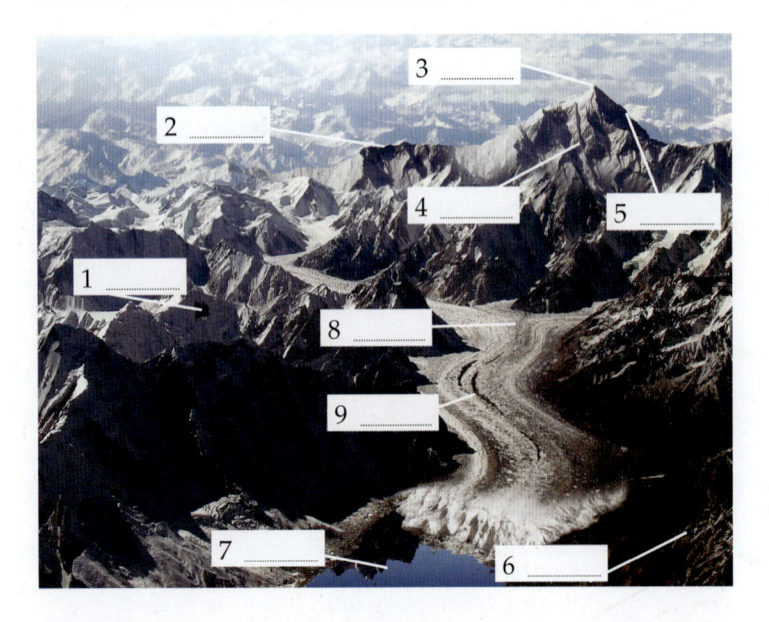

Critical thinking
identifying opinion

5 Read the last paragraph again. Do the following people (1–3) think that Yates made the right decision or the wrong decision?

1 some climbers
2 Simpson
3 the author of the article

6 Do you think Yates made the right decision? Why? / Why not?

Vocabulary *in*, *on* or *at* for time expressions

7 Look at these time expressions from the story. Then complete the rules (1–4) with *in*, *on* or *at*.

> in May 1985   on Day 1
> three days later   at the last second
> at four o'clock in the afternoon
> in the middle of that night   in 1988

1 We use _____ with months, years, seasons, decades, centuries and parts of the day.
2 We use _____ with days, dates and special days such as *her birthday*, *New Year's Day*.
3 We use _____ with times and special expressions such as *night*, *the weekend*, *the final moment*.
4 We don't use _____, _____ or _____ with time expressions such as *yesterday, last week, two days later*.

Speaking

8 Work in pairs. Match the time expressions in Exercise 7 to these events from the story. Then tell the main parts of the story using the time expressions.

> stood at the top of the mountain
> cut the rope   wrote a book
> heard his name
> crawled near to base camp
> started climbing Siula Grande

50

The RIGHT DECISION?

In May 1985 two climbers, Joe Simpson and Simon Yates, left their base camp by a lake and started climbing the north face of a mountain called Siula Grande in the Peruvian Andes. This climb was incredibly dangerous but the two men were experienced climbers and physically fit. On Day 1, the weather was good and the climb began well. At night they made a snow cave and slept on the side of the mountain.

Three days later, after some very difficult climbing and bad weather, the two men stood at the summit. Unfortunately, the weather was getting worse so they didn't stay long. As they were going down a mountain ridge, a disaster happened. Simpson fell and broke his knee. Quickly, Yates tied a rope to himself and then to his friend. He began lowering Simpson down the mountain and, for hours and hours, Yates helped Simpson get down the mountain. They were getting close to the glacier at the bottom of the mountain but suddenly Simpson slipped. This time he went over the edge of a cliff. He was hanging in mid-air. Simpson shouted up to Yates, but the wind was blowing loudly and Yates couldn't hear him.

Yates didn't know it but Simpson was – unbelievably – still alive inside the crevasse.

Yates didn't know what was happening below. He waited for an hour but the rope was too heavy and it was pulling Yates down the mountain towards the cliff. He had two choices: hold the rope but then both of them might die, or cut the rope and survive. It was an impossible decision for Yates but, at the last second, Yates cut the rope and saved himself. Immediately, Simpson fell thirty metres into a crevasse.

The next day, while Yates was desperately looking for Simpson, he found the crevasse. He called for Simpson but he heard nothing. Sadly, he decided that Simpson was dead. Yates didn't know it but Simpson was – unbelievably – still alive inside the crevasse.

Simpson waited for hours but when he realised Yates wasn't coming, he decided to take a risk. He had some rope so he abseiled to the bottom of the crevasse. He managed to find a way out. For three days, Simpson drank water from the snow and ice. He crawled back towards the base camp and at four o'clock in the afternoon of Day 7, Simpson was very near.

In the middle of that night, Yates was sleeping in his tent at base camp when he woke up. He was sure someone was shouting his name. Excitedly, he ran outside and looked around. Finally, after searching and searching he found Simpson. He was lying on the ground, not moving, but he was still breathing.

After a few days, the two men returned home and their story became famous. Unfairly, some climbers criticised Yates for cutting the rope. But, in 1988, Simpson wrote a book about the events and defended Yates. Simpson believed Yates made the right decision.

---

edge (n) /edʒ/ the place where something stops
abseil (v) /ˈæbseɪl/ to lower yourself down a mountain on a rope
crawl (v) /krɔːl/ to move on your hands and knees

real life telling a story • pronunciation intonation for responding

4d A happy ending

Real life telling a story

1 🔊 **1.26** Listen to a conversation between two friends about a camping trip. Answer the questions.

1 Was the start of the weekend good or bad?
2 When did Mark and the others leave?
3 Where did the car break down? Who fixed it?
4 Why couldn't they find the campsite at first?
5 What happened after they found the campsite?
6 Where did they go instead?

2 🔊 **1.26** Listen again and complete the conversation.

A: Hi Mark. How was your camping trip?
B: It was great in the end but we had a terrible time at the beginning.
A: Why?
B: ¹_____, we left the house early on Saturday morning but after only half an hour the car broke down.
A: Oh no!
B: ²_____, there was a garage nearby and the mechanic fixed the problem. But ³_____ we arrived at the forest, it was getting dark. ⁴_____ we drove around for about an hour, we ⁵_____ found the campsite but it was completely dark by then. ⁶_____, it started raining so we found a nice hotel down the road!
A: That was lucky!
B: Yes, it was a great hotel and ⁷_____ _____ we stayed there for the whole weekend.
A: ⁸_____ _____!

3 Match the words and expressions (1–8) in Exercise 2 with the correct section in the box.

> ▶ **TELLING A STORY**
>
> **Sequencing the story**
> At the beginning …   Then …   Next …
> While …
>
> **Introducing good and bad news**
> Luckily …   But …
>
> **Reacting to good and bad news**
> Why?   That was a good idea!   Oh no!

4 Pronunciation intonation for responding

🔊 **1.27** Listen to the expressions in 'Reacting to good and bad news' in the box. Notice how the listener uses intonation to show interest. Then listen again and repeat.

5 Work in pairs. Read the conversation in Exercise 2 aloud. Take turns to be person A. Pay attention to your intonation when you are responding.

6 Practise telling another story with your partner. Student A cycled to work and these events happened.

- You had a terrible journey to work.
- You were cycling and it started raining.
- A car hit your bicycle.
- You weren't hurt.
- The driver was very nice. He owns a bicycle shop.
- He gave you a new bike! It's much better than your old bicycle!

Tell your story to Student B. Student B listens and responds. Then change roles and repeat the story.

7 Think of a bad journey you had. Did it have a happy ending? Make a list of the events. Then tell your partner the story.

TALK ABOUT ▶ YOUR PAST ▶ EVENTS YOU REMEMBER ▶ THE MAIN EVENTS ▶ A HAPPY ENDING   WRITE ▶ A TRUE STORY

writing a true story • writing skill using -ly adverbs in stories   Unit 4 Adventure

4e A story of survival

Writing a true story

1 When you read the news, is it always bad news? Are there ever any news stories with good news or happy endings?

2 True stories in the news often include some or all of this information. Read the story and find out which of this information is included.

> the location   the weather   the people
> why they were there   any sudden or unexpected events that changed the situation
> how the situation ended   a happy or sad ending

BOYS SURVIVE
50 DAYS LOST AT SEA

It's an amazing story and it's true! Fifty days ago, three teenage boys suddenly disappeared from the island of Atafu in a small boat. Immediately, rescue boats went to look for them but sadly there was no sign of their boat. Eventually, a fishing boat in the middle of the Pacific Ocean safely pulled them from the sea. The boys were badly sunburned and dehydrated but doctors said they were in surprisingly good health. Now, they are back happily with their families.

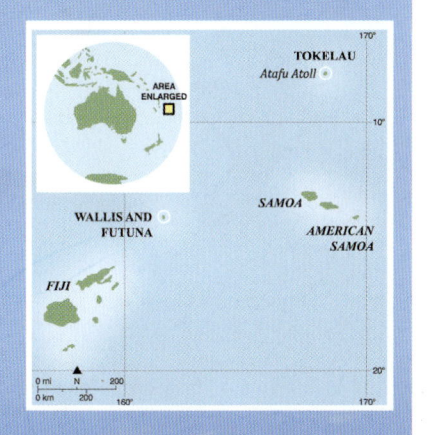

3 Writing skill using -ly adverbs in stories

Look at the sentence from the story in Exercise 2. We often use -ly adverbs to make a story more interesting. Underline the other -ly adverbs in the story.

Fifty days ago, three teenage boys <u>suddenly</u> disappeared from the island of Atafu in a small boat.

4 Match the adverbs you underlined in Exercise 3 with the rules (1–3).

> ▶ **-LY ADVERBS**
> We often use -ly adverbs to:
> 1 comment on the whole clause or sentence.
>   **Eventually**, they saw another ship in the distance.
> 2 describe the verb (how someone did something or how it happened).
>   He **slowly** swam towards the island. (Also He swam towards the island **slowly**.)
> 3 describe an adjective.
>   The three survivors were **amazingly** healthy.
>
> Many adverbs are adjectives + -ly, e.g. sudden – suddenly.

5 Make these sentences from short stories more interesting using the adverbs.

1 The climb was dangerous. (incredibly)
   The climb was incredibly dangerous.
2 The sun was shining. (brightly)
3 The man jumped into the car. (quickly)
4 They were nearly at the top of the mountain but one of them slipped. (suddenly)
5 It started raining. Gill had an umbrella. (fortunately)
6 The Amazon river was long and they were lost for days. (amazingly)
7 They walked back and looked into each other's eyes. (slowly)
8 They were lost in the forest for hours but they found the road again. (eventually)

6 You are going to write a true story. It can be from your own life or a story you read in the newspaper. Think about these questions and make notes.

- Where did it happen?
- What was the weather like?
- Who was there and what were they doing?
- What unexpected event happened?
- What happened next?
- Did it have a happy or sad ending?

7 Write your story. Use -ly adverbs to make it more interesting.

8 Work in pairs. Exchange stories. Use these questions to check your partner's story.

- What information in Exercise 6 does your partner include?
- Does he/she use -ly adverbs effectively?

TALK ABOUT ▶ YOUR PAST ▶ EVENTS YOU REMEMBER ▶ THE MAIN EVENTS ▶ A HAPPY ENDING   WRITE ▶ A TRUE STORY   53

4f Alaskan ice climbing

It's hard work climbing the glacier.

Unit 4 **Adventure**

Before you watch

1 Work in pairs. Look at the photo and discuss the questions.

1. Where is the woman?
2. What is she doing?
3. Do you think this is a dangerous activity?
4. How do you think she is feeling?

2 What do you think these words mean? Try to match the words (1–3) with the correct meaning (a–c).

1. serac
2. crevasse
3. ice fall

a. a narrow, deep hole in ice
b. an area with many seracs
c. large piece of glacial ice that sticks up in the air

While you watch

3 Watch the video and check your answers from Exercise 2.

4 Watch the video again and put the events from the climbers' trip in order (1–8).
a. It was a very special feeling for the woman when she got to the top.
b. They drove to the Matanuska glacier.
c. They hiked across the glacier.
d. When they arrived at Talkeetna, the weather was so bad that they couldn't fly to Mount McKinley.
e. A woman slipped, but the rope saved her.
f. After a long walk they reached solid ice at the heart of the glacier.
g. When they arrived at the glacier, the guides explained how to use the equipment.
h. They started climbing the ice wall.

5 Watch the video again and make notes about these topics.

the weather on the trip	
the glacier	
the guides	
the equipment	
the dangers	

After you watch

6 **Roleplay** telling a friend about a trip

Work in pairs.

Student A: You are one of the people who went to the glacier. You are now back at home. Tell a friend about your trip. Use the ideas below to make notes.

Student B: Your friend went on a trip to a glacier in Alaska. Use the ideas below to prepare questions to ask your friend.

- the journey to the glacier
- what the glacier was like
- what the weather was like
- the equipment
- what the climb was like
- how it felt to get to the top

Act out the conversation. Then change roles and have another conversation about a different trip.

7 The narrator says Colby and Caitlin are not usually doubtful when they're in the mountains. What does this tell you about them?

8 Work in pairs. Discuss these questions.

1. What kind of people like ice climbing?
2. Would you like to go ice climbing? Why? / Why not?

---

climb (v) /klaɪm/ go up with a lot of effort
climber (n) /ˈklaɪmə/ a person who climbs
crampons (n) /ˈkræmpɒnz/ spikes that climbers put on the bottom of their boots
doubtful (adj) /ˈdaʊtfl/ not feeling certain about something
glacier (n) /ˈglæsiə/ a large mass of ice
guide (n) /gaɪd/ a person who shows a place to visitors
heel (n) /hiːl/ the back part of the foot
hike (n) /haɪk/ a walk in a wild place
rope (n) /rəʊp/ a thick string used for tying things
stable (adj) /ˈsteɪbl/ not likely to fall or move in the wrong way
unsafe (adj) /ʌnˈseɪf/ dangerous
weather (n) /ˈweðə/ atmospheric conditions like rain, snow, sun, temperature

UNIT 4 REVIEW

Grammar

1 Work in pairs. Look at the photo. What can you see? Where do you think it is?

2 Read about two adventurers and check your ideas in Exercise 1. Then complete the text with the past simple form of the verbs.

Steve O'Meara ¹ _____ (meet) Donna in Boston in 1986. On their second date, Steve ² _____ (take) Donna in a helicopter to Hawaii. That sounds romantic but they ³ _____ (not / fly) to a beach. They ⁴ _____ (go) to the Kilauea volcano. A year later, they ⁵ _____ (visit) to the volcano again and this time they ⁶ _____ (get) married on the volcano. It ⁷ _____ (not / be) only for romantic reasons. Steve and Donna both ⁸ _____ (become) volcanologists and they ⁹ _____ (travel) all over the world to study volcanoes. But they really ¹⁰ _____ (want) to spend more time by the Kilauea volcano and some years later they ¹¹ _____ (buy) a house there. Donna explains why: 'This volcano can still kill you but for me to live on the volcano is exciting every day.'

3 Work in pairs. Make questions about Steve and Donna O'Meara using these prompts. Then take turns to ask and answer using information from the text.

Student A: When / meet?
Where / get married?   What / want to do?

Student B: Where / take Donna?
What / become?   What / buy?

I CAN
talk about past events and important moments in my life
ask questions about the past

Vocabulary

4 Choose the correct option (a–c) to complete the sentences.

1 My biggest _____ at school was passing my mathematics exam. I got an A grade in the end!
   a achievement   b challenge   c decision
2 Don't get angry when things don't happen as fast as you'd like. Learn to be _____.
   a patient   b reliable   c experienced
3 Probably the most _____ person in history was Albert Einstein. He had an amazing brain.
   a ambitious   b careful   c intelligent
4 You dropped water everywhere. Please try to be more _____!
   a ambitious   b careful   c determined

I CAN
talk about challenge and personal qualities

Real life

5 Look at the pictures (1–5) and write sentences about what happened in each part of the story.

6 Work in pairs. Take turns to tell each other your stories from Exercise 5. The person telling the story has to include the words on the left. The person listening uses the words on the right.

| then   next | Why?   Oh no! |
| while   luckily | Good idea! |

I CAN
sequence the stages of a story
introduce good and bad news in a story
respond to a story

Speaking

7 Write down five years when something important happened in your life. Show the years to your partner. Take turns to guess why each year was important.

Unit 5 The environment

An artist with his sculpture made from recycled parts of old computers
Photo by Peter Essick

FEATURES

58 Recycling
The real story behind recycling our rubbish

60 The Greendex
A new online survey finds out how green the world is

62 A boat made of bottles
How one environmentalist is trying to raise awareness

66 Coastal clean-up
A video about a plan to improve the US coastal environment

1 George Sabra is an artist and sculptor. What do you think of his sculpture in the photo? Which of these materials did he use?

| cardboard | glass | leather | metal | paper | plastic | wood |

2 🔊 1.28 Listen to part of a documentary about George Sabra. Answer the questions.
   1 What everyday objects does the speaker talk about?
   2 What does George Sabra do with these objects?
   3 What does he want us to think about?

3 Look at the highlighted expressions for talking about objects. Make sentences about these everyday objects in a similar way.

A dictionary is made of paper. You use it for looking up words.

| dictionary | mobile phone | pen | scissors | tin can |

4 Work in pairs. Think of other everyday objects. Don't tell your partner the object but describe what it's made of and what it is for. Your partner has to guess the object.

TALK ABOUT ▸ RECYCLING ▸ A GREENDEX SURVEY ▸ AN INTERVIEW ▸ AN ONLINE ORDER WRITE ▸ AN EMAIL   57

vocabulary household items • listening a radio phone-in show • grammar quantifiers • reading e-rubbish • speaking your opinions on recycling

5a Recycling

Vocabulary household items

1 How much do you recycle or reuse items in the house or at work? How easy is it to recycle where you live?

2 You can recycle all these objects. Match each object with the correct recycling bin above.

| aluminium foil   carton |
| cereal box   coffee   eggshell |
| yoghurt pot   jar   tin can |
| envelope   newspaper   bottle |
| plastic bag   vegetable peel |

3 Look at the grammar box. Which of the nouns in Exercise 2 are countable (C) and which are uncountable (U)?

▶ **COUNTABLE and UNCOUNTABLE NOUNS**

Countable nouns have singular and plural forms: *a bottle, two bottles*.
Uncountable nouns are singular and have no plural forms. You cannot use them with numbers: *milk*.

For further information and practice, see page 88.

Listening

4 🔊 1.29 Listen to two callers on a radio phone-in show about recycling. Answer the questions.
  1 Which caller (Reg or Sandra) thinks more people need to recycle?
  2 Which caller doesn't think recycling helps the environment?

Grammar quantifiers

5 🔊 1.29 Listen to the radio show again. Match the two parts of the sentences.

1 There aren't any —   a people on my street recycle.
2 Are there any   b bags.
3 There are some   c recycling bins.
4 They don't recycle much   d recycling bins there?
5 Not many   e rubbish every week.
6 They throw away a lot of   f minutes every day.
7 Some people recycle a little g recycling centres in my town.
8 You only need a few   h stuff.

6 Find these quantifiers in the sentences in Exercise 5. Which of the quantifiers do we use to talk about small quantities?

| any   a few   a little   a lot of   not many   not much   some |

▶ **QUANTIFIERS**

Countable nouns
We use *some*, *a lot of* and *a few* in affirmative sentences. We use *any* or *many* in negative sentences or questions.

Uncountable nouns
We use *some*, *a lot of* and *a little* in affirmative sentences. We use *any* or *much* in negative sentences or questions.

Note: *a lot of* = *lots of* (there is no difference in meaning or use)

For further information and practice, see page 88.

7 Work in pairs. Look at the grammar box. Then make sentences about what you recycle and throw away using the table.

| I / We (don't) | recycle / throw away | a lot of / many / much / any / a few / a little | metal / newspapers / plastic / glass / tin cans / cardboard / ink cartridges / food / other? |

Unit 5 The environment

Reading

8 Read the article about e-rubbish. Answer the questions using quantifiers.

1. How many of us know where our e-rubbish goes?
2. Did Peter Essick follow the rubbish to lots of countries?
3. How many of the computers do sellers resell?
4. How much metal do the parts of the computers contain?
5. Why is the process of recycling these parts so dangerous?
6. How much e-rubbish does Peter Essick think we should export? Why?

> ▶ **WORDBUILDING**
> **hyphenated words**
>
> We often join words or parts of other words with a hyphen to make new words: *e-rubbish, out-of-date, eco-friendly*.
>
> For further information and practice, see Workbook page 135.

E-RUBBISH

Nowadays, every household produces electronic rubbish (or e-rubbish) – an old TV or computer printer, or an out-of-date mobile phone we no longer need. But when we throw these everyday items away, not many of us know where these objects go. The journalist and photographer, Peter Essick, decided to follow this e-rubbish to several different countries around the world.

In particular, Essick found a lot of e-rubbish goes to Ghana. There, he saw mountains of old computers in the local markets. The sellers resell some of them but not much equipment works. Instead, they recycle the broken computers by melting the parts inside. These parts contain a little metal such as copper or even gold sometimes. However, this process of recycling is dangerous for the workers because it produces a lot of toxic chemicals.

As a result of his journey, Peter Essick thinks it's important to stop exporting e-rubbish. It's bad for the environment and it's bad for people's health. Instead, he believes manufacturers need to produce more eco-friendly electronics in the future; in other words, electronic products which you can recycle cheaply, safely and in the country where they were made.

melt (v) /melt/ to heat an object until it turns to liquid
toxic (adj) /ˈtɒksɪk/ poisonous

9 Complete these sentences about the article. Then compare your sentences with the class.

I knew *a little / a lot* about this topic before reading this.

This article *is / isn't* surprising for me because …

I *agree / partly agree / don't agree* with Essick because …

Speaking

10 Work in pairs. Imagine you are talking on a radio phone-in programme.

Student A: You are the radio presenter. Turn to page 81 and follow the instructions.

Student B: You are a caller. Turn to page 82 and follow the instructions.

TALK ABOUT ▶ RECYCLING ▶ A GREENDEX SURVEY ▶ AN INTERVIEW ▶ AN ONLINE ORDER WRITE ▶ AN EMAIL

59

5b The Greendex

Reading and speaking

1 We describe people and their behaviour as 'green' when they help the environment. How green are you? Answer the questions.

1 Do you …
- recycle your rubbish?
- ever buy second-hand goods?
- switch computers and TVs off before you go to bed?
- use public transport or share car journeys?

2 Can you think of more ways to be green in your daily life?

2 Work in groups. Read the first paragraph in the article about the 'Greendex'. Then discuss the questions.

1 What is the purpose of the 'Greendex'?
2 Is your country in the survey?
3 What kinds of cost do you think each of the four categories includes (e.g. housing = electricity, gas)?

3 Read the latest results from the 'Greendex'. Label the pie charts (1–5) with the correct country.

The Greendex

The 'Greendex' is a survey of 17,000 consumers in 17 different countries. It finds out how these people regularly spend their money. The four categories for spending are: housing, food, transportation and 'other goods' (such as electronic items and household appliances).

LATEST RESULTS FROM THE 'GREENDEX':

- About ninety per cent of people in Argentina eat beef nearly every day.
- Exactly half of all Russians use public transport every day or most days.
- Just over two thirds of people in Germany drink a bottle of water daily and most of them also recycle the bottle.
- Consumers in the United States have the most TVs at home. Well over two thirds have four or more.
- Nearly half of all Canadians regularly recycle electronic items.

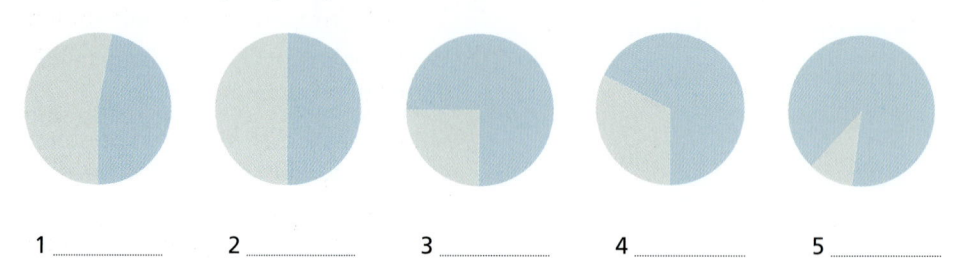

1 _____ 2 _____ 3 _____ 4 _____ 5 _____

Unit 5 The environment

Vocabulary results and figures

4 Look at these words from the results in Exercise 3. Choose the correct percentage (a–c).

1. about ninety per cent
   a 89%   b 90%   c 99%
2. exactly half
   a 49%   b 50%   c 51%
3. just over two thirds
   a 64%   b 66%   c 69%
4. well over two thirds
   a 66%   b 69%   c 75%
5. nearly half
   a 48%   b 50%   c 52%

5 Approximately, what percentage of your money do you spend on housing, food, transport and 'other goods'? Divide the pie chart to show the percentages.

transport   housing

'other goods'   food

6 Work in pairs. Present your pie chart using words from Exercise 4.

I spend about half my money on …

Well over eighty per cent is on …

Grammar definite article (*the*) or no article

7 Complete the text with *the* or Ø (no article). Then check your answers in the 'Greendex' results in Exercise 3.

- Just over two thirds of people in ¹_____ Germany drink a bottle of water daily and most of them also recycle ² _____ bottle.
- ³ _____ consumers in ⁴ _____ United States have ⁵ _____ most TVs at ⁶ _____ home.

8 Look at the grammar box. Then match the rules (a–f) with the gaps (1–6) in Exercise 7.

> ▶ **DEFINITE ARTICLE (*THE*) or NO ARTICLE**
>
> Use the **definite article** (*the*):
> a with something or someone you mentioned before.
> b when it is part of the name of something (e.g. *The United Kingdom*).
> c with superlative phrases (e.g. *the best*).
>
> Use **no article**:
> d with most countries.
> e to talk about people and things in a general way.
> f with certain expressions (e.g. *at night, at school*).
>
> For further information and practice, see page 89.

9 Look at these sentences from the 'Greendex' survey. Delete *the* where it isn't necessary.

1. ~~The~~ European houses do not have air conditioning.
2. Countries such as the Brazil are using the electric cars more and more.
3. Many people around the world are trying to use less energy at the home.
4. The fish and seafood is the most common dish in the Japan.
5. The people in the United Kingdom are sharing the cars more and more to save costs.

10 Pronunciation /ðə/ **or** /ðiː/

a 🎧 **1.30** Listen to the difference in the pronunciation of *the* before a consonant sound and a vowel sound.

/ðə/   /ðiː/
the TV   the internet

b 🎧 **1.31** Listen and write /ðə/ or /ðiː/. Then listen again and repeat.

1 the bottle   5 the electricity
2 the phone   6 the gas
3 the fuel   7 the insurance
4 the apple   8 the water

Writing and speaking

11 Work in groups. You are going to prepare a 'Greendex' report about the class. Follow these steps:

1. Write eight to ten questions to find out how 'green' everybody is.
2. Each group member meets students from the other groups and interviews them using the questions.
3. Work with your first group again. Collect the information from your questions and summarise the results.
4. Present your conclusions to the class, using pie charts to help your presentations.

TALK ABOUT ▶ RECYCLING ▶ A GREENDEX SURVEY ▶ AN INTERVIEW ▶ AN ONLINE ORDER   WRITE ▶ AN EMAIL

61

reading the Plastiki • critical thinking close reading • word focus *take* •
speaking an interview with an environmentalist

5c A boat made of bottles

Reading

1 Look at these words from the article on page 63. What do you think it is about? Read the article. Were your predictions correct?

| boat   plastic bottles   recycle   sail   San Francisco |
| Sydney   the Pacific Ocean |

2 Read the article again. Complete the fact file about the Plastiki. Write the information as figures.

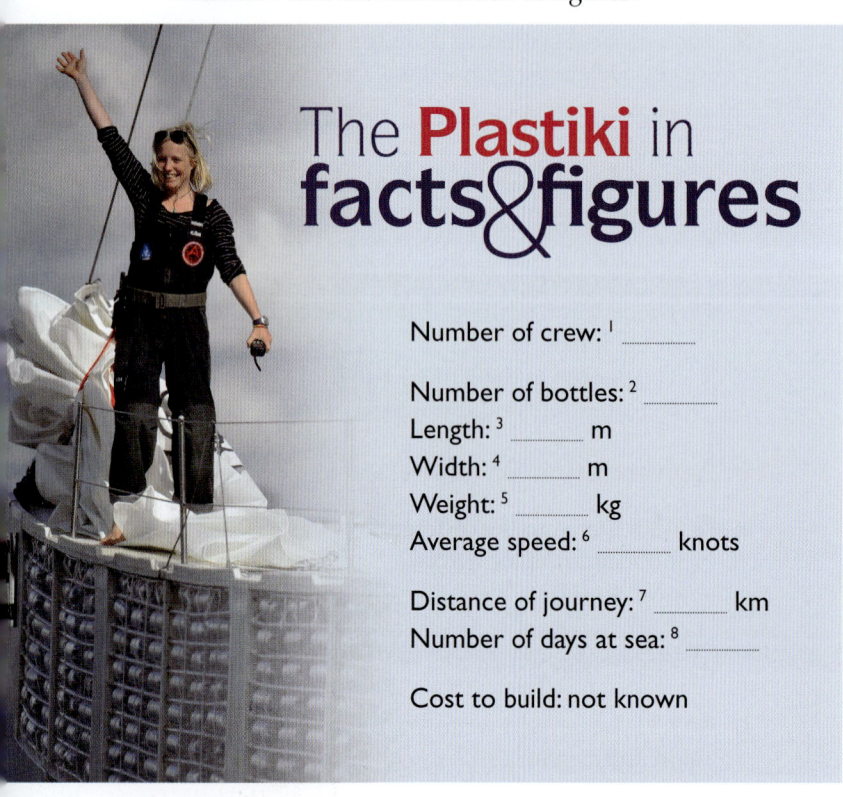

The Plastiki in facts & figures

Number of crew: [1] _____

Number of bottles: [2] _____
Length: [3] _____ m
Width: [4] _____ m
Weight: [5] _____ kg
Average speed: [6] _____ knots

Distance of journey: [7] _____ km
Number of days at sea: [8] _____

Cost to build: not known

Critical thinking close reading

3 Read sentences 1–8. Write answers A, B or C.

A = The sentence is true. The information is in the text.
B = The sentence is false. The information is in the text.
C = We don't know if it's true or false. The information isn't in the text.

1 The *Plastiki* is made of the same material as other boats.
2 Nowadays, humans recycle most of their plastic bottles.
3 The boat doesn't use renewable energy.
4 The crew only ate vegetables for the whole journey.
5 Plastic in the sea is killing animals.
6 The size of the 'Great Garbage Patch' is growing.
7 Some people criticised De Rothschild and his journey.
8 De Rothschild wants to sail the Plastiki again one day.

4 Do you think the *Plastiki* made a difference to people's attitude to rubbish? Will De Rothschild's journey make people change their behaviour? Why? / Why not?

Word focus *take*

5 Find five expressions with *take* in the article on page 63. Then match them with the correct category (1–4).

take /teɪk/
1 transport: *take a taxi*
2 daily routines: *take a walk*
3 lengths of time: *take a few days*
4 idioms: *take time (to do something)*

takeaway /ˈteɪkəweɪ/
1 food: *we ordered some Chinese*

6 Complete the sentence with *take* and these phrases.

| regular breaks   many days   care |
| a plane   time |

1 Most people _take a plane_ from San Francisco to Sydney so they don't know about the pollution in the ocean.
2 The journey across the Great Garbage Patch _____.
3 The journey was tiring and the crew needed to _____.
4 For this kind of project, it's important to _____ to plan everything.
5 The Pacific Ocean can be dangerous so everyone on the ship had to _____.

Speaking

7 Work in pairs. Imagine you are going to interview David De Rothschild about the *Plastiki*. Prepare six to eight questions using the information in the article and any other questions you would like to ask him.

> How long did the whole journey take?

> How do you think you made a difference?

8 Change partners with another pair. Take turns to roleplay the interview and ask each other your questions. When you are De Rothschild, use information from the article or create new answers with your own ideas and opinions.

Unit 5 The environment

A boat with a difference

The *Plastiki* looks similar to many other boats or yachts in Sydney harbour. It's eighteen metres long, six metres wide and it weighs about twelve thousand kilogrammes. It carries a crew of six people and has an average speed of five knots. However, once you get near to the *Plastiki* you realise there's a big difference. It's made of twelve thousand five hundred reclaimed plastic bottles.

How did the *Plastiki* begin?

One day, the environmentalist David De Rothschild was reading some information about all the plastic in the seas and oceans. He couldn't believe what he was reading. For example, humans throw away four out of every five plastic bottles they use and plastic rubbish causes about eighty per cent of the pollution in the sea. Soon afterwards, Rothschild decided he wanted to help the fight against pollution in the sea. To create publicity for the problem, he started building a boat made of plastic bottles.

Designing the *Plastiki*

As well as building the boat with recycled plastic, it was important for him to make the boat environmentally-friendly and user-friendly. The boat uses renewable energy sources including wind power and solar energy. The crew can make meals with vegetables from the small garden at the back of the boat. They can take a break from work and get some exercise by using the special exercise bicycle. The energy from the bike provides power for the boat's computers. And if anyone needs to take a shower, the boat's shower uses saltwater from the sea.

The journey

De Rothschild sailed the *Plastiki* across the Pacific Ocean from San Francisco to Sydney. That's fifteen thousand three hundred and seventy two nautical kilometres. On the way, De Rothschild took the special boat through the 'Great Garbage Patch'. It is a huge area in the Pacific with 3.5 billion kilogrammes of rubbish. You can see every kind of human rubbish here: shoes, toys, bags, toothbrushes, but the worst problem is the plastic. It kills birds and sea life.

How well did the *Plastiki* survive the journey?

The journey wasn't always easy and De Rothschild and his crew had to take care during storms. There were giant ocean waves and winds of over one hundred kilometres per hour. The whole journey took one hundred and twenty nine days. Originally, De Rothschild thought the boat could only travel once but it survived so well that he is planning to sail it again one day.

A BOAT *made of* BOTTLES

knot (n) /nɒt/ measurement of speed at sea (1 knot = 1.8 km/hr)
garbage (n) /ˈgɑːbɪdʒ/ (US Eng) rubbish (UK Eng)
patch (n) /pætʃ/ area

TALK ABOUT ▶ RECYCLING ▶ A GREENDEX SURVEY ▶ AN INTTERVIEW ▶ AN ONLINE ORDER ▶ WRITE ▶ AN EMAIL

reading a company website • real life phoning about an order • pronunciation sounding friendly

5d Online shopping

Reading

1 Do you normally go shopping or do you prefer shopping online?

2 Read the website and email order. What did the customer order? What is the problem?

WWW.TECOART.COM

| HOME | MY ACCOUNT | SHOPPING CART | CHECKOUT |

Unusual clocks, Office clocks, Unique Clocks, Computer clocks, Computer art and Vintage clocks all from recycled computers!

Computer Hard Drive Clock with Circuit Board.
£39.00

Apple iPod Hard Drive Clock on a Circuit Board.
£35.00

Order number: 80531A
Order Date: 20 March

Thank you for your order. Unfortunately, the model you ordered is currently not available. We expect delivery in seven days. We apologise for the delay. For further information about this order, speak to a customer service assistant on 555-01754.

Ms Jane Powell
90 North Lane

Item Number	Description	Quantity	Price
HCV1N	Hard drive clock	1	£35

Real life phoning about an order

3 🔊 1.32 Jane Powell telephones customer services about her order. Listen to the conversation. Answer the questions.

1 What information does the customer service assistant ask for and check?
2 Why does Jane want the clock quickly?
3 How much does the other clock cost?
4 What does Jane decide to do?
5 What will the customer service assistant email her?

4 🔊 1.32 Look at the expressions for phoning about an order. Then listen to the conversation again. Tick the sentences the customer service assistant uses.

▶ **PHONING ABOUT AN ORDER**

Telephone expressions
Good morning. Can I help you?
I'm calling about an order for a clock.
Can I put you on hold for a moment?
Is there anything else I can help you with?

Talking about an order
Do you have the order number?
Would you like to order a different product?
Would you like to cancel the order?
Would you like a refund?
Would you like confirmation by email?

Checking and clarifying
Is that A as in Alpha?
Let me check.
So that's F for Freddie.
That's right.

5 **Pronunciation** sounding friendly

a 🔊 1.33 Listen to the sentences from a telephone conversation. Does the customer services assistant sound friendly (F) or unfriendly (U)?

1 Good morning. Can I help you?
2 Can I put you on hold?
3 Is that A as in Alpha?
4 I'm calling about an order.
5 Is there anything else I can help you with?
6 Do you have an order number?

b 🔊 1.34 Listen to the sentences again but now they are all friendly. Listen and repeat with a similar friendly intonation.

6 Work in pairs. Practise two phone conversations similar to the one in Exercise 3.

Student A: Turn to page 81 and follow the instructions.

Student B: Turn to page 82 and follow the instructions.

TALK ABOUT ▶ RECYCLING ▶ A GREENDEX SURVEY ▶ AN INTERVIEW ▶ AN ONLINE ORDER   WRITE ▶ AN EMAIL

writing **emails** • writing skill **formal language**　　　　　　　　　　　　　　Unit 5 The environment

5e Problem with an order

Writing emails

1 Read the correspondence between a customer and a customer service assistant. Put the emails in order (1–5).

A Dear M Cottrell

I would like to inform you that the e-book reader you ordered is now in stock. I would be delighted to deliver this item immediately. Please reply to confirm you still require this item.

Charlotte Lazarro

B Dear Sir or Madam

I recently ordered an 'e-book reader'. However, I received an email which said this was not currently available. Please refund my money back to the credit card.

Yours sincerely

Mr M Cottrell

C Thanks, but I bought the same product at a shop yesterday. Therefore, please cancel the order and, as requested, send me my refund.

M Cottrell

D As requested here is the order number: 80531A

E Dear M Cottrell

Thank you for your email. I apologise for the difficulties with your order. In order to provide you with the necessary assistance, could you please send the order number?

Best regards

Charlotte Lazarro

Customer Service Assistant

2 Read the emails in Exercise 1 again. Underline any phrases and expressions that request something or give instructions to do something.

3 Writing skill formal language

a The language in the emails in Exercise 1 is fairly formal. Match the formal verbs in the emails to these less formal verbs and phrases (1–9).

1 get　　　　　　　*receive*
2 be happy
3 asked for
4 give
5 give back (money)
6 help
7 say sorry
8 tell
9 want

b Work in pairs. Make these sentences more formal.

1 I want my money back.
2 I'm writing to tell you that I didn't get the delivery.
3 Do you want any help?
4 Please give us your credit card details.
5 Sorry, but I can't give you your money back.

4 You ordered a printer but it doesn't work. Write an email to the supplier and request a refund.

5 Work in pairs. Exchange emails with your partner. Write a formal reply from the supplier to your partner's email.

6 Use these questions to check the emails in Exercise 5.

- Did the writer make polite requests and give clear instructions?
- Did the writer use formal language?

TALK ABOUT　▶ RECYCLING　▶ A GREENDEX SURVEY　▶ AN INTERVIEW　▶ AN ONLINE ORDER　　WRITE　▶ AN EMAIL　　65

5f Coastal clean-up

> The aim of this clean-up is to make the coastlines beautiful again.

Unit 5 **The environment**

Before you watch

1 Work in groups. Look at the photo and the title of this video. Discuss the questions.

1 Where are the people?
2 What do you think they are doing? Why?
3 What are they thinking?

While you watch

2 Watch the video and check your ideas from Exercise 1.

3 Watch the video again and number the actions in the order you see them.

a writing information on a form
b getting off a bus
c swimming underwater
d picking up tin cans
e putting bags of rubbish on a boat

4 Watch the video again. Are these sentences true (T) or false (F)?

1 The government pays the people who collect the rubbish.
2 They collect a lot of the rubbish along the coast.
3 The Ocean Conservancy makes a note of every piece of rubbish it collects.
4 Most of the rubbish comes from boats at sea.
5 They cleaned everything up along the river, so there isn't any more to do there.

5 Watch the video again. What do these numbers and dates refer to?

1 half a million
2 3,500,000 kilos
3 35
4 1986
5 1,000 kilos

6 Complete what the people say with these words.

| amazing | disgusting | litter | shocked | trash |
| twice | | | | |

'It's ¹_____ all this stuff that's out here. I was so ²_____ when I came out here. I thought 'oh, you know people don't ³_____ that much.' You see stuff on the side of the road, but when you come here it's just everywhere.'

'Yeah it is pretty ⁴_____, actually. We can pick a lot of it up one day and the next day we come back and there's ⁵_____ as much as the day before. So it seems like there is no end to the ⁶_____.'

7 According to the narrator, what two reasons are there for doing the clean-up?

After you watch

8 **Roleplay** a conversation between a coastal clean-up volunteer and a member of the public

Work in pairs.

Student A: You are a coastal clean-up volunteer. You want to get more volunteers. Make a list of reasons for helping with the coastal clean-up.

Student B: You live near the coast but you enjoy your free time and don't want to help with the coastal clean-up. Make a list of reasons why you are busy and can't volunteer.

Act out the interview. Student A must convince Student B to volunteer. Then change roles and repeat the conversation.

9 Jay says: 'we are getting there.' What does he mean?

10 Work in pairs. Discuss these questions.

1 Are there places in your country where there is a lot of rubbish?
2 Would you do voluntary work like this?
3 How can you stop people littering?

---

amazing (adj) /əˈmeɪzɪŋ/ very surprising
cigarette end (n) /ˈsɪgəˈret end/ the part of the cigarette people throw away after they finish smoking it
coast (n) /kəʊst/ the place where the sea meets the land
clean-up (n) /ˈkliːn ʌp/ the process of making something clean
collect (v) /kəˈlekt/ pick up
disgusting (adj) /dɪsˈgʌstɪŋ/ very unpleasant
litter (v) /ˈlɪtə/ leave things like paper and plastic bags in public places after you finish using them

rubbish (n) /ˈrʌbɪʃ/ things people throw away when they don't need them (British English)
search (v) /sɜːtʃ/ look for
shocked (adj) /ʃɒkt/ surprised in a negative way
trash (n) /træʃ/ things people throw away when they don't need them (American English)
twice (adv) /twaɪs/ two times
volunˈteer (n) /vɒlʌntɪə/ a person who does something without being paid

67

UNIT 5 REVIEW

Grammar

1 Choose the correct options to complete the article about recycling. (Ø = no article)

Recycling around the World

New statistics give a view of recycling around the world. Here are three of the countries in the report.

Switzerland
[1] *A / The* Swiss score well at recycling. With so many different types of recycling bins, local people only have to throw away [2] *a little / a few* household items. For example, they recycle 80% of their plastic bottles. That's much higher than other countries in [3] *Ø / the* Europe with plastic recycling levels of only between 24–40%.

United States of America
Overall [4] *Ø / the* USA doesn't recycle as [5] *many / much* rubbish as a country like Switzerland but it's introduced [6] *a lot of / any* new projects in recent years and so its record is really improving quickly. This year it recycled 48% of its paper, 40% of its plastic bottles and 55% of its cans.

Senegal
Senegal only recycles [7] *a few / a little* of its waste industrially. However, people don't throw away [8] *any / much* items that they can use for something else. For example, you can buy shoes made from old plastic bags and drinking cups from tin cans. Here, everything has another purpose.

2 Work in pairs. Discuss these questions about the countries in the article.

1 Which country recycles the most?
2 Which country reuses items the most?
3 Which country do you think your country is most similar to?

3 Complete the questions with *many*, *much* or *any*. Then ask your partner the questions.

1 How _____ of your rubbish do you recycle? 70% or more? Between 30 to 69%? 29% or less?
2 How _____ newspapers and magazines do you buy a week?
3 Do you reuse _____ of your household items for something else? For example, glass jars to put other items in, or vegetable peel for compost?

4 Can you name three different countries in each of these regions?

| South America | Europe | Asia | Africa |
| The Middle East | | | |

I CAN
talk and ask about quantities
talk about countries and different regions in the world

Vocabulary

5 Match the percentages from the article in Exercise 1 with the definitions (1–5).

1 just over half
2 four fifths
3 about a quarter
4 two fifths
5 nearly half

6 Work in pairs. Make two sentences about your weekly life using percentages. Talk about:

- the amount of time you spend at work a week.
- the percentage of your money you spend on food.

Then say the same sentences using descriptions (e.g. a quarter, over a half).

I CAN
talk about results and figures

Real life

7 Work in pairs. Practise making a telephone call.

Student A: You want to speak to the Customer Service Manager at an online shop. You bought a TV but it doesn't work. You want the company to collect and replace it. Telephone the customer helpline and explain your problem.

Student B: You work on the customer helpline for an online company. Your manager is not available so take the caller's name, number and write down the details of the complaint.

I CAN
make a telephone call and leave a message
answer a telephone call and take a message

Speaking

8 Write three sentences about your country or another in the world. Two sentences are true facts and one sentence is false.

Example:
1 *The United Kingdom has a population of well over sixty million people.*
2 *The average person in the UK works about forty hours a week.*
3 *70% of the population in the UK is below the age of 30.*
(Sentence 3 is false)

9 Work in pairs. Take turns to say your three sentences and guess which of your partner's sentences is false.

Unit 6 Stages in life

The Egyptian Sphinx
Photo by Bill Ellzey

FEATURES

70 Changing your life
How one couple left their day-to-day world for a life of adventure

72 World party
Join in some of the world's biggest and most colourful parties this year

74 Masai rite of passage
A special week of ritual in the Masai tribe as boys become men

78 Steel drums
A video about the steel drums of Trinidad and Tobago

1 The Sphinx is from ancient Greek and Egyptian mythology. The Sphinx in the photo is the most famous sphinx in the world. Where is it? What else do you know about it?

2 Read this story about the Sphinx. Do you know the answer to the Sphinx's question?

> In Greek history, the Sphinx was a giant monster with the body of a lion, the wings of a bird and a human head. When travellers wanted to enter the city of Thebes, the Sphinx asked them a question: 'What goes on four legs in the morning, on two legs at noon, and on three legs in the evening?' The Sphinx killed any traveller who didn't answer correctly.

3 **1.35** Listen to an explanation of the story and find out the answer. Did you guess correctly?

4 Look at these different life events. Answer the questions.

> get a pension   get engaged   get married
> get your driving licence   go to college or university
> learn to ride a bicycle   leave home   start a family
> start your career   take a career break

1 At what age do people in your country do these things?
2 Do you think it's important to do each one at a particular age?

TALK ABOUT ▸ A LIFE-CHANGING DECISION ▸ PLANNING A CELEBRATION ▸ EVENTS IN THE YEAR ▸ AN INVITATION
WRITE ▸ A DESCRIPTION

vocabulary stages in life • reading how a couple changed their life •
grammar and listening verb patterns with *to* + infinitive • pronunciation /tə/ • speaking a life-changing decision

6a Changing your life

Vocabulary stages in life

1 Put these stages of life into the correct order (1–7) from youngest to oldest.

| adolescent | child | infant | middle aged |
| pensioner | teenager | young adult | |

2 What age do you think these stages begin and end? What is your current stage of life?

Reading

3 Read the article on page 71 about Rich and Amanda. What was their stage of life? Why did they decide to leave their jobs?

4 Read the article again. Underline the answers to these questions.

1 What did they intend to do at the weekend?
2 What did they realise they wanted to do?
3 Why did they buy a campervan?
4 Where did they plan to travel to by container ship?
5 What did colleagues at work find difficult?
6 What did friends think they were crazy to do?
7 What did Rich and Amanda start to do after they left home?

5 Who do you think you are most similar to in the article: Rich and Amanda, or their work colleagues and friends? Explain your answer.

Grammar and listening verb patterns with *to* + infinitive

6 Look at the sentences (a–c). Match the sentences to the verb patterns (1–3).

a We intend to leave our jobs.
b Let's buy a camper to travel in.
c It's difficult to understand your decision.

1 a verb followed by the *to* + infinitive
2 an adjective followed by the *to* + infinitive
3 the *to*-infinitive explains the purpose of the main verb

> **VERB PATTERNS WITH *TO* + INFINITIVE**
>
> 1 **verb + *to* + infinitive**: *We intend/plan/want/hope/'d like to travel across Africa.*
> 2 **adjective + *to* + infinitive**: *It isn't easy to learn. That's good to know.*
> 3 **infinitive of purpose**: *Save your money to buy something special.* (= in order to do something)
>
> For further information and practice, see page 89.

7 🔊 1.36 Listen to three people talking about their plans and intentions. What is their stage in life? Match the two parts of the sentences.

1 One day I plan to
2 I want to take a year off to
3 I'd like to travel to
4 I intend to
5 I'll be happy to
6 These days, it's really difficult to
7 It's hard not to

a get some work experience abroad.
b do all the things I wanted to do but never had time.
c buy a house.
d go to university.
e leave my job.
f feel sad about it.
g somewhere like Australia.

Unit 6 **Stages in life**

CHANGING your life

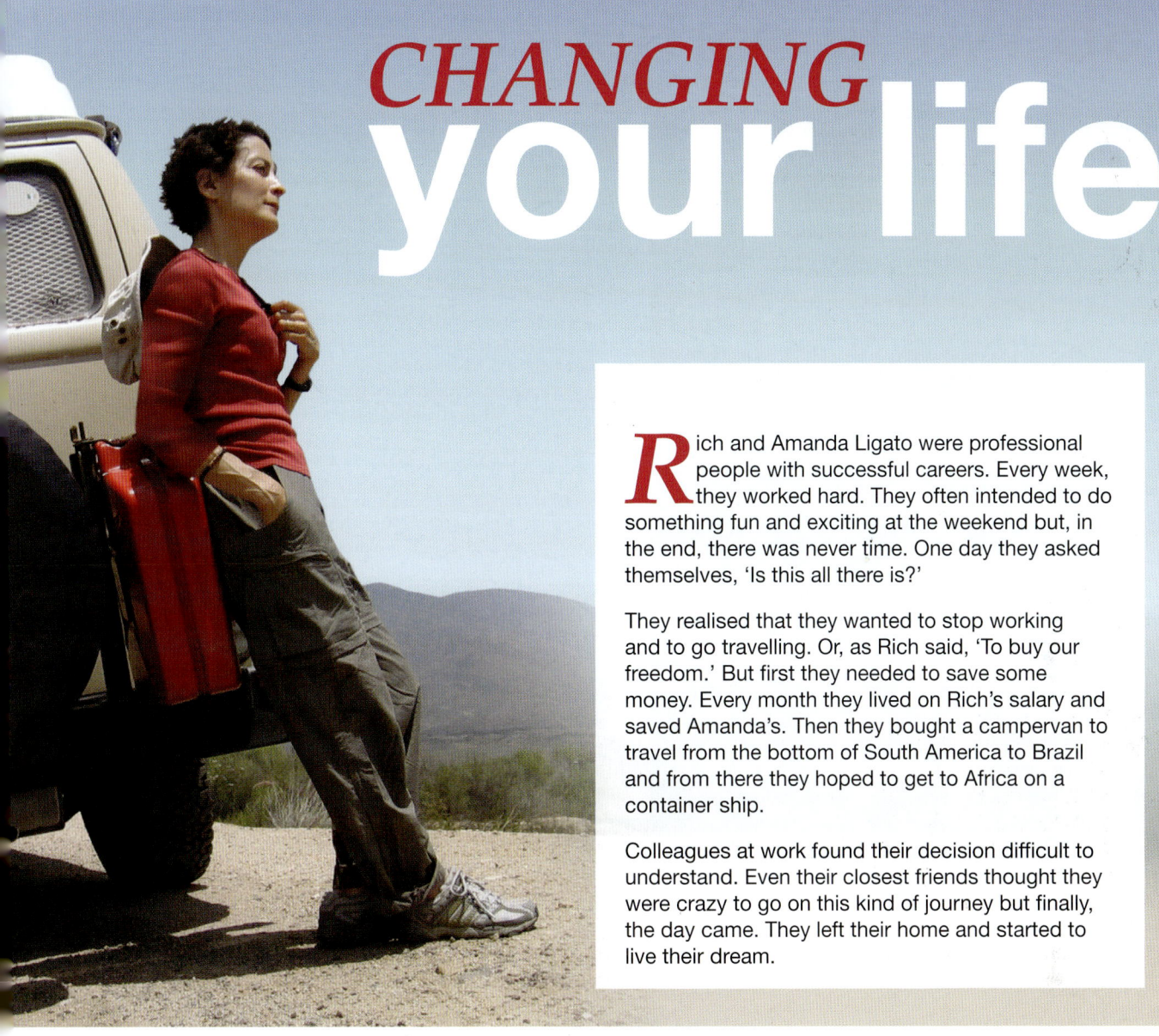

Rich and Amanda Ligato were professional people with successful careers. Every week, they worked hard. They often intended to do something fun and exciting at the weekend but, in the end, there was never time. One day they asked themselves, 'Is this all there is?'

They realised that they wanted to stop working and to go travelling. Or, as Rich said, 'To buy our freedom.' But first they needed to save some money. Every month they lived on Rich's salary and saved Amanda's. Then they bought a campervan to travel from the bottom of South America to Brazil and from there they hoped to get to Africa on a container ship.

Colleagues at work found their decision difficult to understand. Even their closest friends thought they were crazy to go on this kind of journey but finally, the day came. They left their home and started to live their dream.

8 Pronunciation /tə/

🔊 **1.37** Listen to the sentences in Exercise 7. Notice how *to* is not stressed /tuː/ but pronounced /tə/. Listen again and repeat.

9 Write your own sentences using the sentence beginnings (1–7) in Exercise 7. Then compare your sentences with your partner.

Speaking

10 Work in groups of three or four. Imagine you are one of the people on the right. Read about your current situation and make plans for the future. Is there anything you need to do or buy in order to change your life?

11 Present your plans and intentions to your group. Do they think it's a good idea to do these things or do they find them difficult to understand?

Marie (45) and Javier (43)
This couple are both accountants and they own a small apartment in a city. They love skiing but they never have time because the mountains are so far away.

Ahmed (25)
When he was young, he wanted to star in films but his parents said it was difficult to be an actor. So he studied engineering at university and he got a good job. However, sometimes he still dreams about being in films.

Lucy (68)
She's a retired teacher and gets a good pension, but life at home is boring. She never travelled when she was younger but she likes watching travel programmes on TV.

TALK ABOUT ▶ A LIFE-CHANGING DECISION ▶ PLANNING A CELEBRATION ▶ EVENTS IN THE YEAR ▶ AN INVITATION
WRITE ▶ A DESCRIPTION

reading and vocabulary celebrations • listening preparing for a festival • grammar future forms • pronunciation contracted forms • speaking planning a celebration

6b World party

WORLD PARTY

People in different countries celebrate Mardi Gras with live music, costumes, fireworks, parades and lots of good food. The most famous celebrations are in New Orleans, Venice, Rio de Janeiro and Port-of-Spain.

New Orleans, USA
Small parties for Mardi Gras began in the 1700s. By the 1800s they were huge events with masks, costumes and jazz bands. Visitors also have to try 'King Cake' with its gold, purple and green decorations.

Venice, Italy
Mardi Gras is called *Carnevale* in this beautiful city. The first celebrations were in the 11th century and you can still enjoy the costumes, candles and fireworks at night from a gondola in Venice's canals.

Rio de Janeiro, Brazil
The world famous parades started in the mid-1800s with decorated floats and thousands of people dancing to samba. There is also the famous meat and bean stew called *Feijoda*.

Port-of-Spain, Trinidad
The French landed here in the 18th century and brought Mardi Gras with them. Nowadays, everyone enjoys the parties and concerts with the famous steel drums from morning to midnight.

Reading and vocabulary
celebrations

1 Which events do you celebrate in your country? When do you have parties?

> When a child is born, everyone in the family has a party.

2 Look at the first paragraph of the article. Why is it called 'World party'?

3 Read the article. Match the sentences (1–6) to the place described.

1 There were no Mardi Gras celebrations here before the mid-1800s.
2 It has the oldest celebration.
3 One type of food is decorated with different colours.
4 One type of musical instrument is especially important.
5 One type of music is especially important.
6 People can travel to the party on a type of boat.

4 Find words in the article for these pictures.

5 Work in groups. Describe your favourite festival or celebration in your country. Think about these things.

- History: When and why did it begin?
- Traditional food: Is there any special food like cakes with candles?
- Clothes: Do people wear special costumes or masks?
- Parades: Do people walk round the streets or ride on floats? Do you have fireworks in the evenings?
- Live music: Is music important? What kind of music do people play?

Unit 6 **Stages in life**

Listening

6 🔊 **1.38** Listen to a news item about Mardi Gras. At which celebration in the *World party* article is the presenter?

7 🔊 **1.38** Listen again. Answer the questions with *Yes*, *No* or *Don't know*.

1. Are a lot of people going to come?
2. Is the woman riding on the float on her own?
3. Is she wearing her mask when the interview starts?
4. Does she think she'll have a good time?

Grammar future forms

8 Look at the sentences (a–c) from the interview in Exercise 6. Answer the questions (1–3).

a *Are you going to* be in the parade this afternoon?
b *I'm meeting* everyone at the float in a few minutes.
c Interviewer: And do you have a mask? Lorette: Sure. Here it is. *I'll put* it on.

1. Which sentence is about a plan or future intention? (It was decided before the conversation.)
2. Which sentence is a decision during the conversation?
3. Which sentence is about an arrangement with other people at a certain time in the future?

> ▶ **FUTURE FORMS**
>
> **going to**
> I'm
> he's/she's/it's   *going to* + verb
> you're/we're/they're
>
> **'ll (will)**
> I/he/she/it/you/we/they   *'ll* + verb
>
> **Present continuous for future**
> She's leaving next Friday.
> When are they arriving?
>
> For further information and practice, see page 90.

9 Look at the grammar box. Then choose the correct options to complete the sentences.

1. A: Did Geoff email the times of the parade?
   B: I don't know. *I'll check / I'm checking* my inbox right away.
2. *You'll go / You're going* to visit New Orleans! When did you decide that?
3. A: Hey, this costume would look great on you.
   B: Maybe. *I'm trying / I'll try* it on.
4. A: I forgot to tell you. I'm travelling back home today.
   B: Oh, so *I won't see / I'm not seeing* you later?
5. One day when I'm older, *I'm visiting / I'm going to visit* Venice.
6. A: What time *will we meet / are we meeting* everyone for the parade?
   B: At two in the main square.
7. A: *Are we going to give / Will we give* Mark the present tonight?
   B: No, because his birthday isn't until tomorrow.
8. A: What time *will you leave / are you leaving*?
   B: Straight after the firework display.

10 Pronunciation contracted forms

🔊 **1.39** Listen to sentences 1–5 in Exercise 9. Notice how the contracted forms are pronounced. Listen again and repeat.

Speaking

11 Work in groups. Next year, your town is five hundred years old. Have a town meeting to plan and prepare a celebration. Discuss this list. Decide what you need and who is in charge of organising each thing.

- type of celebration? (e.g. a party, floats, parade, fireworks)
- type of food?
- music?
- where? (e.g. indoors, outdoors)
- date and time?
- items to buy? who will buy them?
- anything else?

> *We're celebrating the town's birthday next year …*
>
> *I'll buy the food!*

12 Present your final plans to the whole class. Explain what you are going to do.

> *We're going to …*

| TALK ABOUT | ▶ A LIFE-CHANGING DECISION | ▶ PLANNING A CELEBRATION | ▶ EVENTS IN THE YEAR | ▶ AN INVITATION |
| WRITE | ▶ A DESCRIPTION | | | |

reading celebrating change • critical thinking identifying the key information • word focus get • speaking events in the year

6c Masai rite of passage

Reading

1 Discuss these questions.

1 At what age can people legally do these things?

> drive a car   get married   buy cigarettes
> leave home   buy fireworks
> open a bank account

2 At what age do you think teenagers become adults?
3 Do you have special celebrations in your country for young people as they become adults?

2 Look at the photo and the title of the article on page 75. What do you think the expression 'rite of passage' means? Choose the correct option (a or b). Then read the article and check.

a a long journey from one place to another
b a traditional celebration where you move from one stage of life to the next

3 There are six paragraphs in the article. Each paragraph answers one of these questions. Read the article again and number the questions 1 to 6. Then answer the questions.

a How is hair important in Masai culture?
b Where do the Masai live? 1
c Why are the Masai more famous than other tribes?
d What is the 'Osingira'?
e Who are the warriors?
f How does 'Eunoto' end?

Critical thinking identifying the key information

4 Write notes about the 'Eunoto'. Use these headings and only write down the most important information from the article.

- Location
- Purpose
- Special clothing or appearance
- Special places
- Responsibilities of older men and women

5 Work in pairs. Compare your notes from Exercise 4. How similar are they? Did you include the same information?

Word focus *get*

6 *Get* has different meanings. Underline examples of *get* in the article with these meanings.

> arrive   become   receive

7 Read the description of a wedding. Notice the different ways we can use *get*. Replace the bold words with these words.

> ~~become~~   catch   meet and socialise   prepare
> receive   return   wakes up and gets out of bed

Once the couple ¹ **get** *become* engaged, people start to ² **get ready** _____ for the big day! On the morning of the wedding, everyone ³ **gets up** _____ early. Family and friends sometimes have to travel long distances but it's always a great chance for everyone to ⁴ **get together** _____ again. After the main ceremony, the couple ⁵ **get** _____ a lot of presents. Nowadays, many couples go abroad on their honeymoon so they leave to ⁶ **get** _____ their plane. When they ⁷ **get back** _____, they move into their new home.

Speaking

8 Work in pairs. Choose one of these events. Describe it to your partner and try to use the word *get* three times in your description.

> a birthday   a religious day or period
> New Year's day   your country's national day
> Valentine's day   another special occasion

Unit 6 **Stages in life**

MASAI RITE OF PASSAGE

The Masai are an African tribe of about half a million people. Most of them live in the country of Kenya, but they are also nomadic. Groups of Masai also live in other parts of east Africa, including north Tanzania and they move their animals (cows, sheep and goats) to different areas of the region.

There are many other African tribes but, for many people, the Masai are the most well-known. They are famous for their bright red clothing and their ceremonies that include lots of music and dancing. Probably, one of the most colourful ceremonies is the festival of 'Eunoto'. This is a rite of passage when the teenage boys of the Masai become men.

'Eunoto' lasts for many days and Masai people travel across the region to get to a special place near the border between Kenya and Tanzania. The teenage boys who travel with them are called 'warriors'. This is a traditional name from the past when young men fought with other tribes. Nowadays, these warriors spend most of their time looking after their cattle.

At the beginning of the ceremony, the teenagers paint their bodies. Meanwhile, their mothers start to build a place called the 'Osingira'. It is a sacred room in the middle of the celebrations. Later, the older men from different tribes will sit inside this place and, at different times, the boys go inside to meet them. Later in the day, the boys run around the 'Osingira', going faster and faster each time. It is another important part of the ritual.

The teenagers also have to change their appearance at 'Eunoto'. Masai boys' hair is very long before the ritual but they have to cut it off. In Masai culture, hair is an important symbol. For example, when a baby grows into an infant, the mother cuts the child's hair and gives the child a name. At a Masai wedding, the hair of the bride is also cut off as she becomes a woman. And so, at Eunoto, the teenage boy's mother cuts his hair off at sunrise.

On the final day, the teenagers meet the senior elders one more time. They get this advice: 'Now you are men, use your heads and knowledge.' Then, people start to travel back to their homes and lands. The teenagers are no longer 'warriors'. They are adult men and now they will get married, have children and buy cattle. Later in life, they will be the leaders of their communities.

tribe (n) /traɪb/ large group of families living in the same area
nomadic (adj) /nəʊˈmædɪk/ moving from one place to another and not staying in one place
warrior (n) /ˈwɒriə(r)/ soldier or someone who fights for the tribe
ritual (n) /ˈrɪtʃuəl/ formal ceremony with different stages
sunrise (n) /ˈsʌnraɪz/ when the sun comes up and the day starts
elder (n) /ˈeldə(r)/ older and experienced person in a tribe or community

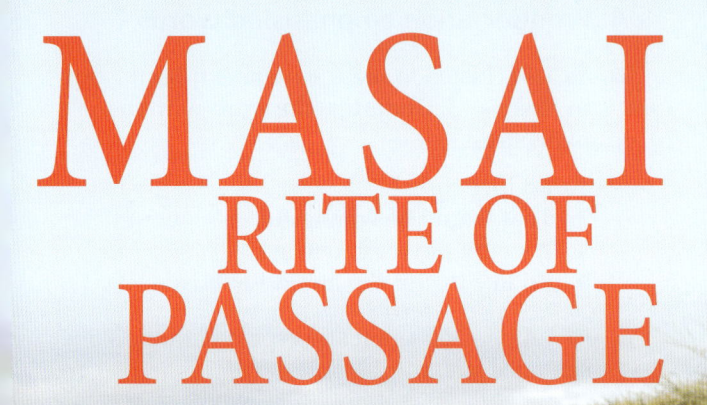

TALK ABOUT ▶ A LIFE-CHANGING DECISION ▶ PLANNING A CELEBRATION ▶ EVENTS IN THE YEAR ▶ AN INVITATION
WRITE ▶ A DESCRIPTION

speaking formal and informal events • real life inviting, accepting and declining • pronunciation emphasising words

6d An invitation

Speaking

1 Which of these events are very formal? Which are less formal?

> an end-of-course party
> an engagement party
> a barbecue with family and friends
> a leaving party for a work colleague
> your grandfather's ninetieth birthday party
> going out for dinner with a work client

Real life inviting, accepting and declining

2 🔊 1.40 Listen to two conversations. Answer the questions.

Conversation 1
1 What event does Ian invite Abdullah to?
2 Why does Abdullah decline the invitation at first?
3 How does Ian convince Abdullah to come?
4 Does Abdullah need to get anything?

Conversation 2
5 When is Sally leaving?
6 Where does Joanna invite Sally?
7 Does Sally accept the invitation?
8 Do you think this conversation is more or less formal than conversation 1? Why?

3 🔊 1.40 Look at the expressions for inviting, accepting and declining. Listen to the conversations again. Tick the expressions the speakers use.

▶ GOING ON A JOURNEY		
	Less formal	More formal
Inviting	Do you want to …? How about -ing? Why don't you …?	Would you like to come to …? I'd like to take you to …
Accepting	It sounds great/nice. Thanks, that would be great. Yes, OK.	I'd like that very much. That would be wonderful. I'd love to.
Declining	Thanks, but … Sorry, I can't. I'm …	I'd like/love to, but I'm afraid I … It's very nice of you to ask, but I …

4 **Pronunciation** emphasising words

a 🔊 1.41 Listen to these sentences from the box in Exercise 3. Underline the word with the main stress.

1 I'd love to.
2 That would be wonderful.
3 It's very nice of you to ask.
4 I'd like to, but I'm afraid I'm busy.

b 🔊 1.41 Listen again and repeat with the same sentence stress.

5 Work in pairs. Take turns to invite each other to different events. (Think about how formal you need to be.) Practise accepting and declining.

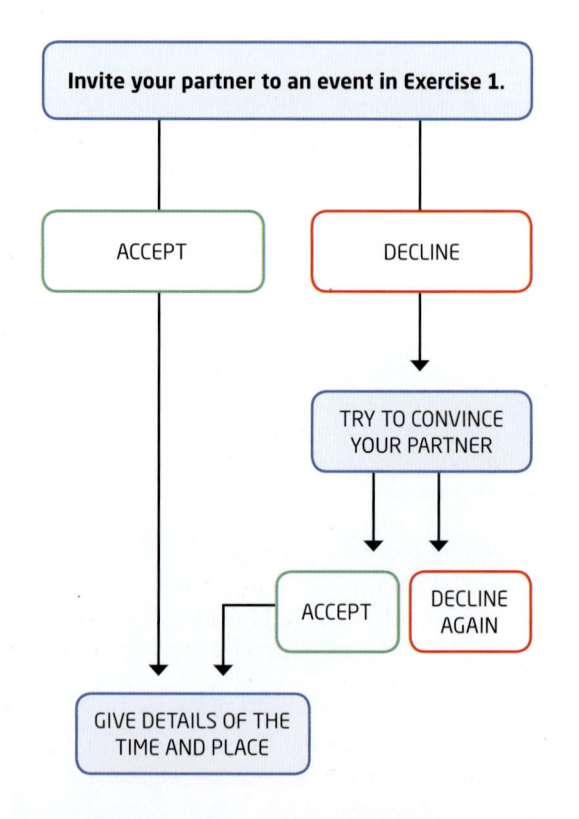

Invite your partner to an event in Exercise 1.
→ ACCEPT / DECLINE
DECLINE → TRY TO CONVINCE YOUR PARTNER → ACCEPT / DECLINE AGAIN
→ GIVE DETAILS OF THE TIME AND PLACE

TALK ABOUT ▶ A LIFE-CHANGING DECISION ▶ PLANNING A CELEBRATION ▶ EVENTS IN THE YEAR ▶ AN INVITATION
WRITE ▶ A DESCRIPTION

writing a description • writing skill descriptive adjectives   Unit 6 Stages in life

6e A wedding in Madagascar

Writing a description

1 On the website *Glimpse*, people write descriptions of their experiences abroad. Read this post. Which of the things in the box does the writer describe?

| food and meals   clothes   festivals and ceremonies |
| nature and geographic features   people |
| towns, cities and buildings   transport |

glimpse YOUR STORIES FROM ABROAD

I was staying in Madagascar with a family and they invited me to their daughter's wedding. On the big day, I arrived outside an **enormous** tent. There was a zebu at the entrance and it looked **miserable**. Inside the tent, there were **beautiful** decorations and over 300 excited relatives and guests were waiting for the bride and groom to arrive. The women wore **colourful** dresses. The older men wore **smart** suits but the younger men were less formally dressed. I even saw jeans and T-shirts. Finally, the ceremony began with some very long and sometimes **dull** speeches. But the crowd listened politely and sometimes they laughed and applauded. Finally, it was dinner and I suddenly realised what the zebu was for. We ate from **massive** plates of meat. I felt sorry for the zebu but the meat was the best part of the ceremony! It was **delicious**!

2 Writing skill descriptive adjectives

a In the description, the writer uses interesting adjectives. Match the highlighted adjectives to these less descriptive adjectives (1–4).

1 big   *enormous*, ...
2 unhappy ....
3 nice   *beautiful*, ..., ..., ...
4 boring   ....

> **WORDBUILDING synonyms**
> Some words have the same meaning as another word. These are called synonyms: *historic* = *old*, *big* = *huge*, *boring* = *dull*.
>
> For further information and practice, see Workbook page 143.

b Work in pairs. Improve the sentences with more descriptive adjectives. You can use words from the description in Exercise 2 or your own ideas.

              beautiful   *historic*
1 Venice is a ~~nice~~ city with lots of ~~old~~ buildings.
2 In the USA, you can buy big burgers.
3 The parade was a bit boring after a while.
4 The crowd was happy because the nice fireworks started.
5 All the costumes were nice.
6 I was very sad to leave Paris.
7 I tried sushi for the first time and it was really good.
8 The view of the mountains was nice.

c Work in pairs. Look back at the list of subjects in Exercise 1. Think of two or three interesting adjectives to describe each one. Use a dictionary to help you. Then join another pair and compare your adjectives.

Example:
food and meals – delicious, tasty, disgusting

3 Choose one of these topics and write a short description (one paragraph) for the *Glimpse* website.

- a day you remember from a holiday
- your favourite place in the world
- a special occasion in your life
- a festival or celebration

4 Work in pairs. Read your partner's descriptions. Does he/she use interesting adjectives?

TALK ABOUT ▶ A LIFE-CHANGING DECISION ▶ PLANNING A CELEBRATION ▶ EVENTS IN THE YEAR ▶ AN INVITATION
WRITE ▶ A DESCRIPTION

6f Steel drums

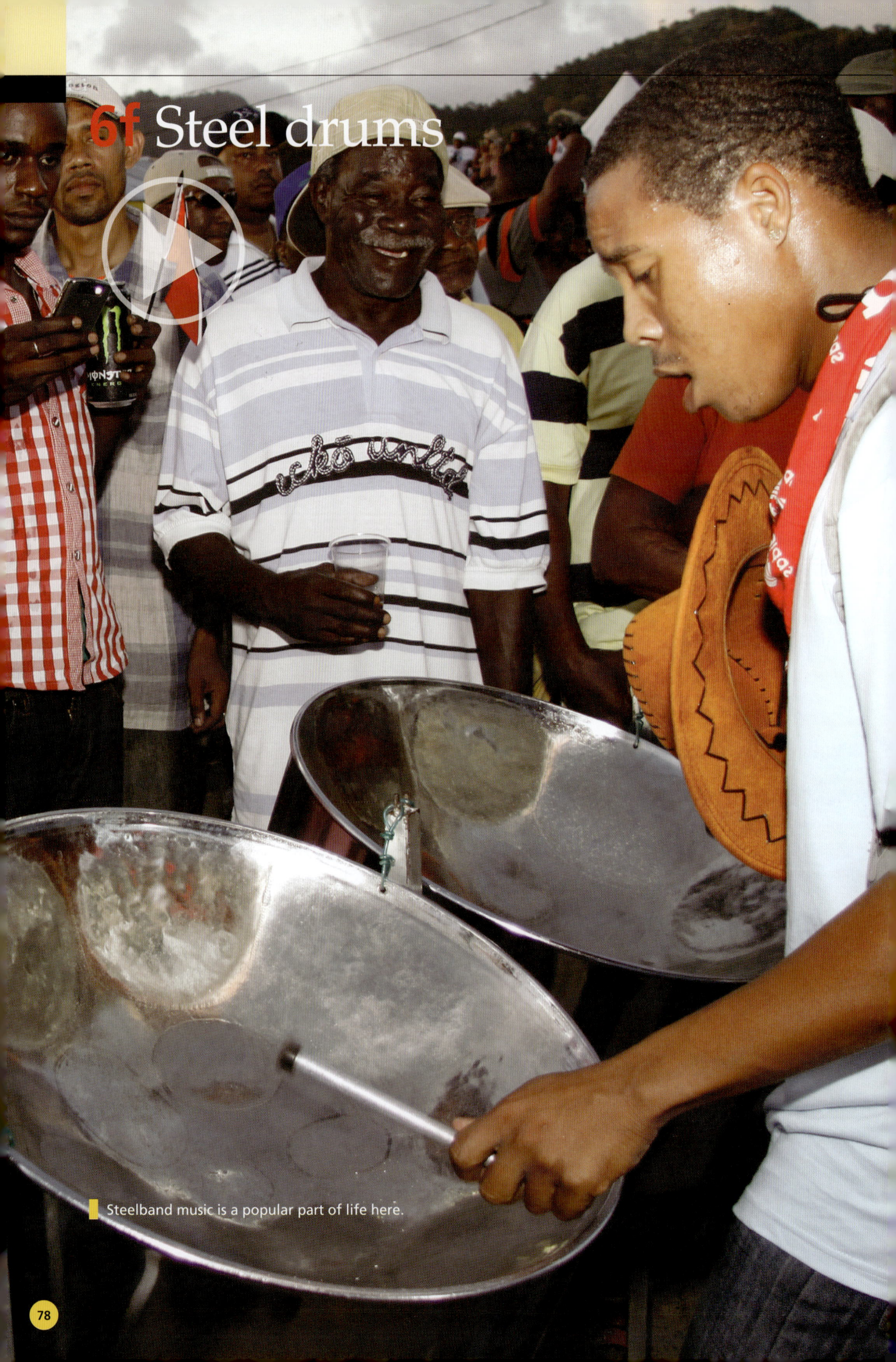

Steelband music is a popular part of life here.

Unit 6 **Stages in life**

Before you watch

1 Work in groups. Look at the photo and discuss the questions.

  1 Where do you think these people are from?
  2 What kind of musical instrument are they playing?
  3 Why do you think this music is important for them?

While you watch

2 Watch the video and check your answers from Exercise 1.

3 Watch the video again. Put these actions in the order you see them.

  a Beverley and Dove learn to play the drums.
  b A steel band with children and adults play together.
  c A person runs into the sea.
  d Honey Boy tunes a drum.
  e A man makes an oil drum into a steel drum.
  f People sell food in a market.

4 Watch the video again and answer the questions.

  1 What are the islands of the Caribbean region famous for?
  2 Is the 'steelband' or 'pan' native to all the islands?
  3 When did people invent this musical instrument?
  4 Why did Trinidad have many oil drums?
  5 Is the music of the island old? Where did it come from?
  6 Do most people play by reading music?
  7 What is the name of a person who tunes the drums?
  8 Who do you find in a 'panyard'?

5 Match the people (1–4) with the comments (a–d).

  1 Beverly
  2 woman in market
  3 Tony Poyer
  4 Dove

  a You got that!
  b It's part of our culture.
  c It's the music of my country so I should learn it.
  d This is ours. We made it. We created it.

6 Complete the summary with words from the glossary.

Everywhere you go on the island of Trinidad and Tobago, you can't ¹_____ the sound of the steel drum. It's ²_____ to the island. It was the only new musical instrument of the twentieth century. Because the county produces oil, it has lots of ³_____. During the Second World War, people made them into steel drums or '⁴_____'. However, the music of the region is much older and originally it came over with the African people. Today, the drums still give pleasure to children and adults. Most people play the drums by ⁵_____ and every night places call '⁶_____' are full of musicians, learning to play and enjoying part of their country's culture.

After you watch

7 Roleplay a conversation with Tony Poyer

Work in pairs.

Student A: You are Tony Poyer, the expert on steel drums in the video. A journalist is going to interview you. Look at the information below and think about what you are going to say to the journalist about the drums.

Student B: You are a journalist. You are making a documentary about steel drums in Trinidad and Tobago. Use the information below to prepare questions about the drums.

- its history
- how it's made
- how people learn to play it
- the importance of the drum in local culture

8 Work in groups. Discuss these questions for each of your countries.

  1 What is the most important or popular musical instrument in your country?
  2 What is the most common musical instrument that people play in your country?
  3 What is an important symbol of your culture? Does it have a special type of music?
  4 Do you think symbols are important for a country or culture? Why? / Why not?

---

escape (v) /ˈɪskeɪp/ run away from
be native to (v) /bi: neɪtɪv tu:/ be from somewhere originally
oil drums (n) /ɔɪl drʌmz/ round metal containers for oil
play by ear (expression) /pleɪ baɪ i:ə/ play musical instrument by listening and not by reading music
pans (n) /pænz/ local word in Trinidad and Tobago meaning 'steel drums'
panyards (npl) /ˈpænjɑːdz/ local word in Trinidad and Tobago meaning place to play steel drums

79

UNIT 6 REVIEW

Grammar

1 Add the word *to* in six of these sentences. One sentence is correct.

1 I intend ^to find a new job.
2 It's difficult learn a musical instrument.
3 Save your money have a nice holiday this year.
4 We're going meet everyone later.
5 Do you want join us for a drink?
6 I'll see you at the parade.
7 Would you like come for dinner?

2 Choose the correct option (a–c) to complete the sentences.

1 We _____ visit my family this weekend but we aren't sure yet.
  a hope to
  b 're going to
  c 'll
2 A: I need someone to carry these books for me.
  B: I _____ you!
  a 'm going to help
  b 'm helping
  c 'll help
3 It isn't easy _____ the lottery.
  a win
  b to win
  c will win
4 A: When _____ bring the cake?
  B: In a few minutes.
  a are you going to
  b will you
  c are you
5 Rachel _____ a party tonight. She arranged it months ago.
  a will have
  b plans to have
  c is having

3 Work in pairs. Tell each other:
• your plans for this weekend.
• your future career intentions.

I CAN	
talk about my future plans and intentions	
talk about decisions and arrangements	

Vocabulary

4 Complete the text about the Notting Hill Carnival with these words.

| costumes | decorations | drums | floats | ~~parades~~ |

Every year at the end of August, the London neighbourhood of Notting Hill is full of colourful ¹ *parades* for the biggest carnival in Europe. Over 40,000 volunteers help by putting up ² _____ along the streets of west London and welcoming over one million visitors to the party. Many of them make and wear their own ³ _____. The Caribbean community of London started the event in 1966 so you'll see many decorated ⁴ _____ and hear loud music and traditional steel ⁵ _____.

5 Match the verbs (1–6) with the nouns (a–f).

1 start   a home
2 get   b a pension
3 leave   c a mask
4 take   d a career break
5 wear   e a family
6 ride   f on a float

I CAN	
talk about stages and events in life	
talk about parties and celebrations	

Real life

6 Replace the words in bold with these phrases.

| I'd like you to | I'd like to | that sounds | would you like |

1 **Do you want** to go for a coffee?
2 **Why don't you** come with me to the cinema?
3 **It's nice of you to ask** but I'm out this evening.
4 Thanks. **That'd be** great.

7 Work in groups. Invite each other to do something this week. Accept or decline the invitations.

I CAN	
invite people	
accept and decline invitations	

Speaking

8 Work in groups. You are halfway through this course. Discuss and plan a mid-course party for your class.

UNIT 5a Exercise 10, page 59

Student A
Ask the caller about his/her views on recycling and what we need to do about the problem. It's your job to ask extra questions and argue with the caller about his/her views. Before you begin, prepare some of your questions for the caller. You can use some of the questions and ideas from the audioscript on page 93.

UNIT 5d Exercise 6, page 64

Student A
Conversation 1
You ordered some clothes online. You received an email from the company. The clothes are not in stock. Telephone the customer service helpline.

- Say why you are calling.
- Your order number is EI3304A.
- Spell your surname.
- Find out how long you have to wait for the clothes.
- Ask for a refund. The price was $149.50.

Conversation 2
You are a customer service assistant for a book supplier. Answer the telephone.

- Ask for the customer's order number and the title of the book.
- The book isn't in stock. You don't know when the book will arrive.
- Offer the caller a second-hand copy of the same book. It's £3.50.

Communication activities

UNIT 5a Exercise 10, page 59

Student B
Speak to the radio presenter. Explain your views about recycling and what we need to do about the problem in the future. Before you begin, prepare some of your comments and opinions. You can use some of the expressions and ideas from the audioscript on page 93.

UNIT 5d Exercise 6, page 64

Student B
Conversation 1
You are a customer service assistant for a clothing company supplier. Answer the telephone.

- Ask for the customer's order number and his/her surname.
- The clothes aren't in stock but they will be in two weeks.
- Offer some different clothes at the same price.

Conversation 2
You ordered a book online called *Learn Spanish in One Week*. You received an email from the company. The book is not in stock. Telephone the customer service helpline.

- Say why you are calling.
- Your order number is AZE880.
- Find out how long you have to wait for the book.
- Ask for the price of the second-hand copy.
- Buy the second-hand book.

Grammar summary

Grammar summary

UNIT 1
Present simple and adverbs of frequency
Form

Affirmative	Negative	Interrogative
I/you/we/they **work** he/she/it **works**	I/you/we/they **don't work** he/she/it **doesn't work**	**do** I/you/we/they **work**? **does** he/she/it **work**?

Use
We use the present simple to talk about:
- habits and routines. *I **eat** an apple every day.*
- things that are always true. *Lions **eat** meat.*

We often use adverbs of frequency (*always, usually, often, sometimes, rarely, never*) and expressions of frequency (*once a week, on Fridays, at the weekend, in the summer, every Saturday*) with the present simple to talk about how often we do something.

Adverbs of frequency usually go before the main verb or after the verb *to be*.
*I **sometimes** watch football on TV.*
*I am **always** very happy.*

Expressions of frequency usually go at the beginning or end of a sentence.
***At the weekend** they visit their grandparents.*
*They visit their grandparents **at the weekend**.*

Practice
1 Complete the sentences with the present simple form of the verbs and the adverbs / expressions of frequency.

1. I *walk* (walk) into town every Saturday.
2. Emily _____ (ride / often) her bike to work in summer.
3. When _____ he _____ (be / usually) at home?
4. I _____ (not be / often) in the office on Mondays.
5. He _____ (do / never) exercise at the weekend.
6. _____ the doctor _____ (work / every weekend)?

Present continuous
Form
We form the present continuous with the present simple of the verb *to be* plus the *-ing* form of the verb.

Affirmative	Negative	Interrogative
I **am** / you **are** / he **is** / she **is** / it **is** / we **are** / they **are** washing	I **am not** / you **are not** / he **is not** / she **is not** / it **is not** / we **are not** / they **are not** washing	**Am** I / **are** you / **is** he / **is** she / **is** it / **are** we / **are** they **washing**?

Use
We use the present continuous to talk about:
- things happening now. *He's **watching** the news on TV at the moment.*
- things happening around now, but not necessarily at the moment. *Vicky's **travelling** to several African countries this year.*
- current trends and changing situations. *Fewer people **are buying** cars this year.*

We don't usually use stative verbs (*be, have, like, love, hate, want*) in the present continuous.

Notes
Notice the spelling rules for the *-ing* form:
- for most verbs, add *-ing* (*walk → walking, play → playing, read → reading*).
- for verbs ending in a consonant + vowel + consonant, double the last letter of the verb and add *-ing* (*sit → sitting, run → running*).
- for verbs ending in *-e*, delete the final *e* and add *-ing* (*make → making, write → writing*).

Practice
2 Complete the sentences. Use the present continuous and present simple form of the verbs.

| ~~cook~~ | not cycle | do | go | play | prepare |

1. Carl usually *cooks* on Wednesday.
2. The boys often _____ hiking in the holidays.
3. _____ David _____ tennis at the moment?
4. She _____ to work today – it's raining.
5. Please wait. The pharmacist _____ the medicine.
6. We always _____ gardening at the weekend.

84

Grammar summary

UNIT 2
Verb + -ing forms
Form
We add -ing to the main verb. The spelling rules are the same as for the present continuous.

verb	-ing form
walk	walking
swim	swimming
give	giving

Use
We use the verb + -ing form:
- as the subject of the sentence. The -ing form is often a noun. **Eating** *a lot of fruit is important.*
- after verbs such as *like, love, enjoy, prefer, don't like, hate, can't stand, (not) mind* as an object. *I love* **walking** *in the mountains.*
- after a preposition. *I'm very good at* **playing** *tennis.*

Practice
1 Complete the sentences with the -ing form of these verbs.

| ~~cycle~~ | eat | go | shop | sit | visit | watch |
| write |

1 I'm listening to a radio programme about _cycling_.
2 Do you enjoy _____ sport on TV?
3 _____ at home all day is boring!
4 We don't like _____ this football stadium.
5 Jenny is very good at _____ sports reports.
6 _____ for new football boots is always difficult.
7 He hates _____ to matches when his team loses.
8 _____ a lot before a game is bad for you.

like + -ing / 'd like to
Form
like + -ing

Affirmative	Negative	Interrogative
I/you/we/they **like watching** old films.	I/you/we/they **don't like watching** old films.	Do I/you/we/they **like watching** old films?
He/she/it **likes playing** in the park.	He/she/it **doesn't like playing** in the park.	Does he/she/it **like playing** in the park?

'd like to (= would like to)

Affirmative	Negative	Interrogative
I**'d**/you**'d**/he**'d**/she**'d**/it**'d**/we**'d**/they**'d like to** go there tomorrow.	I/you/he/she/it/we'd/they **wouldn't like to** go there tomorrow.	**Would** I/you/he/she/it/we/they **like to** go there tomorrow?

Use
like + -ing
We use *like + -ing* to talk about a general feeling which is true now.
Richard **likes skiing** *a lot.*
Ella **doesn't like listening** *to rap music.*

'd like to (= would like to)
We use *'d like to* to talk about a future ambition.
I'd **like to visit** *Kenya next year.*
She **wouldn't like to work** *in an office when she leaves school.*

Practice
2 Complete the sentences with *like + -ing* or *'d like to* and the verbs.

1 Andy _likes playing_ (like / play) football every Saturday.
2 The boys _____ (like / learn) how to swim next year.
3 _____ Mike _____ (like / drive) his new car?
4 I _____ (not like / compete) in this competition every week!
5 _____ you _____ (like / sit) here, sir?
6 Jo _____ (not like / travel) round the world next year.
7 My father _____ (like / cook) lunch for all the family every Sunday.
8 She _____ (like / watch) the match with us next week.

Modal verbs for rules
Form

I/you/he/she/it/we/they **must** wear goggles.	I/you/he/she/it/we/they **can** play here.	I/you/he/she/it/we/they **have to** hit the ball.
I/you/he/she/it/we/they **mustn't** (= must not) wear goggles.	I/you/he/she/it/we/they **can't** (= cannot) play here.	I/you/he/she/it/we/they **don't have to** hit the ball.

85

Grammar summary

Notes
There are two important differences between *must* and *can* and regular verbs in the present simple:
- There is no third person *-s* with modal verbs.
  *She **must** go. I **can** stay.*
- There is no auxiliary *do* with modal verbs.
  *I **mustn't** lose. He **can't** play.*

Have to is a regular verb. *I **have to** go. He **has to** help. I **don't have to** play. She **doesn't have to** compete.*

Use
We use different modal verbs to talk about rules.
- When something is necessary and an obligation, we use *must*, *have to* and *mustn't*. *You **must** be home at eleven o'clock. You **have to** finish your homework tonight. He **mustn't** leave the house.*
- When something is allowed according to the rules, we use *can*. *Yes, you **can** go to the cinema on Friday.*
- When something is not necessary (but allowed), we use *don't have to*. *You **don't have to** wear a suit at the meeting.*
- When something is not allowed, we use *mustn't* and *can't*. *She **mustn't** tell anybody. He **can't** play football tomorrow.*

Practice
3 Put the words in the correct order.

1 get up he must tomorrow early
   He must get up early tomorrow.
2 competition finish at must ten o'clock the
3 send my have today application I to
4 tomorrow to don't they have to go work
5 argue referee team with the the can't
6 five o'clock to game have doesn't finish at the
7 for wear Tim can clothes casual the game
8 sports kit they forget their mustn't

UNIT 3
Comparatives and superlatives
Form

Adjective	Comparative	Superlative
▶ REGULAR		
new	newer	newest
hot	hotter	hottest
nice	nicer	nicest
easy	easier	easiest
interesting	more interesting	most interesting
▶ IRREGULAR		
good	better	best
bad	worse	worst

We add *-er* to regular short adjectives to form the comparative and we add *-est* to regular short adjectives to form the superlative:
new → newer → newest

We add *more* and *most* to form the comparative and superlative forms with longer adjectives:
*interesting → **more** interesting → **most** interesting*

Notice the spelling rules for comparative and superlative adjectives:
- for regular short adjectives, add *-er / -est*:
  long → longer → longest
- for adjectives ending in *-e*, add *-r / -st*:
  large → larger → largest
- for adjectives ending in *-y* (after a consonant), change the *-y* to *-i*: *happy → happier → happiest*
- for adjectives ending in consonant–vowel–consonant, double the final consonant:
  big → bigger → biggest; hot → hotter → hottest

We use *than* after a comparative adjective.
*My bicycle is newer **than** yours.*

We usually use *the* before a superlative adjective.
*It's **the** quickest way to get to the station.*

We use *much* to add emphasis to a comparative adjective.
*Petrol cars are **much** more expensive than electric cars.*

Use
We use comparative adjectives to compare two things.
Cars are faster than buses.

We use superlative adjectives to compare three or more things.
Blues whales are the biggest animals in the world.

Practice

1 Write sentences. Use the comparative (C) and superlative (S) forms.

1. India / Norway / hot (C)
   India is hotter than Norway.
2. cars / bikes / dangerous (C)
3. James / friendly / person / in our class (S)
4. Helena / good athlete / in the country (S)
5. cheetahs / tigers / fast (C)
6. Naomi / happy / person / in the office (S)
7. skiing / exciting sport / in the world (S)
8. sports cars / family cars / difficult to drive (C)

as … as
Form

Affirmative	Negative	Interrogative
An elephant is **as** heavy **as** a car.	A bus **isn't** (is not) **as** comfortable **as** a car.	Is a horse **as** strong **as** an elephant?

Use

We use *as* + adjective + *as* to compare two things and say they are the same or equal.
*Robbie is **as** tall **as** his brother.*

We use *not as* + adjective + *as* to compare two things and say they are different or not equal.
*Paul is **not as** clever **as** Anna.*

Practice

2 Write comparative sentences and questions using *as … as* (+) and *(not) as … as* (–).

1. Rosa / old / Maria (+)
   Rosa is as old as Maria.
2. Alaska / cold / Canada (+)
3. cars / cheap / bicycles (–)
4. horse riding / healthy / running (?)
5. buses / quiet / trams (–)
6. books / exciting / films (?)
7. our car / clean / an electric car (+)
8. Russia / hot / Brazil (?)

UNIT 4
Past simple
Form

Affirmative	Negative	Interrogative
▶ **REGULAR**		
I/you/he/she/it/we/they walk**ed** all day.	I/you/he/she/it/we/they **didn't** walk all day.	**Did** I/you/he/she/it/we/they walk all day?
▶ **IRREGULAR**		
I/you/he/she/it/we/they **said**	I/you/he/she/it/we/they **didn't** say	**Did** I/you/he/she/it/we/they **say**?

Short answers
Yes, I/you/he/she/it/we/they **did**.
No, I/you/he/she/it/we/they **didn't**.

We add *-ed* to regular verbs to form the past simple: *work → worked, walk → walked, play → played*.

Notice the spelling rules for other regular verbs:
- for verbs ending in *-e*, we add *-d*: *die → died*
- for verbs ending in *-y*, we change the *-y* to *i* and add *-ed*: *try → tried, cry → cried, study → studied*
- for verbs ending in vowel + consonant (not *-w*, *-x* or *-y*), we double the consonant: *stop → stopped*

Some verbs have an irregular affirmative form in the past simple:
be → was / were, do → did, go → went, drive → drove, know → knew, take → took

We use the auxiliary verb *did / didn't* to form negatives and questions.
*Kirsten **didn't** go on the adventure.*
***Did** you live in Peru?*

We also use *did / didn't* to form short answers.
*Did you live in Peru? Yes, I **did**.*
*Did Kirsten go on the adventure? No, she **didn't**.*

Use

We use the past simple to talk about completed actions and events in the past. We often use a time phrase (*yesterday, last week, ten years ago*) with the past simple.
*I visited Paris **in January**.*
*They didn't see his new film **last night**.*

Practice

1 Write questions and answers using the past simple.

1. Where / he / go? go / Spain
   Where did he go? He went to Spain.
2. Where / she / live? live / Rome

87

Grammar summary

3 What / they / do? drive / Norway

4 When / Kerry / travel / the USA? travel / the USA / last year

5 Where / you / find / it? find / it / in South Africa

6 When / they / live / Canada? live / Canada / in 2010

Past continuous
Form
We form the past continuous with the past simple of the verb *to be* plus the *-ing* form of the verb.

Affirmative	Negative	Interrogative
I/he/she/it/ **was working** last week.	I/he/she/it/**wasn't working** last week.	**Was** I/he/she/it/**working** last week?
You/we/they **were working** last week.	You/we/they **weren't working** last week.	**Were** you/we/they **working** last week?

Use
We use the past continuous to:
- describe actions and situations in progress at a particular time in the past. *Paul **was watching** TV. Katy **was reading** a book.*
- talk about the background to a story. *The sun **was shining** and the birds **were singing**.*

We often use the past continuous with the past simple to talk about two actions that happened at the same time in the past. We can join the tenses with the words *when* or *while*.
*Tania **was waiting** at the station **when** the rest of the climbing team arrived. **While** the team **were walking** to the train, she ran to meet them.*
Remember, we don't usually use stative verbs (e.g. *be, like, believe, understand*) in the continuous form.

Practice
2 Complete the sentences with the past simple or the past continuous form of the verbs.

1 Jo *was driving* (drive) and Katya *was reading* (read) the map.
2 She .... (sleep) when a noise .... (wake) her up.
3 The team leader .... (shout) and the wind .... (blow).
4 While the boys .... (make) a fire, it .... (start) to rain.
5 Liz .... (cook) supper and the others .... (talk) about the expedition.
6 As they .... (walk) in the mountains, the weather .... (get) worse.

7 The rescue team .... (arrive) while we .... (decide) where to go.
8 While I .... (swim), I .... (see) a group of dolphins.

UNIT 5
Countable and uncountable nouns
Form and use
Some nouns are **countable**. These are nouns you can count and they have both a singular and a plural form. We use them with an indefinite article (*a/an*) and numbers.
*There is **a bag** on the table.*
*There are **two bags** on the table.*

Some nouns are **uncountable**. These are nouns you cannot count. They are singular and have no plural form. We use them with the definite article or no article. You cannot use them with *a/an* or numbers: *water (two waters), rubbish (two rubbishes).*
*We drink **water** eat every day.*
*The **water** is in the jug.*

Quantifiers
Form

Affirmative	Negative	Interrogative
▶ **COUNTABLE NOUNS**		
I've got **some** books.	I haven't got **any** books.	Are there **any** books?
There are **a lot of** books.	There aren't **many** books.	How **many** books have you got?
She's got **a few** books.		
▶ **UNCOUNTABLE NOUNS**		
I've got **some** water.	I haven't got **any** water.	Have you got **any** water?
There is **a lot of** water.	There isn't **much** water.	How **much** water have you got?
They've got **a little** water.		

Use
We use quantifiers with countable and uncountable nouns to talk about quantity.

Countable nouns
We use *some*, *a lot of* and *a few* in affirmative sentences.
*I've got **some** newspapers.*
*We've got **a lot of** bottles.*
*There are **a few** cans.*

We use *any* or *many* in negative sentences or questions.
*I haven't got **any** books.*
*There aren't **many** boxes.*
*Have you got **any** bags?*
*How **many** photos did you take?*

Grammar summary

Uncountable nouns
We use *some*, *a lot of* and *a little* in affirmative sentences.
*I've got **some** water.*
*They've got **a lot of** food.*
*There is **a little** milk.*

We use *any* or *much* in negative sentences or questions.
*I haven't got **any** information.*
*There isn't **much** bread.*
*Have you got **any** rubbish?*
*How **much** water is there?*

Note: *a lot of* = *lots of* (there is no difference in meaning or use)

Practice
1 Choose the correct option.

1. There's *any* / *some* pollution in the river.
2. There isn't *much* / *many* food on the table.
3. Are there *much* / *any* plastic bags in the park?
4. I've got *a lot of* / *a few* drinking water.
5. How *any* / *many* recycling bins are there here?
6. Do you throw away *many* / *much* plastic?
7. He recycles *much* / *a little* rubbish.
8. How *much* / *many* air pollution is there?

Definite article (*the*) or no article
Form and use
We use the definite article (*the*):
- with something or someone you mentioned before. *Have they done a survey? Yes, They finished **the** survey last week.*
- when it is part of the name of something. ***The** USA introduced 'car pool' lanes.*
- with superlative phrases. *Consumers spend **the** most money on electronic equipment.*

We use no article:
- with most countries. *He lives in Canada and I live in Spain.*
- to talk about people and things in a general way. *People are trying to recycle more rubbish.*
- with certain expressions. *I don't work **at night**.*

Practice
2 Choose the correct option. Choose Ø for no article.

1. There's a black dog in my garden. It's *the* / Ø dog from next door!
2. Have you visited any recycling plants in *the* / Ø Germany?
3. He's *the* / Ø greenest person I know.
4. There were *the* / Ø children everywhere at the festival.
5. What time do you go to *the* / Ø work?
6. I'm going to a meeting about the environment in *the* / Ø Netherlands.
7. He is staying in London on *the* / Ø business.
8. How much did *the* / Ø computer cost?

UNIT 6
Verb patterns with *to* + infinitive
Form
We use *to* + infinitive after several structures. The form of the verb is always the same.

They intend/plan	**to go** to South America.
It's difficult	**to learn** Chinese.
She worked hard	**to buy** a new car.

Use
1 verb + *to* + infinitive
After certain verbs we use the *to* + infinitive form of another verb. This is often to talk about hopes, intentions and decisions.
*He decided **to stop** work.*
*She agreed **to travel** round the world.*
Common verbs which are followed by the *to* + infinitive form are: *intend, plan, want, hope, 'd like, decide, agree, refuse, promise*.
We don't use *to* + infinitive after modal verbs.
*She can't **play** tennis. We will **stay** here.*

2 adjective + *to* + infinitive
We use *to* + infinitive after certain adjectives, often to express a feeling about something.
*It's **fun to play** a musical instrument.*
*It's **difficult to live** on $50 a day.*

3 infinitive of purpose
We can use *to* + infinitive to explain the purpose of the main verb or an action (= in order to do something).
*Marco moved to New York **to go** to college.*
*They visited Greece **to learn** about Ancient Greece.*

Practice
1 Put the words in the correct order.

1. planning summer go diving to this we're
   We're planning to go diving this summer.
2. would like Australia Emma and Pip visit to
3. medicine get job she to studied good a
4. have pension to it's important a
5. wants his my brother leave job to
6. isn't to your save it easy money
7. promised email Brenda every to week
8. fun holiday a it's plan to

89

Grammar summary

Future forms: *going to, will* and present continuous

Form

1 *going to*

Affirmative	Negative	Interrogative
I'm/you're/he's/she's/it's/we're/they're **going to** come to the party.	I'm not / you aren't / he isn't / she isn't / it isn't / we aren't / they aren't **going to** come to the party.	Am I / are you / is he / is she / is it / are we / are they **going to** come to the party?

2 *will*

Affirmative	Negative	Interrogative
I/you/he/she/it/we/they **'ll (will) go** home later.	I/you/he/she/it/we/they **won't (will not) go** home later.	**Will** I/you/he/she/it/we/they **go** home later?

3 Present continuous

For the present continuous form see page 84.

Use

1 *going to*

We use *going to* + infinitive to talk about a plan or a future intention.
I'm **going to make** a costume.
She **isn't going to take part** in the celebrations.

2 *will ('ll)*

We use *will* to talk about a decision which is made during the conversation.
Tim: Oh no! There isn't any sugar left.
Sue: Don't worry. I**'ll buy** some when I go into town.

3 Present continuous for future

We use the present continuous to talk about an arrangement with other people at a certain time in the future.
I'**m leaving** for the party at five o'clock.
We'**re moving** house next month.
We usually use the present continuous, not *going to*, with the verbs *go* and *come*.
I'**m going** to the parade later.
He'**s coming** to the festival with us.

Practice

2 Choose the correct option (a–c).

1 We ___ to Costa Rica on holiday next year.
   (a) are going   b   are going to go   c   will go
2 I've decided to do an evening class. I ___ Italian.
   a   am studying   b   am going to study
   c   will study
3 Alex: I've left my money at home.
   Thomas: Never mind. I ___ the tickets.
   a   am buying   b   am going to buy   c   'll buy
4 What ___ next weekend?
   a   are you doing   b   are you going to do
   c   will you do
5 I'm so excited! We ___ for Athens in a week!
   a   are leaving   b   are going to leave
   c   will leave
6 Sam ___ in London next year.
   a   's working   b   's going to work
   c   'll work
7 I don't know when it starts. I ___ out now.
   a   am finding   b   am going to find
   c   will find
8 ___ to stay with you?
   a   Is he coming   b   Is he going to come
   c   Will he come

Audioscripts

Unit 1

1.1

People sometimes think Mary and Gerald are married but in fact they're just good friends. They have known each other for forty years because they regularly go ballroom dancing. Every week they meet and practise dancing. Mary Hall is eighty-five years old and Gerald Kavanagh is eighty. So, after all these years, why do they dance? Probably because it's good for their health for two reasons. It's good physical exercise, but dancing is also about learning new movements so it's good for your mental health as well. Dancing is one good reason for their long and happy life.

1.2

This quiz is a good way for people to find out how they sleep. It shows them what kind of person they are. People with mostly A answers usually sleep very well. They have regular routines and they are hardly ever tired. People with B answers sleep fairly well. Most adults wake up once or twice a night and that's normal. But these people probably have busy working lives or families so they always want extra hours in bed. Try to go to bed earlier and sleep for an extra hour at weekends. People with mostly C answers have the biggest problems. These people don't relax before bedtime. They regularly work in the evening or do exercise. Don't misunderstand me. Sport is good for your health but not late at night.

1.4

P = Presenter, D = David McLain

P: No one knows exactly the reason why some people live longer than others. Why are they so healthy? Is it their diet? Do they go to the gym more than others? Well, one man is trying to answer these questions and that man is explorer and journalist David McLain. He's currently travelling to places and regions with large numbers of people aged a hundred and over and asking the questions: Why are they so healthy? What are they doing that the rest of us aren't? At the moment he's working on the Island of Sardinia in Italy but he's speaking to us right now on the phone. David, thank you for joining us today.
D: Hello.
P: So, first of all. Tell us why you decided to visit Sardinia.
D: Well, Sardinia is an interesting place because men live the same amount of time as women. That isn't normal for most countries. Men normally die younger.
P: And does anyone know the reason why people live longer in Sardinia?
D: There are different ideas about this but possibly one explanation is that the family is so important here. Every Sunday the whole family meets and they eat a huge meal together. Research shows that in countries where people live longer, the family is important. But also on Sardinia, the older mother or grandmother often has authority in the family. As men get older, they have less responsibility in Sardinian culture. So, perhaps the older men have less stress, which means they're living longer.
P: I see. So, do you think people live longer in traditional societies?
D: That's an interesting question. It's true that even on Sardinia the younger generation are eating more food like chips and burgers. Also young people are moving to the city, so they are doing less exercise because of their lifestyle. So, it will be interesting to come back to Sardinia in twenty years and see if people are still living longer …

1.6

Conversation 1
C = Customer, P = Pharmacist
C: Hello. I've got a sore throat and a runny nose. I feel terrible.
P: Have you got a temperature as well?
C: No, it's normal.
P: Well, you should take this medicine twice a day. It's good for a sore throat.
C: Thanks.
P: And try drinking hot water with honey and lemon. That helps.
C: OK. I will.
P: Oh, and you need a box of tissues. If you still feel ill in a few days, see a doctor.

Conversation 2
P = Patient, D = Doctor
P: I've got an earache in this ear. I couldn't sleep last night because it was so painful.
D: Let me have a look. … ah … yes, it's very red in there. What about the other one?
P: It feels fine.
D: Hmm. It's a bit red as well. Do you feel sick at all?
P: No, not really.
D: Let me check your temperature. … Yes, it's higher than normal. I'll give you something for it. You need to take one of these pills twice a day for seven days. Drink lots of water and come back if you don't feel better.

Unit 2

1.7

The swimming race in the photo is one part of three races in total. The competitors swim for 3.86 kilometres (that's two point four miles), cycle for 180 kilometres and run a marathon at the end. It's called the Ironman triathlon and the men swimming in the photo are all competing at the annual Ironman world championship in Hawaii. Hundreds of people compete but thousands of spectators also watch the famous contest. They all want to see someone win the ultimate test of fitness.

1.9

M = Meg, P = Paul, K = Kirsty

M: I love getting up early every morning and going to the pool. It's really quiet at this time and there are only one or two other people. I'm not very good at swimming but I've got problems with my back so it helps with that.
P: I prefer watching sports to doing them. Especially running. We have to do sport at school on Tuesdays and Fridays with our teacher Mr Sykes. He tells us to run round and round the school field. Running is really boring exercise and I'm always last. I hate losing.
K: I like playing tennis so much that currently I'm working with a tennis coach to improve my game. I've got my first competition in a month. I'm very excited about competing because one day I'd like to become a professional player and this is an opportunity to see how good I really am against other players.

1.11

Well, here we are in a place called Banner Elk. Yes, I'd never heard of it either. Anyway, it's in the mountains of North Carolina, USA and it is cold! But that doesn't stop hundreds of competitors coming here every October for the town's annual Woolly Worm Race. The rules for the competition are easy. Anyone of any age can enter but you must have a woolly worm. You can bring your own or you can buy one before the race. Each race has twenty people and twenty woolly worms. You have to put your worm on a piece of string at the start. Then they're off! The only rule is that you mustn't touch your worm during the race. During the day, there are lots of races and if your woolly worm beats the others in the race, you take part in the grand final in the afternoon. And the prize money is one thousand dollars! Well worth it I'd say …

1.12

A: Hey! Have you seen this?
B: What?
A: This advert. You're really good at doing that.
B: Yes, but I have so much work at the moment, I don't have time.
A: So this is a good way to relax.
B: I can take a good one of friends and family but I'm not very creative with it.
A: Alright. Well, what about joining something else? Er, this one! Are you interested in acting?
B: You're joking. I hate standing up in front of people. You're more of a performer than me.
A: Yes, but it's a musical. I'm not very good at singing.
B: Let's have a look at that. But it says here enthusiasm is more important than talent. Go on. I think you'd enjoy it.
A: Emm, well maybe but I think I'd prefer to join this on Wednesday evenings.
B: What? You? Do exercise?
A: What do you mean? Me? Anyway, it looks fun. Why don't you come too?
B: Me? But I can't even walk twenty kilometres, never mind run it.
A: No, but that's the point. Look, there's even a beginner's group. You should do it with me.

Unit 3

1.14

This photo is on a train in Bangladesh. It was the end of Ramadan and lots of people travel home at that time of year. Train tickets sell out quickly so you often see people riding on top of the trains and the carriages. In this picture the woman is sitting between the carriages because there isn't space on top of the train. It looks a bit dangerous but she doesn't look very worried.

1.15

A: One day I'd like to buy an electric car. They're much cleaner than petrol cars. But I'm not sure if I'll see many on the road in the near future.
B: But you can already buy them.
A: Really?
B: Sure, and they have the most efficient type of engine. Unfortunately they're much more expensive than petrol cars. When they're cheaper, more people will buy them.

Audioscripts

A: I'm not sure if that's better or worse! With more people on the road, we'll have more traffic jams.
B: Especially at eight in the morning. It's the worst time of the day.
A: Yes. I try to avoid the rush hour now. I leave home before seven.
B: Well, I'd like to leave the car at home but every other type of transport is slower. This town needs better public transport. The buses don't go to the right places. And they are always late. Last week I waited for a number twenty-nine for over an hour …

1.17

Documentary 1
On a beautiful summer morning in Thailand, guests are arriving for a wedding. Some are arriving in cars but the most special guests are riding, in traditional style, on the backs of elephants. Elephants are as heavy as cars but they aren't as fast, and most people also think elephants aren't as comfortable as cars. However, in Thailand these animals have great importance. The Asian elephant became a domestic animal 5,000 years ago. In the past they transported soldiers to wars and worked in the forests pulling up trees and carrying wood. Nowadays, it's more common to see them transporting tourists and people on special occasions, but they are as important as ever in Thai society.

Documentary 2
Lester Courtney and his wife spend a lot of time with their horses, not for leisure but for work. They are traditional tree loggers who cut trees in traditional ways. They also transport the trees traditionally – with horses. Once the trees are down, Dan and Maddy pull them away. They're Lester's two horses. Lester has always used horses. Horses aren't the fastest form of transportation but Lester doesn't believe modern machines are as good. It's true that horses aren't as strong as lorries, or as fast, but Lester prefers working with animals. For one thing a horse isn't as heavy as modern machinery so it doesn't damage the old forests. Lester also prefers horses because horses aren't as noisy.

1.19

1 J = Javier, D = Driver
J: Hello? Are you the next taxi?
D: Yes, that's right.
J: I'd like to go to the station, please.
D: Bus or train?
J: Oh sorry. The train station.
D: OK. Get in then.

2 D = Driver, J = Javier
D: There are road works up by the entrance.
J: You can drop me off here. It's fine. How much is that?
D: Six pounds thirty.
J: Sorry, I only have a twenty-pound note. Do you have change?
D: Sure. So, that's thirteen pounds seventy. Do you want a receipt?
J: No, it's OK thanks. Bye.

3 S = Shelley, D = Driver
S: Hi. Do you stop at the airport?
D: Yeah, I do. Which terminal is it? North or south?
S: Err. I need to get to the … north terminal.
D: OK. A single or return ticket?
S: Single, please.
D: That's two pounds.

4 J = Javier, T = Ticket office clerk
J: A return ticket to the airport, please.
T: OK. The next train goes in five minutes.
J: Right. That one, please.
T: First or second class?
J: Second.
T: OK. That's fourteen pounds fifty.
J: Wow! Can I pay by cheque?
T: Sorry. Cash or credit card.
J: Oh no … Oh, one moment. Maybe I have enough left.
T: OK. Here you are.
J: Which platform is it?
T: Err, platform six.

5 A = Attendant, S = Shelley, J = Javier
A: Hello. Can I see your passport?
S: Here you are. I don't have a ticket because I booked online.
A: That's OK. How many bags are you checking in?
S: None. I only have this carry on.
A: OK. Window or aisle?
S: Err, I don't mind but can I have a seat next to my friend?
A: Has he already checked in?
S: No, I'm waiting for him.
A: Well, I can't …
J: Shelley!
S: Where have you been?
J: It's a long story.

Unit 4

1.21

My name's Vic and I live in the state of Tennessee. During the week I work in a bank but at the weekends I go caving. Colleagues at work think I'm a bit crazy because it's dangerous and sometimes you have to take risks, but I like the challenge. Every cave is a new adventure. I think my biggest achievement so far was reaching Rumbling Falls Cave. It's a really challenging cave because you climb down a hole that's about twenty metres into the ground. Then you go up two waterfalls and through a cave on your hands and knees for nearly a mile so you need to be physically fit. But at the end, you suddenly come to what we call the Rumble Room. It's an incredible place. It's a gigantic room – and it's like a different world.

1.23

1 Where did Edurne Pasaban live? In the mountainous Basque region of Spain.
2 When did she climb her first mountain? When she was fourteen.
3 What did she study at university? Engineering.
4 When did Steven Shoppman and Stephen Bouey drive round the world? From 2007 to 2010.
5 What did they go across? A minefield.
6 What did they find? That the world wasn't as dangerous as they thought.

1.24

I = Interviewer, W = Sandy Weisz
I: Normally we only hear bad news so it's good to have some good news from time to time. For example, did you hear in the news about Maria Garza? She was sitting on an aeroplane in Denver airport with her one-year-old child when she saw a fire from the window. It was coming from one of the engines. Did you read that? No? It was amazing. While the other passengers were running to the exits, Maria climbed out of the window and onto the wing of the plane. She saved her daughter's life and she was pregnant at the time! So, in fact she saved three lives.
In today's programme we're talking about why some people are survivors. We want to know what makes these people so special. For example, what are their personal qualities? Here to help us answer that question is Doctor Sandy Weisz. Sandy is a doctor of psychology and an expert in survival skills. So Sandy, what kind of person is a survivor?
W: Well, the story of Maria Garza is a good one because she showed a personal quality that all survivors have.
I: Which is?
W: They are always decisive. They always think and move very quickly and so she saved three lives. It's an important quality in a difficult situation. Another important quality they need is determination. For example, did you read about thirteen-year-old Bethany Hamilton? She showed real determination. One day when she was surfing a shark attacked her and she lost an arm. It was an incredible story. With one arm, she swam back to the beach.
I: Incredible, and there was another recent similar story … err that couple … the Carlsons.
W: Sorry, what were they doing?
I: They were sailing their boat when a wave hit them. The boat sank and they were at sea for thirty-one days.
W: Oh yes, I remember that story. But they were experienced with boats so skill and knowledge probably saved them more than anything else.
I: Right. So, what if I don't have special personal qualities or skills? Is there anything I can do?
W: Yes, there is. Most survivors don't normally take risks.
I: What do you mean?
W: Well, on an aeroplane, the survivors usually wear seat belts. At sea, you take extra food and water. On a mountain, a climber always wears warm clothes …
I: Right. I suppose we normally think survivors are risk-takers but in fact most of them are quite careful.
W: Exactly. We all take risks – even when we walk across the road – but most survivors don't take unnecessary risks.

1.26

A: Hi Mark. How was your camping trip?
B: It was great in the end but we had a terrible time at the beginning.
A: Why?
B: First, we left the house early on Saturday morning but after only half an hour the car broke down.
A: Oh no!
B: Fortunately, there was a garage nearby and the mechanic fixed the problem. But when we arrived at the forest, it was getting dark. After we drove around for about an hour, we finally found the campsite but it was completely dark by then. Unfortunately, it started raining so we found a nice hotel down the road!
A: That was lucky!
B: Yes, it was a great hotel and in the end we stayed there for the whole weekend.
A: Sounds great!

Audioscripts

Unit 5

1.28

Every day we use objects like computers, mobile phones and household appliances such as washing machines and cookers without thinking. So, when you see a sculpture by the artist George Sabra, it's surprising because he uses these objects in new ways. Take the sculpture in the photo, for example. It looks like a strange animal and it's made of wood, metal and plastic. The body is wood from a beach. The round head is made of metal and the hair is made of metal and plastic computer parts. George makes these sculptures because he wants people to think about the environment and about recycling and reusing everyday objects.

1.29

P = Presenter, R = Reg, S = Sandra
- **P:** OK. So, this week on Radio Talk, we're talking about recycling. We want to know: How much do you recycle? And do you think it's important? The phone lines are open … and our first caller this morning is Reg from Cambridgeshire. Reg, you're on Radio Talk. Go ahead. Reg? Are you there?
- **R:** Hello? Can you hear me?
- **P:** Yes, Reg, I can hear you and so can about half a million other people. What did you want to say, Reg?
- **R:** Well. A lot of people talk about recycling these days and they say it's good for the environment, but I'm not so sure. Take where I live, for example. There aren't any recycling centres in my town.
- **P:** Really, Reg? But what about at your local supermarket? Are there any recycling bins there?
- **R:** OK, yes there are some recycling bins I admit and a lot of people take their rubbish there. But listen to this. A lorry comes every single week to take it all away. I ask you! How is that good for the environment? Think about all the fuel it uses. No, I'm not convinced. And another thing …
- **P:** Actually Reg. I'm going to stop you there because on line two I have another caller. Line two? Are you there?
- **S:** Hello, yes I'm here.
- **P:** And what's your name?
- **S:** Sandra.
- **P:** OK Sandra. You are live on Radio Talk.
- **S:** Well, I'm really angry with the man who was just on.
- **P:** You mean Reg?
- **S:** Yes. He's just like all the people who live round me. They don't recycle much stuff either.
- **P:** What? None of them?
- **S:** Well, not many people on my street recycle. I don't know about other parts of the town. Every week I see them. They throw away a lot of bags. I suppose some people recycle a little rubbish every week. They don't think they have time for recycling.
- **P:** And do you ever say anything to them?
- **S:** Yes, I do! I tell them. You only need a few minutes every day to separate your glass, plastic and paper. And there are a lot of places where you can take recycling. There's no excuse at all.
- **P:** That's an interesting opinion Sandra and so what I want to do is bring back Reg who's waiting on line one … Reg?
- **R:** Hello?
- **P:** Reg, I'd like to you reply to Sandra because she says it's easy to recycle. What do you say to that?
- **R:** Well, she might be right but where I live you can't …

1.32

V = recorded voice, C = Customer care assistant, J = Jane
- **V:** Thank you for calling Teco Art dot com. Your call is important to us. For information about our latest products, press one. For orders, press two. For problems with your order, press three. … All our customer service assistants are busy. We apologise for the delay. Your call is important to us. One of our customer service assistants will be with you as soon as possible.
- **C:** Good morning. Can I help you?
- **J:** Hi, I'm calling about an order for a Computer Circuit Board Clock from your website but I received an email saying I have to wait seven more days.
- **C:** One moment … Do you have the order number?
- **J:** Yes, it's 8-0-5-3-1-A.
- **C:** Is that A as in Alpha?
- **J:** That's right.
- **C:** Is that Ms Jane Powell of 90 North Lane?
- **J:** Yes, it is.
- **C:** Hmm. Can I put you on hold for a moment?
- **J:** Sure.
- **C:** Hello?
- **J:** Yes, hello.
- **C:** I'm very sorry but this product isn't in stock at the moment. We'll have it in seven days.
- **J:** I already know that. But it's my husband's birthday tomorrow.
- **C:** I see. Well, would you like to order a similar clock? We have an Apple iPod one for thirty-five pounds.
- **J:** Hmm. I really liked the one I ordered.
- **C:** Oh, I'm sorry about that. Would you like to cancel the order?
- **J:** Yes, I think so. How does that work?
- **C:** Well, we'll refund the amount of thirty-nine pounds to your credit card.
- **J:** OK. Thanks.
- **C:** And would you like confirmation by email?
- **J:** Yes, please.
- **C:** Let me check. Your email is J – powell at S-mail dot com.
- **J:** That's right.
- **C:** Is there anything else I can help you with?
- **J:** No, thanks. That's everything.
- **C:** OK. Goodbye.
- **J:** Bye.

Unit 6

1.35

In the story of the Sphinx, the answer to the question is 'man'. This is because, a baby moves using two hands and two feet. An adult walks on two legs and an old person walks on two legs but also needs a walking stick. In the question the Sphinx also talks about three different parts of the day: morning, noon and evening. These parts of the day represent the different stages of our life. Morning is childhood. Noon is the middle of our life. Evening is old-age. In the original Greek story, the Sphinx killed many travellers because they didn't know the answer. Finally, one man answered the question correctly. He was Oedipus and when he answered 'man', the Sphinx killed itself.

1.36

Speaker 1
One day I plan to go to university but first I want to take a year off to get some work experience abroad. So, at the moment I'm working at a local supermarket and I'm going to save all my money. Then I'd like to travel to somewhere like Australia if I can afford it.

Speaker 2
People seem to think this stage in life means looking after grandchildren and playing golf. Well forget that! I intend to do all the things I wanted to do but never had time. And as for work! Well, I'll be happy to leave my job, I can tell you.

Speaker 3
We hope to get a place of our own but these days it's really difficult to buy a house. House prices are so high so we're still living with my husband's parents. It's hard not to feel sad about it.

1.38

R = Reporter, L = Lorette
- **R:** It's about six o'clock in the morning here in New Orleans and the streets are very quiet. But in about six hours the city is going to have the biggest party in the world and thousands of visitors from all over are going to fill the streets. However, Mardi Gras is really about the local communities in the city. So, I've come to the traditional Tremé neighbourhood of New Orleans where there are already some people preparing for the big day. So, I'll try to speak to some of them … Hello? Hello?
- **L:** Hello?
- **R:** Hello. What's your name?
- **L:** Lorette.
- **R:** Hi Lorette. You're wearing a fantastic costume. Are you going to be in the parade this afternoon?
- **L:** That's right. I'm meeting everyone at the float in a few minutes and then we're riding through the city.
- **R:** As I say your dress looks amazing. Did you make it?
- **L:** Yes, we all make our own costumes for Mardi Gras.
- **R:** And do you have a mask?
- **L:** Sure. Here it is. I'll put it on.
- **R:** Wow. That's perfect. So tell me. How important is Mardi Gras for the people in Tremé?
- **L:** It's the most important part of the year. It brings people together.
- **R:** Well, good luck this afternoon. You're going to have a great time, I'm sure!

1.40

Conversation 1
I = Ian, A = Abdullah
- **I:** Hi Abdullah. How's it going?
- **A:** Good. I finished all my courses today so I can relax.
- **I:** Great. Maybe you'll have time for some travelling and sightseeing now.
- **A:** Maybe. But I think I'll take it easy this weekend.

Audioscripts

I: Oh! Well, why don't you come to my house? My family is coming over. We're having a barbecue in the back garden. It'll be fun.
A: Thanks, but I have a few things to do at home and it's with your family so you probably don't want other people there …
I: No, really. Don't worry because I'm inviting a few people from our class as well. So you'll know people. I'd really like you to come.
A: OK. Thanks, that would be great. Is it a special occasion?
I: Well, my oldest sister has a new baby girl so it's a bit of a celebration for that.
A: Oh! So I should bring something.
I: No, please don't. It isn't like that. There's no need …

Conversation 2

J = Joanna, S = Sally

J: Hello Sally. How are you?
S: Fine, thanks. It's been a busy week.
J: Yes, I imagine. When do you finish?
S: Tomorrow.
J: Oh, really. I didn't realise it was so soon.
S: Well actually, my flight home is on Saturday.
J: But you're staying for another week?
S: No.
J: Oh. Well, what are doing tonight?
S: Nothing at the moment. I'll be at my hotel.
J: Well, would you like to come out for dinner? Let's go somewhere this evening.
S: Really? I'd love to.
J: Of course. I'd like to take you to my favourite restaurant.
S: That would be wonderful. I'd like that very much.
J: Great. Let's go straight after work. I'll meet you downstairs in reception.
S: OK. What time?
J: I finish at six. Is that OK for you?
S: Sure. I'll see you then. Bye.

Life

PRE-INTERMEDIATE
WORKBOOK

John Hughes

Unit 1 Health

1a Global health

Grammar present simple

1 Complete the article about Nathan Wolfe with the present simple form of the verbs.

How one scientist fights for global health

Nathan Wolfe is a scientist and he [1] _____ (work) all over the world. He [2] _____ (specialise) in virus and diseases and he often [3] _____ (go) to places with health problems. In particular, he [4] _____ (study) viruses and diseases from animals. It's an important job because he [5] _____ (want) to know how these viruses move from animals to humans and how we can stop them in the future. As a result, Nathan [6] _____ (spend) a lot of time in regions with wildlife.

In the modern world, humans [7] _____ (not / stay) in one place anymore and so new viruses also [8] _____ (travel) more easily. When humans [9] _____ (visit) regions with wildlife (for example, in Africa), they [10] _____ (not / realise) how easy it is to bring a new kind of disease back with them.

However, the modern world with its technology also [11] _____ (help) Nathan with his work. For example, in central Congo many people [12] _____ (not / have) electricity or running water, but a mobile phone allows Nathan to continue his life-saving work.

Glossary
disease (n) /dɪziːz/ an illness that affects humans and animals
virus (n) /vaɪrəs/ a small living thing that enters a human body and makes you ill

▶ **SPELL CHECK present simple (he / she / it) verb endings**

We normally add *-s* to most verbs in the present simple third person. However, note these exceptions:
- Add *-es* to verbs ending in *-ch*, *-o*, *-s*, *-ss*, *-sh* and *-x*: watch → watches.
- For verbs ending in *-y* after a consonant, change the *-y* to *-i* and add *-es*: study → studies.
- *have* and *be* have irregular forms.

2 Look at the spell check box. Then rewrite the verbs in the present simple third-person form.

1 start _____
2 watch _____
3 fly _____
4 pass _____
5 live _____
6 study _____
7 finish _____
8 relax _____

3 Pronunciation /s/, /z/ and /ɪz/

🔊 **1.1** Listen to the final *-s* and *-es* in these verbs. Write the verbs in the table. Listen again and repeat.

| has | helps | is | realises | specialises | spends |
| stays | studies | travels | visits | wants |

/s/	/z/	/ɪz/

4 Write questions about Nathan Wolfe and his work using the present simple.

1 (where / Nathan / work)
   _____?
   All over the world.
2 (where / he / often / go)
   _____?
   To places with health problems.
3 (what / he / find and study)
   _____?
   Virus and diseases from animals.
4 (where / he / spend / a lot of time)
   _____?
   In regions with wildlife.
5 (why / new viruses / travel more easily)
   _____?
   Because humans travel all over the world.
6 (what / he / need / for his work)
   _____?
   Modern technology.
7 (many people / have / electricity and running water)
   _____?
   No, they don't.
8 (how / Nathan / communicate)
   _____?
   With a mobile phone.

Grammar adverbs of frequency

6 Put the words in order to make sentences.

1 do always in the evening I exercise
2 it in the winter always colder is
3 take twice a day I this medicine
4 they don't go often on holiday
5 at weekends we sometimes busy are
6 eats out rarely she during the week
7 on time are never for work you
8 do check you your emails always at lunchtime?

Listening healthy living quiz

5 🔊 1.2 Look at the quiz. Then listen to a conversation between two people at work. Choose the correct option (a, b or c).

Stress is bad for your health – both physical and mental

Find out how stressed you are with this quick quiz.

1 I worry about money _____.
   a every day   b at least once a week   c once a month
2 I _____ have problems sleeping at night.
   a never   b sometimes   c always
3 I _____ find it difficult to concentrate.
   a rarely   b sometimes   c often
4 Which of these sentences describes your lunchtimes?
   a I often eat lunch at my desk and answer calls or send emails.
   b I often eat lunch at my desk and read the newspaper or relax.
   c I often leave my desk, go for a walk or eat my lunch somewhere else.

1b Mobile medicine

Reading community health

Mobile medicine

Sarubai Salve goes to work twice a day. She leaves her home once at nine o'clock in the morning and then again at six o'clock in the evening to visit people in her village of Jawalke. The village has about 240 families and, with another woman called Babai Sathe, Sarubai is responsible for the health of the village. The women visit pregnant women and give medicine to some of the older people. Today they are visiting their first patient. Rani Kale doesn't come from Jawalke. She lives about an hour away but her village doesn't have anyone like Sarubai to help mothers-to-be. Sarubai is checking Rani and she is worried about the position of the baby. Rani might need to go to hospital.

Half an hour later, Sarubai and Babai visit another mother with a three-month-old baby. While they are checking the baby, Sarubai also gives the mother advice on nutrition and vaccinations. Jawalke is a very different place because of the two women. They regularly deliver babies and continue to help as the child grows up. There is a shortage of doctors in this region, so village health workers are important because they can give preventative medicine and advice about health.

New health workers go for two weeks of intensive training and then they receive ongoing training. A mobile team visits Jawalke once a week. The team includes a nurse and a doctor. The mobile team meets with Sarubai and they look at any of her patients with serious medical problems. The health workers are an important connection between the mobile team and the local people. Currently there are 300 village health workers in the region and the number is growing.

1 Read the article and answer the questions. Choose the correct option (a, b or c).

1 How often does Sarubai visit people in the village?
   a once a day
   b twice a day
   c twice a week

2 How many doctors are there in the village of Jawalke?
   a one
   b two
   c none

3 Where does Rani Kale come from?
   a Jawalke
   b another village near Jawalke
   c we don't know

4 Sarubai meets Rani because she is
   a ill.
   b pregnant.
   c sick.

5 Which of these statements is true about the health workers?
   a They only deliver babies.
   b They do the same job as doctors.
   c They have many different responsibilities.

6 How much training do they receive?
   a None. They learn it all from books.
   b Two weeks only on a course.
   c Two weeks and then more training while they are working.

7 What is the purpose of the mobile team?
   a To do the job of the health workers.
   b To provide more medical help.
   c To train the health workers.

8 How do we know from the article that the village health project is successful?
   a Because they are training more health workers.
   b Because patients say they are happy with their health workers.
   c Because the region doesn't need any more doctors.

2 Find words in the article for these definitions.
1. a person with a medical problem who sees a doctor (n) ....
2. women who are going to have a baby (n) ....
3. a place for people with medical problems (n) ....
4. food that keeps you healthy (n) ....
5. medicine you put in the body to stop disease (n) ....
6. not enough of something (n) ....
7. stopping something bad before it happens (adj) ....
8. opinion about the best thing to do in a situation (n) ....
9. a lot of teaching in a short time (adj) ....
10. continuing and never stopping (adj) ....

Grammar present continuous

3 Look at the article again. Underline the verbs in the present continuous.

4 Choose the correct option to complete the sentences.
1. At the moment *I drive / I'm driving* towards the city. Is that the right direction?
2. London *has / is having* a population of about eight million people.
3. Where *do you come / are you coming* from originally?
4. Sorry, I can't hear you because a plane *flies / is flying* overhead.
5. *I never cycle / I'm never cycling* to work in the winter.
6. Someone *stands / is standing* at the front door. Can you see who it is?
7. *Do you understand / Are you understanding* what I mean?
8. It was warm earlier today but now *it gets / it's getting* colder and colder.
9. We *don't stay / aren't staying* very long. It's just a short visit.
10. *Do you work / Are you working* now or *do you take / are you taking* a break?

5 Pronunciation contracted forms

🔊 1.3 Listen to the sentences. Write the number of words you hear. Contracted forms (*I'm, we're, aren't, isn't* etc.) count as one word.

a _5_   d ....
b .... e ....
c .... f ....

> ▶ **SPELL CHECK present continuous -*ing* endings**
> - With verbs ending in -*e*, delete the -*e* then add -*ing*: dance → danc**ing**
> - With verbs ending in -*ie*, delete the -*e* and change the *i* to a *y*: die → dying
> - With some verbs ending in one vowel and a consonant, double the final consonant: stop → sto**pp**ing, run → ru**nn**ing

6 Look at the spell check box. Then write the verbs below in the -*ing* form.
1. live ....   6. lie ....
2. drop ....   7. take ....
3. let ....   8. travel ....
4. swim ....   9. get ....
5. have ....   10. jog ....

Dictation my typical day

7 🔊 1.4 The man in this photo is describing his typical day. Listen and write down the words you hear.

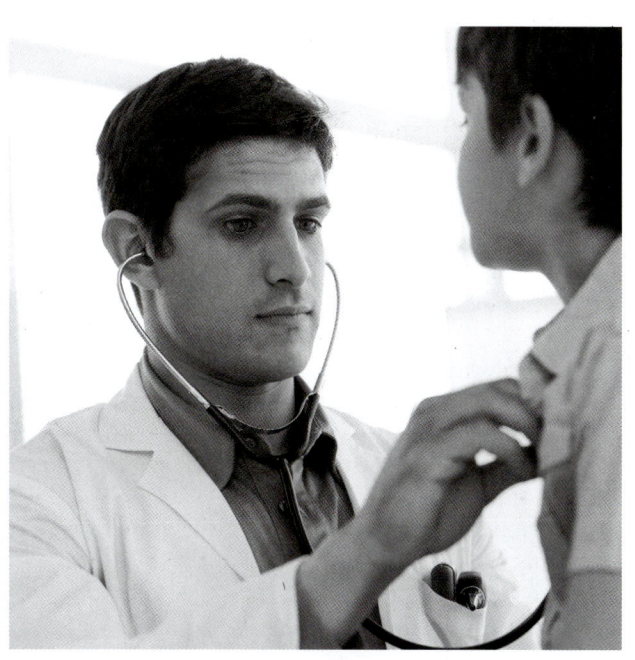

1c Happy and healthy

Listening an interview with Elizabeth Dunn

1 🎧 **1.5** Listen to an interview with Elizabeth Dunn. Complete the sentences.

1 Elizabeth is interested in what makes us feel _____ .
2 She does research on happiness and how _____ affects this.
3 As part of her research she did an experiment with a group of _____ .
4 She thinks that experiences like visiting a new country are good for you _____ .

2 🎧 **1.5** Listen again. Read these sentences and choose the correct response (a–c).

a Elizabeth agrees.
b Elizabeth disagrees.
c Elizabeth doesn't say.

1 Coffee with friends is better than having lots of money. _____
2 Money is the most important thing in the world. _____
3 Money doesn't make you feel happier. _____
4 Giving money to other people makes you happy. _____
5 Spending money on other people makes you happier. _____
6 Spending money on experiences makes you feel happy. _____

Word focus *feel*

3 Match the sentences (1–6) with the uses of *feel* (a–f).

1 I feel like going out for dinner tonight.
2 I don't feel this is the right thing to do.
3 My daughter feels ill.
4 I feel much happier today.
5 The sun feels warm. It felt much colder yesterday.
6 I feel like a coffee.

a Talking about your emotions
b Talking about sickness
c Giving a view or an opinion
d Refers to the weather
e Wanting something
f Wanting to do something

4 Match the questions (1–5) with the answers (a–e).

1 How are you today?
2 Do you feel like something to eat?
3 What do you think about my work in general?
4 Do you feel like helping me with this?
5 What's the weather like?

a Actually, I feel you need to do more.
b It feels freezing out there!
c Sorry, I'm really busy at the moment.
d Yes, a sandwich, please.
e I'm feeling much better, thanks.

5 Write seven different questions with the word *feel*. Use the words in the box. You can use words more than once.

| a coffee | doing something | like |
| how do you | OK | 's | weather | what |

1 _____ ?
2 _____ ?
3 _____ ?
4 _____ ?
5 _____ ?
6 _____ ?
7 _____ ?

100

1d At the doctor's

Vocabulary medical problems

1 Complete the conversations with these words.

| back | ear | head | mouth | nose | stomach |
| throat | tooth | | | | |

A: Sorry, I've got a really runny ¹_____ today.
B: It's OK. Here's a tissue if you need one.

A: I've got really bad ²_____ ache.
B: Is the problem in the left or the right?
A: Both!

A: It's too painful to eat.
B: It sounds like you have ³_____ ache. You should go to the dentist.

A: What's that noise?
B: They're digging up the road outside.
A: It's giving me a terrible ⁴_____ ache.

A: I can hardly talk today.
B: Why? Have you got a sore ⁵_____?

A: Can you pick this up for me? I've got a bad ⁶_____ at the moment.
B: Sure. But maybe you should lie down for a while.

A: My throat is very red, doctor.
B: Well, let's have a look. Open your ⁷_____, please.

A: Where's the problem?
B: It's in my ⁸_____. I feel a bit sick.

2 Pronunciation sound and spelling

🔊 1.6 Listen to these groups of words. Cross out the word in each group that has a different vowel sound.

1 ~~bad~~ said head bed
2 sore ear or saw
3 love off cough soft
4 ate wait late eat
5 here ear see near
6 try why play fly

Communication talking about illness

3 🔊 1.7 Listen to a conversation at the doctor's. Complete the form.

Patient's medical problems
1 **Medical problem:** sore throat _____ headache _____ stomach ache _____ earache _____ cough _____ other _____
2 **Temperature:** low _____ normal _____ high _____
3 **Details of prescription:** medicine _____ pills _____
4 **Advice:** _____

4 🔊 1.7 Complete the conversation with these phrases. Then listen again and check.

They are good	Have you got
How do you feel	If you still feel ill
Do you feel	take this prescription
Let me have a	You need to
try drinking	Let me check

Doctor: ¹_____ today?
Patient: Not very well. I've got a terrible sore throat.
Doctor: I see. ²_____ look. Open wide. Yes, it's very red in there.
Patient: I've also got a bad cough.
Doctor: ³_____ sick at all?
Patient: No, not really.
Doctor: ⁴_____ a temperature?
Patient: I don't think so. I don't feel hot.
Doctor: ⁵_____ it … Yes, it's a bit high. Do you have anything for it?
Patient: I bought some pills at the pharmacy, but they didn't do any good.
Doctor: Well, ⁶_____ to the pharmacy. ⁷_____ take some different pills. ⁸_____ for your throat. Take one every four hours. You need to go to bed for a couple of days, and ⁹_____ lots of water.
Patient: OK. Thanks.
Doctor: ¹⁰_____ in a few days, come back and see me, but I think it's flu. Everyone has it at the moment.

Glossary:
flu (n) /fluː/ a common illness which makes patient feel hot or cold with a temperature.
prescription (n) /prɪˈskrɪpˈʃən/ a piece of paper from the doctor with medicine on. You give it to the pharmacist.

Listen and respond giving advice

5 🔊 1.8 Listen to five different friends, each with a different medical problem. Respond each time with some advice. Then compare your advice with the model answer that follows.

> I've got a headache.

> You need to take some pills.

101

1e Online advice

Writing online advice

1 Read the messages asking for advice from different forums. Match the messages with the forums. There is one extra forum.

| Career | Computer | Food | Love | Sport | Town |

1 My boyfriend's mother is coming for dinner tonight. It's the first time she's tried my cooking. I need a simple but tasty meal. Do you have any advice?

2 I love my current job but my company wants me to become a manager. I know I should take the opportunity but I'm happy with my life. What can I do?

3 This new version of Digital XZ version 9.1.2 doesn't work. Can anyone help?

4 I'm new here and I don't know many people. What kinds of activities do people do in the evenings or at weekends? Does anyone have any good advice?

5 There's a girl at school. I really like her but I don't know how to ask her out. What should I do?

2 Read the messages again. Underline the useful question for asking for advice in each message.

3 Choose three of the messages. Write a short reply to each one. Start your message with the words given.

1 In my opinion, you should ....

2 My advice is to ....

3 It's a good idea to ....

Grammar extra should / shouldn't

▶ **GRAMMAR should / shouldn't**

We use *should* for giving strong advice. For example:
You **should** tell her how you feel.
You **shouldn't** cook her anything. Buy it from a shop!

should is a modal verb, so remember:
It doesn't have a third person -s: *He should tell her / it.*

Don't use the auxiliary *do* for negatives or questions: *She ~~don't~~ shouldn't cook it.*

Should isn't followed by the *to* + infinitive: *You should ~~to~~ tell her.*

4 Write advice for these situations. Use *should* or *shouldn't* and the words in brackets.
1 I feel ill. (take / pills / twice a day)
  You should take these pills twice a day.
2 I want a cigarette. (you / smoke)
3 I'm watching TV all weekend. (do / some exercise)
4 I usually work about fourteen hours a day. (work / eight hours)
5 I like coffee but I can't sleep. (drink / caffeine / in the evening)

Writing skill conjunctions (*and, or, so, because, but*)

5 Connect these sentences with one of these conjunctions: *and, or, so, because, but*.
1 If you want to lose weight, you could start running. You could go cycling.
2 Take some of this medicine. Take two of these pills.
3 I do sports such as tennis or golf. I don't like team sports.
4 Drink lots of water. Your body needs about two litres per day.
5 Your body needs about two litres per day. Drink lots of water.

6 Complete these sentences with your own words.
1 I can't sleep if I .... and ....
2 I prefer team sports such as .... or ....
3 My favourite hobby is .... because ....
4 Sometimes I get bored at the weekend, so I ....
5 Some people think money makes you happy, but I ....

Unit 1 Health

Word building verb + noun collocations

1 Match the verbs with the nouns to make collocations. Then complete the sentences.

| **Verbs** | check | do | go | have | play |
| read | run | take | | |

Nouns books   a coffee   emails   exercise   hiking   a marathon   the piano   public transport

1 I'm training to ....
   .... next year. So far I can do about twenty kilometres.
2 I like to ....
   in the mountains at weekends. It's very relaxing.
3 I .... when I have time. Mozart is my favourite composer.
4 I like to ....
   Fantasy or science fiction are my favourites.
5 I .... about twice a week at the local gym.
6 I .... to work instead of driving a car.
7 I never .... my personal .... at work. My boss doesn't want me to.
8 Can I .... with milk, please?

2 Write down other verb + noun collocations. Use the verbs in Exercise 1.

Example:
take time, take a break, take a taxi

Learning skills recording new vocabulary

3 When you write down a new English word, how do you record it? Tick the techniques you use.

a the meaning
b the translation into your language
c the pronunciation (the sounds and the stress)
d the type of word (verb, adjective, noun, preposition, etc.)
e collocations
f any common phrases or expressions using this word

4 Which techniques do you use in your notebook?

a   **Word groups**

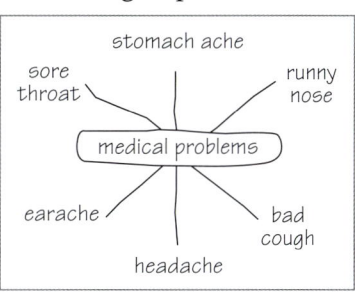

medical problems: stomach ache, sore throat, runny nose, earache, bad cough, headache

b   **Drawings**

go hiking

c   **Diagrams**

always   often   sometimes   rarely   never
100% ←————— 50% —————→ 0%

5 Look at some of the new words from Unit 1.
1 Try recording some new information about the words. Use a dictionary to help you.
2 Try different techniques for learning the new words. Decide which techniques work well for you.

Check!

6 Complete the crossword. You can find the answers in Unit 1 of the Student's Book.

Across
3   A large Italian island
6   You do this with plants and flowers
7   Measurement of how hot your body is
8   A person who lives to 100 years or more
10 The noun form of 'happy'

Down
1   You can give this to a friend if they have a problem
2   Something a pharmacist or doctor gives you for an illness
4   A place on the internet for leaving and replying to messages
5   A Japanese island with some of the oldest people in the world
9   A short sleep

103

Unit 2 Competitions

2a Sports and leisure activities

1 Vocabulary extra talking about likes and dislikes

a Match the highlighted verbs in the speech bubbles with the emoticons (a–f).

> I **enjoy** swimming when I have time.

> I **love** winning!

> I **really like** watching sport on TV.

> I **hate** boxing.

> I **can't stand** losing!

> I **don't mind** playing cricket but I **don't like** watching it.

a ☺☺☺ _____
b ☺☺ _____
c ☺ like, _____
d 😐 _____
e ☹ dislike, _____
f ☹☹ _____, _____

b Complete the sentences for you.
1 I love playing _____ .
2 I enjoy _____ when I have time.
3 I don't mind _____ .
4 I don't like watching _____ on TV.
5 I can't stand _____ .

Grammar verb + -ing forms

2 Complete the sentences with the -ing form of these verbs.

be	compete	cycle	fly	learn	lose
~~play~~	sit				

1 _Playing_ tennis is fun and it's very good for your health.
2 _____ in a match is only fun if you win.
3 We love _____ because you get fit and see the countryside.
4 _____ to play the piano takes years of practice.
5 When I play games, I'm not good at _____ . I get really angry.
6 _____ in front of the TV all day isn't good for you.
7 Are you interested in _____ in our team?
8 I don't like travelling by plane because I'm afraid of _____ .

Vocabulary talking about sport

3 Read the clues in the quiz and write the words.

SPORTS QUIZ

1 You hit the ball with it in baseball and table tennis. _____
2 You race round it in Formula One and cycling. _____
3 You wear them over your eyes in skiing and also underwater. _____
4 You hit a ball over it in volleyball, badminton and tennis. _____
5 There are two of them, but you only wear one in golf. _____
6 You play on this in cricket, rugby and football. _____
7 It's the name of a sport with balls and a table, but it's also the name of something you swim in. _____
8 You hit the ball with this in golf, but you can also be a member of one. _____

104

4 Pronunciation vowel sounds

🔊 **1.9** Listen to these pairs of words. Do they have the same or different vowel sounds? Write *S* or *D*.

1 club   glove   ....
2 ball   bat   ....
3 play   race   ....
4 court   course   ....
5 bat   track   ....
6 sport   golf   ....

Grammar *like -ing / 'd like to*

5 Choose the correct options to complete the sentences.

1 *I like playing / I'd like to play* golf later today.
2 *They like playing / They'd like to play* against us. Is that OK with you?
3 No one *likes finishing / would like to finish* last, but someone always has to.
4 One day in the future, my family *likes going / would like* to go on a trip to Antarctica.
5 *I like parachuting / I'd like to parachute*. It's a lot of fun.
6 At some point in their life, everyone *likes being / would like to become* famous.
7 We *don't like playing / wouldn't like to play* on a concrete court. We prefer grass.
8 What *do you like doing / would you like to do* when you leave school?

6 Match the two halves of the sentences.

1 Every day, Richard likes
2 I'd like to
3 Do you like
4 She'd like
5 Would you like to
6 They always like

a be in my team?
b playing tennis?
c running a few miles before breakfast.
d to compete in the Olympics one day.
e visit New Zealand one day.
f competing against each other.

7 Dictation Kristi Leskinen

🔊 **1.10** Listen to part of a documentary about the skier Kristi Leskinen. Write the missing words.

Kristi Leskinen is a famous skier. She [1] ....
.... but her favourite place is Mammoth Mountain in the USA. [2] ....
such as kayaking but she [3] ....
....
Recently she was in a TV show called *The Superstars*. In the show, famous [4] ....
....
that [5] ....
Kristi won [6] ....
But soon it's winter again so she needs to go back to the mountains and start training again. This year [7] ....
a lot more medals.

105

2b Paddleboard racing

Reading adventure sport

1 Read the article. Are the sentences true (T) or false (F)?

1. Paddleboarding is a combination of two other sports.
2. Competitive paddleboard races are usually on rivers.
3. The most important race is on the ocean around Hawaii.
4. Jamie Mitchell completed the Molokai to Oahu race in the fastest time.
5. The prize money for first place in the race is three thousand dollars.
6. The writer says paddleboard racing is a famous sport.
7. Jamie is a full-time professional sportsperson.
8. Jamie loves the sport and visiting Hawaii with friends.

Paddleboard racing

Paddleboarding is a mixture of two water sports, surfing and rowing. Paddleboarding uses a surfboard and the paddleboarder 'rows' the board. However, there are two big differences. In surfing, you have to stand but in paddleboarding you can kneel or lie on the board. In rowing you use oars, but in paddleboarding you mustn't use oars. You have to use your arms to move along.

You can do the sport on rivers, but most of the big competitions are on the ocean. The main competition for paddleboarders is the annual race from Molokai to Oahu in Hawaii. The distance is 50 kilometres. On a good day, with the right kind of waves, you don't always have to use your arms because the water carries you some of the way but, on a bad day, you are using your arms the whole way.

Competitors must be very strong and athletic. One of paddleboarding's most famous competitors is the Australian Jamie Mitchell. Not many people know about Mitchell, but he is the eight-time winner of the Molokai to Oahu race. He also has the record time of four hours, fifty-eight minutes and twenty-five seconds.

Because the sport isn't well known, the prize money for winning paddleboarding is small compared to other sports – Mitchell only received $3,000 for winning the race this year. But Mitchell obviously loves the sport because he trains two or three times a day, six days a week, for the four months before the race. At the same time, he has to earn money, so he does anything including working in bars or building work.

So how does Mitchell stay interested in such a sport? He says, 'I just love paddleboarding. It's not about winning. It's about coming to Hawaii and spending time with my good friends in a place that I love.'

Unit 2 Competitions

2 Match these words from the article with the definitions.

| athletic | kneel | oars | rowing | surfing | waves |

1 sport of riding waves on the sea
 _____ (n)
2 sport of moving a boat through water with oars
 _____ (n)
3 put both knees on a flat surface
 _____ (v)
4 equipment in rowing for moving the boat
 _____ (n)
5 water on the sea that goes up and down
 _____ (n)
6 physically strong and good at sport
 _____ (adj)

Grammar modal verbs for rules

3 Rewrite these sentences with a modal verb for rules. Sometimes you can use more than one verb. Then compare your answers with the same sentences in the article in Exercise 1.

1 In surfing, it's necessary to stand on your board.
 In surfing, you *have to* stand on your board.
2 Paddleboarders are allowed to kneel or lie on the board.
 Paddleboarders _____ kneel or lie on the board.
3 In paddleboarding, you are not allowed to use oars.
 In paddleboarding, you _____ use oars.
4 It's necessary to use their arms to move along.
 They _____ use their arms to move along.
5 On a good day, with the right kind of waves, it isn't always necessary to use your arms because the water carries you some of the way.
 On a good day, with the right kind of waves, you _____ use your arms because the water carries you some of the way.
6 It's necessary for competitors to be very strong and athletic.
 Competitors _____ be very strong and athletic.

4 Pronunciation *n't*

🔊 1.11 Listen and choose the form you hear. Then listen again and repeat.

1 You *must / mustn't* play.
2 They *do / don't* have to win.
3 He *can / can't* lose the match.
4 The team *must / mustn't* score another goal.
5 A player *can / can't* hit the ball twice.

5 Make one rule for each sport (1–5) with the words in the table.

| Each team | The ball | The fighters | You | Players |

| has to / must | can | don't have to |
| can't / mustn't | | |

get a red card.
go over the net.
leave the ring during the fight.
have five people on the court.
use any special equipment.

1 Basketball: *Each team has to / must have five players on the court.*
2 Football: _____
3 Boxing: _____
4 Running: _____
5 Tennis: _____

Vocabulary competitions

6 Complete the sentences with one word. The first letter is given.

1 My local team got this t_____ because they won the final.
2 Winners at the Olympics get a gold medal because they b_____ all the other competitors.
3 The final s_____ in the tennis match was three sets to one.
4 The players came home today and hundreds of their f_____ came to meet and cheer them.
5 The r_____ gave two red cards and six yellow cards during the match.
6 The j_____ at the dancing competition didn't give us a very high score for our performance.
7 How much p_____ money did you receive for winning?
8 There were 48,000 s_____ at the football match.

107

2c Dangerous sports

Listening freediving

1 🎵 1.12 Listen to a sports programme about Annelie Pompe, a freediver. Number the topics (a–d) in the order the presenter talks about them.

   a   Annelie's plans to climb Mount Everest
   b   a definition of freediving
   c   why Annelie Pompe likes freediving
   d   why she likes doing other sports

2 🎵 1.12 Listen again. Choose the correct option (a, b or c).

   1 Freediving is an underwater sport. The diver _____ .
      a   has to use breathing equipment
      b   doesn't have to use breathing equipment
      c   can't use breathing equipment

   2 Annelie's world record is a dive of ___ metres.
      a 120   b 126   c 136

   3 She spends every ___ training in the sea.
      a day   b week   c weekend

   4 She ___ other sports.
      a likes doing
      b doesn't have time for
      c doesn't like doing

   5 If she climbs Mount Everest, she'll be the first woman to go ___ than any other woman.
      a higher
      b deeper
      c higher and deeper

Word focus *like*

3 Match the sentences (1–7) with the different uses of *like* (a–g).

   1 He's like his older brother. He was good at athletics too.
   2 He looks like his older brother. He has black hair, too.
   3 I'd like to win a gold medal one day.
   4 I'd like a cup of coffee, please.
   5 Do you feel like going out later?
   6 I like most sports.
   7 I like watching most sports.

   a to say you feel people or things are good (*like* + noun)
   b to say you enjoy doing something (*like* + *-ing*)
   c use with *would* to say you want to do something in the future (*would like* + *to* + infinitive)
   d use with *would* to say you want something (*would like* + noun)
   e to describe similar behaviour to something or someone
   f used with the verbs *look*, *smell*, *sound* and *taste* to describe similarities with someone or something (*look like*, etc.)
   g use with *feel* to talk about wanting to do something (*feel like -ing*)

4 Rewrite the sentences using the word *like*.

   1 They want to play tennis later.
      They *'d like to play tennis later*. OR
      They *feel like playing tennis later*.

   2 You're very similar in appearance to someone else I went to school with.
      You _____ I went to school with.

   3 She wants to play tennis professionally one day.
      She _____ tennis professionally one day.

   4 We want some ice cream, please.
      We _____ , please.

   5 He isn't similar to his sister. She always worked very hard.
      He _____ his sister. She always worked very hard.

108

2d Joining a fitness class

Reading leaflet for a fitness class

1 Read the leaflet for fitness classes at a local gym. Then match the sentences (1–7) to the classes (A–C).

1. You have to get up early for this class.
2. The person in charge tells you what to do.
3. This class is good after a day at work.
4. This class mixes enjoyment with exercise.
5. Take a break from work and come for some exercise.
6. You will notice a difference very quickly.
7. It lasts for an hour and a half.

Fit for Life Gym

A Boot camp starts at 6 a.m. every morning with your instructor. He shouts orders and you run, jump, lift. It's non-stop exercise for 90 minutes.

'Perfect for people who want fast results.'

B Our evening Pilates classes help your body to recover after a hard day at work. Build strength with an exercise programme suitable for any age and fitness level.

'After a day in the office chair, Pilates is perfect for your muscles.'

C Zumba is a new kind of dance and our classes are a mixture of fun, excitement and high energy levels. Classes are at midday, so you can even join us during your lunch break.

'Zumba is a fun way to get fit – every class feels like a party!'

Real life talking about interests

2 🔊 **1.13** Listen to two friends talking about the leaflet in Exercise 1. Number the fitness classes in the order they discuss them.

Boot Camp   Pilates   Zumba

3 🔊 **1.13** Listen again and complete the conversation.

A: Hey, this looks interesting.
B: What?
A: This leaflet for fitness classes at the gym. Are you ¹_____ _____ doing something like that?
B: Maybe. But I'm ² _____ good at sport.
A: But this isn't competitive. It's for getting fit. This one ³ _____ _____. Boot Camp. What about joining that?
B: What is Boot Camp?
A: It's like the army. You have someone who tells you what to do. I think ⁴ _____ _____ do it.
B: When is it?
A: At six.
B: Great. So we can go after work.
A: No, it's six in the morning.
B: What?! You must be joking. I hate getting up early. ⁵ _____ _____ doing something later?
A: Well, there's one at lunchtime. It's called Zumba. It's a kind of dance, I think.
B: I don't like dancing.
A: ⁶ _____ _____. It looks fun.
B: What about something after work?
A: There's a Pilates class. It doesn't say an exact time, but it says it's after work.
B: Well, ⁷ _____ _____ that to Boot Camp or dancing.
A: Yes, ⁸ _____ _____ good.

4 Listen and respond saying what you are interested in doing

🔊 **1.14** A friend wants you to join one of the classes on the leaflet in Exercise 1. You are only interested in doing Pilates. Listen to your friend and respond each time. Then compare your responses with the answers that follow.

> Are you interested in Boot Camp?

> No, I wouldn't like to do it.

Unit 2 Competitions

109

2e Advertisements

Writing adverts and notices

1 Imagine you are organising a social event for everyone after work. Write a notice for everyone and tell them:

- it's a barbecue in the local park with a 'fun' football match afterwards
- the date and time
- the reason (it's a way for everyone to meet each other)
- your email address (so they can say if they are coming)

2 Grammar extra punctuation rules

Complete the list of rules for punctuation with these words.

apostrophe	capital letter
comma	exclamation mark
full stop	

1 You have to use a _____ when it's the first letter of a sentence; with names of people, places and countries; with days of the week and months; and with people's titles.

2 You must end a sentence with a _____ or you can emphasise something with an _____ .

3 A _____ can separate lists of nouns or adjectives and sometimes two clauses in a sentence.

4 You have to use an _____ with contracted forms and with the possessive 's.

3 Writing skill checking and correcting your writing

Read the piece of writing by a student. Three lines are correct and seven lines have punctuation mistakes. Tick (✓) the correct lines and correct the other lines.

My free time

i have many different hobbies
and interests such as computer
gaming cycling and painting but
my favourite is ice hockey. Its a
very popular sport in my home
country of canada. I practise
every saturday morning at our
local sports centre with my team
and we play matches once a month
We love to win

1 *I (capital letter)*
2 ✓
3 _____
4 _____
5 _____
6 _____
7 _____
8 _____
9 _____
10 _____

Unit 2 Competitions

Wordbuilding word forms

1 Complete the table with the other forms of the words. Use a dictionary to help you, if necessary.

Verb	Adjective	Noun (thing)	Noun (person)
compete	1 *competitive*	2 _____	competitor
3 _____	photographic	photograph	photographer
advertise		4 _____ (also *advert*)	advertiser
	5 _____	interest	
	6 _____	profession	professional

2 Pronunciation word stress

🔊 **1.15** Listen to all the words in Exercise 1. Underline the syllable with the main stress.

com*pete*   com*pe*titive   compe*ti*tion   com*pe*titor

Learning skills using a dictionary (1)

3 Match the different parts of the dictionary entries on the right (1–12) with these words.

adjective	definition
example sentence	first meaning
main stress	noun
past participle	plural form
present participle	pronunciation
second meaning	verb

Check!

4 Complete the sentences with these numbers. You can find the answers in Unit 2 of the Student's Book.

2   4   5   42   60   92   1500   1972

1 Arnold Palmer won _____ golf tournaments.
2 Mark Spitz won seven Olympic gold medals in _____ .
3 A Mud Bowl match lasts _____ minutes.
4 The winner of a Combine Harvester Fights wins _____ dollars!
5 There are _____ syllables in *competition*.
6 At the annual Idiotarod race, there are _____ people in a team.
7 The match was a draw. The score was two – _____ .
8 Competitors in a marathon must run _____ kilometres.

---

compete /kəmˈpiːt/ (v) (competing, competed) [1] take part in a contest or game. *Ten people competed in the race.* [2] try to get something for yourself and stop others getting it. *My company is competing with another for an important customer.*

competition /ˌkɒmpəˈtɪʃən/ (n) (competitions) [1] An event when two or more people take part in a contest or game to find the best at the activity. *Ten people competed in the race.* [2] When two or more people are trying to get something and stop others getting it. *There's a lot of competition for the trophy.*

competitive /kəmˈpetɪtɪv/ (adj) [1] situations or events when people compete with each other. *Professional tennis is a very competitive sport.* [2] a person who wants to be the best at something. *I'm a very competitive person who loves winning!*

111

Unit 3 Transport

3a Choosing greener transport

Reading green transport

1 Read the article below. What is the aim of the article? Choose the correct option (a, b or c).
  a to give an opinion about transport
  b to argue for more public transport
  c to give information about a new type of transport

2 Read the article again. Are the sentences true (T) or false (F), according to the information in the article?
  1 The author thinks walking is better than driving when you visit a city.
  2 Renting bicycles from hotels and hostels can be very expensive.
  3 The author thinks cities need to give more information to visitors.
  4 Buses, trains and ferries are better for the environment than cars or aeroplanes.
  5 All hotels have charging stations for electric cars.

Vocabulary transport (1): nouns

3 Complete the sentences with a compound noun, using a word from each box.

| petrol | road | rush | hour | jam | limit |
| speed | traffic | | station | works | |

  1 The _____ _____ begins around eight and ends at around nine in my city.
  2 There's a huge _____ _____ all the way from the city centre to the airport. Nothing is moving.
  3 This motorway will close for _____ _____ at midnight tonight and open again at six in the morning.
  4 The petrol tank is nearly on empty, so we need to find a _____ _____ soon.
  5 Police are using cameras to catch anyone driving over the _____ _____ .

Choosing greener transport

For tourists and travellers who want a more interesting experience when they arrive in a new city or country, here are some better ways to travel, both for you and for the environment.

Step 1 Get out of the car and walk. It's slower but it's the greenest way to travel. It's also the most rewarding way to see a city, but remember to pack comfortable shoes.

Step 2 Cycling is also a good alternative. Many hotels and hostels now offer free bicycles for guests. Some also provide electric bikes that give you help with hills and on longer journeys. Some cities also have bike stations. You pick up a bicycle from one of these stations and return it after two hours. It costs something but it's much cheaper than a bus or taxi.

Step 3 If you have to take transport in a city, try to take public transport. Most cities now offer lots of information and very clear maps. You'll also get more detailed information by visiting the city website before you go because it'll save a lot of time once you get there.

Step 4 Whenever possible, take buses, trains or ferries for travelling from city to city. They are usually greener than cars and aeroplanes.

Step 5 And when the only way to travel is by car, rent a hybrid or electric car. Many car rental companies now offer this kind of choice so always ask. Look for hotels at your destination with free electric vehicle charging stations. You'll be surprised at how many hotels now offer this facility.

by Jeannette Belliveau, Demand Media

Grammar comparatives and superlatives

4 Look back at the article in Exercise 1 and underline the examples of comparative and superlative forms.

> ▶ **SPELL CHECK comparatives and superlatives**
> - Add *-er* or *-est* to short adjectives: *young – younger – youngest*
> - When the adjectives end in *-e*, add *-r* or *-st*: *large – larger – largest*
> - Change adjectives ending in *-y* (after a consonant) to *-i* and add *-er* or *-est*: *happy – happier – happiest*
> - Double the final consonant of adjectives ending with a consonant + vowel + consonant: *hot – hotter – hottest*
> - Don't double the consonant for adjectives ending in vowel + *-w* or *-y*: *slow – slower – slowest*

5 Look at the spell check box. Then write the comparative and superlative forms of the adjectives.

1 cheap — *cheaper* — *cheapest*
2 angry
3 large
4 big
5 safe
6 funny
7 thin
8 low
9 easy
10 green
11 fit
12 fast

6 Write sentences that give your opinion. Use a comparative form with *-er*, *more* or *less*.

1 travelling by bus / travelling by car (relaxing)
I think *travelling by bus is more relaxing than travelling by car.*

2 cake / bread (tasty)
I think

3 email / letters (fast)
I think

4 teachers / politicians (work hard)
I think

5 trains / aeroplanes (bad for the environment)
I think

7 Complete the world records about transport with the superlative forms of these adjectives.

dangerous	fast	large	long	small	tall

WORLD RECORDS TRANSPORT

- Gregory Dunham built the world's ¹_____ rideable motorbike. It's 3.429 metres high.
- The ²_____ jet aircraft in the world is only 3.7 metres long and 5.7 metres wide (including wings).
- Marek Turowski drove the world's ³_____ motorised sofa! The piece of furniture travelled at a speed of 148 kilometres per hour.
- Emil and Liliana Schmid took the ⁴_____ journey ever. They drove 641,115 kilometres – and they are still driving!
- Billy Baxter broke the record for the fastest speed on a motorbike without seeing. He wore a blindfold over his eyes and reached 265.33 kilometres per hour. So it was probably one of the ⁵_____ journeys ever as well.
- In 2008, 490 Ferraris drove round a track in Japan. That's the ⁶_____ number of Ferraris in one place ever.

8 Pronunciation sentence stress in comparative and superlative sentences

🎵 **1.16** Listen and underline the stressed words in the sentences. Then listen again and repeat.

1 Your car is faster than mine.
2 Bicycles are the greenest transport.
3 Walking is slower than cycling.
4 Trains are cheaper than planes.
5 Hybrid transport is the most efficient.

3b Animal qualities

Grammar as ... as

1 Put the words in order to make sentences. Start with the bold phrases.

1 modern transport / in the forest / good as / **Horses** / are as

2 is always / as this in / my country / **The weather** / as hot

3 expensive / **Silver** / isn't / as / as gold

4 as cars / from / aren't / the sixties / **New cars** / stylish / as

5 **Bicycles** / as / cars / are / in the city centre / as fast

6 as I / used / not as / to be / **I'm** / young

2 Pronunciation /əz/

🔊 **1.17** /əz/ is the sound of *as* in sentences with *as ... as*. Listen to the sentences in Exercise 1 and repeat them using this sound.

3 Vocabulary extra expressions with animals

a Label the animals with these words.

| bat | bee | bird | horse | giraffe | lion |
| owl | mouse | | | | |

1   _____ 2 _____

3  _____ 4 _____

5  _____ 6 _____

7  _____ 8 _____

b The English language has many expressions using *as ... as* and the names of animals to talk about good or bad qualities. Complete the sentences with the name of an animal from Exercise 3a. Look up the adjectives in your dictionary to help you.

1 You need glasses. You're as blind as a _*bat*_ !
2 What's on the menu? I'm as hungry as a _____ .
3 My brother is as tall as a _____ . Why am I so short?
4 I'm as busy as a _____ today. I'm doing some gardening and studying my English.
5 My lecturer at university is as wise as an _____ .
6 Sorry, I didn't know you were in the house. You were as quiet as a _____ .
7 My grandfather died in the war. He was as brave as a _____ .
8 When I stand on the top of a mountain, I feel as free as a _____ .

Word focus *as*

4 You can use *as* in different ways. Match the sentences (1–4) with the uses of *as* (a–d) on page 115.

1 As we're late, we'll take a taxi instead of the bus.
2 That car looks as if it's very old.
3 Travelling to Edinburgh by train is as fast as travelling by plane.
4 As we drove past a field, we saw a horse pulling some logs.

114

a   to compare two things
b   to talk about appearance
c   to talk about two actions happening at the same time
d   to talk about the reason for something

5 Rewrite the sentences using *as*.

1   We stopped for lunch because there was a traffic jam on the motorway.
    We stopped for lunch _____ on the motorway.

2   You look like you had a long journey.
    _____ if you had a long journey.

3   In the city, the speed of a bicycle is the same as a bus.
    In the city, _____ fast as a bus.

4   We saw an elephant when we were driving home!
    We saw an elephant _____ !

Reading beautiful animals

6 Read the article on the right. Choose the correct options (a–c) to complete the gaps.

1	a as	b than	c the
2	a as	b than	c the
3	a much	b more	c many
4	a beautiful	b more beautiful	c most beautiful
5	a as	b than	c the
6	a is	b isn't	c aren't
7	a good	b better	c best

7 Read the article again and answer the questions.

1   Why are camels famous?

2   What are the different ways humans use them?

3   Does everyone agree that camels aren't beautiful?

4   How long does the competition last?

5   How many camels enter the competition?

6   What do the family and friends eat at the party?

Unit 3 Transport

Beauty competitions for camels

Camels are famous because they can walk further across deserts [1] _____ any other kind of animal. They can travel for days in places where temperatures are regularly as high as 40°C and where the rainfall can be as low [2] _____ 20mm per year. They often carry heavy loads in these conditions, but people don't only use them for transportation. They also produce milk, and because they can weigh as [3] _____ as 700 kilogrammes, they also provide a lot of meat. So we can all agree that camels have many great qualities, but how many of us would describe camels as [4] _____ ? Camels have a large hump, strange knees, skinny legs and ugly teeth. They are NOT beautiful. But not everyone agrees.

Once a year, people bring their camels from the countries of Oman, Saudi Arabia, Qatar and even further away, to an area of land in Abu Dhabi. They are here to find [5] _____ most beautiful camel. The competition lasts ten days. There are around 24,000 camels in the competition and the judges have to find two for the final day. The winning camel must have good ears, a high back, shiny hair and a long neck, and long legs are also important. There is a prize for the winner but this [6] _____ as important as family honour.

This year, the winner is a man called Bin Tanaf. Immediately, his family and friends celebrate and the party at his tent lasts all night. Two hundred people are there. They sing songs and tell stories about camels. Bin Tanaf's father says, 'This is the [7] _____ day of my life.' In the middle of the celebration there is a lot of food including rice and meat. Another man brings a large plate into the tent. There is a large piece of yellow meat on it. 'Ah,' says the son. 'The hump.'

Glossary
hump (n) / hʌmp /
honour (n) / ˈɒnə / respect for someone who does something important

115

3c Transport in India

Listening the Golden Quadrilateral

1 🔊 **1.18** Listen to a documentary about a new road in India called 'the Golden Quadrilateral'. Number the topics (a–d) in the order the presenter talks about them.
  a transport and industry on the road
  b a new road will help the economy
  c the length and technology of the new road
  d Indians are buying more and more cars

Glossary
poverty (n) /ˈpɒvəti/ a situation where people are poor and do not have money to pay for basic things
highway (American English) (n) /ˈhaɪweɪ/ **motorway** (British English) (n) /ˈməʊtəweɪ/ a large road with many lanes
symbol (n) /ˈsɪmb(ə)l/ something or someone that represents an idea

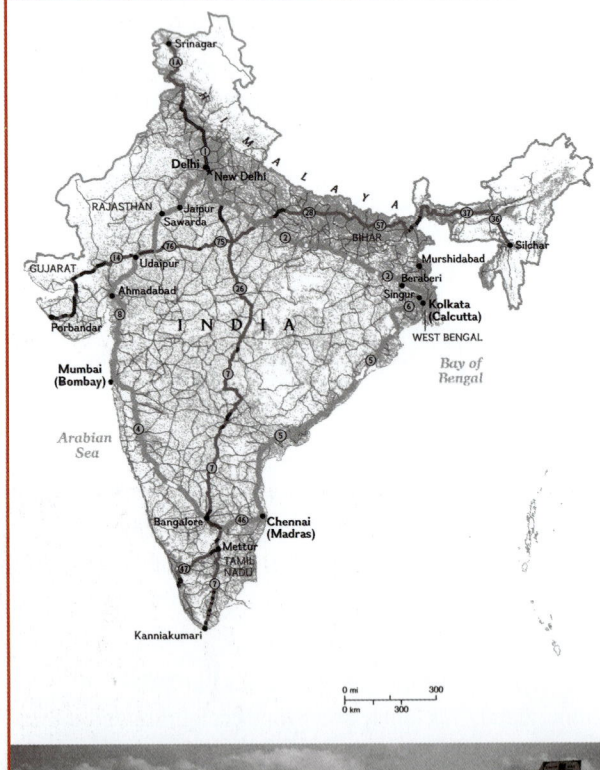

2 🔊 **1.18** Listen again and answer the questions. Choose the correct answer (a–c).
  1 How many new cars will people probably buy in the next few years?
      a 1.5 million
      b two million
      c three million
  2 Where do many of the rich people live?
      a next to the new road
      b in the cities
      c in the countryside
  3 How long is the road?
      a 600 kilometres
      b 6,000 kilometres
      c 60,000 kilometres
  4 What can you see on the computers at the road's headquarters in Delhi?
      a vehicles on the road
      b any problems on the road
      c answers a and b
  5 What types of transport can you see on the road?
      a all types
      b mostly cars
      c the presenter doesn't say
  6 Why does the presenter describe the new road as 'a symbol of India's future'?
      a Because it's the same shape as the country of India.
      b Because it is modern, it is helping the economy to grow.
      c Because India has lots of transport.

Vocabulary transport (2): verbs

3 Cross out the verb which is not possible for each type of transport or commuter (1–6).

  1 *catch / miss / go by / pick up* a train
  2 *drop off / take / catch / pick up* a passenger
  3 *catch / go by / get on / take* a flight
  4 *miss / go in / get / take* a taxi
  5 *ride / go by / get off / go in* a bicycle
  6 *get / take / miss / go* a bus

4 Pronunciation /æ/ or /eɪ/

🔊 **1.19** Match these words with the vowel sounds. Then listen, check and repeat.

| catch | change | day | gate | jam | plan |
| plane | rank | take | taxi | train | |

/æ/ ....
/eɪ/ ....

116

3d Getting around town

Vocabulary taking transport

1 Choose the correct options.

1 What's the bus *price / fare* to the airport?
2 There's a taxi *rank / stop* by the station, so you can get one there.
3 Would you like *a receipt / some change* for that?
4 Which *gate / platform* does the flight to Dublin leave from?
5 I think you should *book / check in* your ticket in advance.
6 Customs will want to look at the visa in your *ticket / passport*.
7 Would you like a window or *a corridor / an aisle* seat?
8 How much does it cost for a *first / return* class ticket?

Real life going on a journey

2 🔊 1.20 Listen to four conversations. Match the conversations (1–4) with the type of transport.
a taxi   b bus   c train   d plane

3 🔊 1.20 Listen again and answer the questions.

Conversation 1
1 Where does the bus stop?

2 What kind of ticket does he buy?

Conversation 2
3 How much is a first-class ticket?

4 What time does it leave?

5 Which platform does it leave from?

Conversation 3
6 How many bags is the person checking in?

7 How much extra does she pay?

8 Can she pay by credit card?

Conversation 4
9 Why can't the taxi stop where the person wants?

10 How much is the taxi fare?

4 Complete the four conversations with these phrases.

Can I have	Can I pay	Do you go
Have you got	How many	How much
I'd like a	Which platform	

Conversation 1
A: Hi. ¹_____ to the centre?
B: Which part?
A: Near the cinema.
B: Yes, we stop outside it.
A: Great. ²_____ a return ticket, please?

Conversation 2
A: ³_____ first-class ticket, please.
B: That's twenty euros fifty.
A: Here you are. ⁴_____ is it?
B: It's at five fifteen from platform twelve.

Conversation 3
A: ⁵_____ bags are you checking in?
B: Two. And I've got a carry-on.
A: I'm afraid your ticket only includes one bag. You'll have to pay an extra ten pounds for that one.
B: Oh, OK. ⁶_____ by credit card?
A: Sure.

Conversation 4
A: It's just up here on the right. You can drop me off over there.
B: I can't stop there. It's a bus stop. But here's OK.
A: OK. ⁷_____ is that?
B: That's thirteen dollars thirty cents.
⁸_____ the right change?

117

3e Quick communication

1 Dictation telephone messages

🎧 **1.21** Listen to three messages on your mobile phone. Write every word you hear in each message.

Message one

WHILE YOU WERE OUT
_____ called at _____ a.m. / p.m.
MESSAGE:

Message two

WHILE YOU WERE OUT
_____ called at _____ a.m. / p.m.
MESSAGE:

Message three

WHILE YOU WERE OUT
_____ called at _____ a.m. / p.m.
MESSAGE:

Writing notes and messages

2 Look at the messages you wrote in Exercise 1. Rewrite them in note form. Remember to miss out words like articles, pronouns, auxiliary verbs and polite forms.

Message one

WHILE YOU WERE OUT
_____ called at _____ a.m. / p.m.
MESSAGE:

Message two

WHILE YOU WERE OUT
_____ called at _____ a.m. / p.m.
MESSAGE:

Message three

WHILE YOU WERE OUT
_____ called at _____ a.m. / p.m.
MESSAGE:

Wordbuilding compound nouns

▶ **WORDBUILDING compound nouns**

Compound nouns are nouns with either:
- two nouns joined together, e.g. *motor + bike = motorbike*.
- two nouns together but as separate words, e.g. *car + parking = car parking*.

There is no rule for when you join the words or keep them separate words so check in your dictionary.

1 Look at the wordbuilding box. Then complete the compound nouns in the sentences with these words.

| centre | credit | driver | seat | snow |
| time | town | transport | | |

1 Sorry, we don't accept .... cards, only cash.
2 He works at night so he often sleeps in the day............ .
3 There are road works in the town .... so you shouldn't drive to the cinema this evening.
4 I know I should take public .... but it's easier to drive my own car.
5 A .... mobile looks like a lot of fun to drive.
6 Do you have any change to pay the taxi .... ?
7 The .... council is meeting tonight to discuss the problem of car parking.
8 I always book a window .... when I travel by plane.

2 Match a word from each box to make compound nouns.

| ~~alarm~~ | bank | boxing | football | letter | mobile |
| tennis | town | | | | |

| account | box | centre | ~~clock~~ | court | gloves |
| phone | pitch | | | | |

1 *alarm clock*
2 ....
3 ....
4 ....
5 ....
6 ....
7 ....
8 ....
9 ....
10 ....

Learning skills remembering new vocabulary

3 Look at the list of ways to remember new vocabulary. Tick (✓) the ones you use now and put an asterix (*) by the ones you would like to use in the future.

Ways to remember new vocabulary

1 After I finish a unit in the Student's Book, I read it again a few weeks later and check any words I don't remember. ○

2 When I find a new word or expression in the unit, I highlight it. ○

3 I write a new word on a piece of paper. On the other side of the paper, I write a definition. Then I test myself a few weeks later. ○

4 When I find a new word, I check in my dictionary for other words that I can build with it, for example, *commute (v), commuter (n)*. ○

5 I write new words in lists with the translations next to them. Then I cover the words and try to translate them from my own language. ○

6 I write the new word in a sentence that is important to me. ○

7 I read more texts on similar subjects to the unit. I usually find some of the new words in the text. ○

8 I choose ten new words and write a short story using them all. ○

4 Do you use other techniques for learning and remembering vocabulary? Write them down and compare your ideas with other students in your next lesson.

Check!

5 Put the letters of these anagrams in the correct order to make words from Unit 3 in the Student's Book. (The clues in brackets will help.)

1 GLEDES (a type of transport) ....
2 LAKATOK (a city in India) ....
3 RODIDTIA (a famous dog race) ....
4 ESIAL (seat on an aeroplane) ....
5 PEALHENT (large animal) ....
6 JETACDIVE (type of word between *as* and *as*) ....

Unit 4 Adventure

4a Risks and adventures

1 Vocabulary extra adventure

Replace the words in bold with these similar words or phrases.

| adventure   ambition   a big challenge |
| my biggest achievement   crazy |
| dangerous   take risks |

1 I don't like to **do things that could be dangerous**.
2 My life is so boring. I want a life of **doing exciting things**.
3 Don't walk so close to the cliff. It looks **unsafe**.
4 Passing my exams at university was **the thing that needed the most hard work and effort** in my life so far.
5 Climbing Mount Everest presents mountaineers with **something that is really difficult to do**, but that's what makes it worth doing!
6 As I get older, I have less and less **I want to achieve**.
7 It's snowing outside. We can't walk a hundred kilometres in this weather! Are you completely **mad**?

Grammar past simple

2 Look at the spell check box. Then write the past simple form of these regular verbs.

> ▶ **SPELL CHECK past simple regular verbs (-ed endings)**
>
> - Add *-ed* to verbs ending in a consonant: watch → watch**ed**
> - Add *-d* to verbs ending in *-e*: dance → dance**d**
> - With verbs ending in *–y* (after a consonant), change the *y* to *i* and add *-ed*: cry → cr**ied**
> - Don't change the *y* to *i* after a vowel: play → pla**yed**
> - Double the final consonant for most verbs ending with consonant + vowel + consonant: stop → sto**pped**

1 visit
2 arrive
3 dry
4 stay
5 jog
6 live
7 study
8 move

3 Complete the article below and on page 121 with the past simple form of the verbs in the boxes.

The TV presenter

| be-born   become   go   start   study   survive |

The circus performer

| grow up   join   learn   play |

The risk takers

The TV presenter

Brady Barr ¹ *was born* in 1963. He ² .... Science Education at university and then he ³ .... a teacher. However, a few years later he ⁴ .... on a scientific expedition to learn more about crocodiles. He joined the *National Geographic* Television channel in 1997 and ⁵ .... presenting TV shows about dangerous animals (including bears!). Recently, a three-and-a-half metre python attacked Brady during filming. Luckily, Brady ⁶ .... and he is currently making another series of the show.

> **Glossary**
> **attack** (v) /əˈtæk/ to use violence against someone or something
> **python** (n) /ˈpaɪθ(ə)n/ a large, dangerous snake

The circus performer

Eskil Ronningsbakken ⁷ _____ in Norway. As a child, he enjoyed climbing trees and he ⁸ _____ on the roofs of houses. He ⁹ _____ to do a handstand when he was five and he studied circus skills when he was eight. Aged seventeen, he ¹⁰ _____ a circus, but two years later he started performing on his own with his balancing act.

4 Read the article again. Are these sentences true (T) or false (F)? Rewrite the false sentences to make them correct.

1. Brady was born in Norway.
   F – Eskil was born in Norway.
2. Both men studied at university.
3. Eskil was interested in the circus when he was a child.
4. Eskil joined a theatre when he was seventeen.
5. Brady joined a TV channel in 1997.
6. Brady attacked a python on his TV show.
7. Eskil started performing with a group of people after he left the circus.
8. Both men took risks in their life.

5 Complete the interview questions for Brady and Eskil. Use the past simple form.

1. _____ born? In 1963.
2. Where _____ ? In Norway.
3. What subject _____ ? Science Education.
4. When _____ to do a handstand? When I was five.
5. _____ National Geographic TV? In 1997.
6. _____ performing on your own? When I was nineteen.

6 Pronunciation past simple irregular verbs

a Write the past simple form of these verbs. (Check your answers in a dictionary.)

1. bite _____
2. buy _____
3. hit _____
4. do _____
5. say _____
6. go _____
7. fight _____
8. bring _____
9. meet _____

b 1.22 Listen to the answers and write the past forms of the verbs in the correct column of the table.

/e/	/ɪ/	/ɔː/

121

4b The survivors

Vocabulary personal qualities

1 Complete the table. Use a dictionary, if necessary.

Adjective	Noun
determined	1 *determination*
ambitious	2
3	care
decisive	4
5	experience
6	intelligence
patient	7
8	reliability

2 Pronunciation word stress

a 🔊 1.23 Listen and check your answers in Exercise 1. Then mark the main stress in each word.

Example:
de<u>ter</u>mined, determi<u>na</u>tion

b 🔊 1.23 Listen again and repeat.

3 Complete the sentences with the adjectives in Exercise 1.

1 Be .... on the side of the mountain. There's a lot of snow out there today.
2 I'm .... to reach the top and nothing is going to stop me!
3 My brother was lazy at school but because he was so .... he passed all his exams anyway.
4 At my company, some people are so .... they will do anything to get a promotion.
5 Don't get angry every time someone is late. You need to learn to be more .... with people.
6 He's so .... in mountaineering that he feels very confident about this next challenge.
7 My car isn't very .... It breaks down all the time.
8 Are you coming out this weekend or not? Please be more .... !

Reading survival stories into books and films

4 Read the article. Then match the stories (A–E) with the statements (1–8) on page 123. Sometimes more than one story matches a statement.

The survivors

Some of the best films and books come from true stories. This is particularly true for stories about mountaineers and explorers. Here are five of the best stories which became books and films.

A In 1996 Jon Krakauer went to Mount Everest. He wanted to climb the mountain and write about how the mountain was changing. However, while he was there, eight people died in terrible weather on the side of the mountain. Krakauer described what happened in his book *Into Thin Air*.

B When a plane was flying over the Andes in 1972, it crashed but some of the passengers survived. Two Uruguayan men, Nando Parrado and Roberto Canessa, walked for many days across the mountains to get help. Their story became a film called *Alive*.

C In 1865, while Edward Whymper and his team were climbing the Matterhorn mountain, one of the men fell. As he fell, his rope pulled others down with him. Whymper survived and wrote a book about the events.

D The climber George Mallory wanted to be the first person to climb Everest in 1924. He never returned, but no one knows if he reached the top. As a result, there are many books about this famous mountaineering mystery.

E While the explorer Ernest Shackleton was sailing around Antarctica his ship, *Endurance*, became stuck in the ice. Eventually, Shackleton and his crew left the ship and they spent sixteen days crossing 1,300 kilometres of ocean in small boats to the island of South Georgia. Shackleton published his famous story of survival in 1919.

Unit 4 Adventure

1 This story isn't about any mountains.
2 The people in the story were not explorers or mountaineers.
3 We don't know if this person achieved his aim.
4 Weather was the problem in this story.
5 The leaders of the teams survived in these stories.
6 These stories include problems with transport.
7 This story became a film.
8 These stories describe long journeys.

Grammar past continuous

5 Underline any examples of the past continuous in the article in Exercise 4.

6 Use the prompts to write past continuous sentences.

1 sun / shine and people / sunbathe on / beach
....
2 phone / ring, but I / leave / the house so I didn't answer it
....
3 we / not / study when the teacher walked in
....
4 we / walk past the building when the fire started
....
5 she / not / think / about her exam results when the envelope arrived
....
6 it / not / rain, / so we went for a picnic
....

7 Choose the correct forms to complete the conversations.

Conversation one
A: ¹ *Did you see / Were you seeing* all those police cars this morning?
B: No. Where were they?
A: They ² *followed / were following* a red sports car, but I don't know if they caught him.
B: I ³ *saw / was seeing* on the news that there was a bank robbery, so it was probably something to do with that.
A: I can't believe you ⁴ *didn't hear / weren't hearing* them as they went past.
B: I ⁵ *listened / was listening* to music with my headphones on, so I couldn't hear anything else.

Conversation two
A: ⁶ *Did you have / Were you having* a bad journey?
B: No, not too bad. My normal train ⁷ *didn't arrive / wasn't arriving* today, so I had to wait for the later train.
A: So you were fifteen minutes late.
B: Sorry. Yes, I was. Why? ⁸ *Did you wait / Were you waiting* for me?
A: No, but you were late yesterday. And the day before! It's becoming a problem.

Word focus was/were

8 We use *was/were* in different ways. Match *was/were* in the sentences (1–5) with the uses (a–c).

1 I was born on a farm in 1966.
2 Our journey was long and dangerous.
3 What were they doing?
4 Why were you so late?
5 He wasn't driving too fast, so why did the police stop him?

a as an auxiliary verb to form the past continuous .... , ...
b with certain fixed expression, e.g. talking about your birth ....
c to talk (and ask) about the subject of the sentence .... , ...

9 Complete the sentences with *was, were, wasn't* or *weren't*.

1 The book .... really good, but the film version ....
2 Where .... you born?
3 We went to the Scottish mountains and there .... another person anywhere. It .... incredibly quiet.
4 We live in London, but we .... born in England. Originally we came from Poland.
5 Why .... you at the party? I .... looking for you all night.

123

4c Survival stories

Vocabulary geographical features

1 Complete the extract from an explorer's diary with these words.

> cave   crevasse   face   glacier   lake
> ridge   summit

Day one
We put up our tents next to an enormous ¹ _____ . The water was blue and very cold. Up above, I could see the north ² _____ of the mountain disappear behind clouds.

Day two
The next morning, it was sunny. We ate a large breakfast and packed our bags. We walked a few kilometres across the huge ³ _____ of rock and ice that moves down the valley about a centimetre a year. At one point in the journey, there was a deep ⁴ _____ . It was too big to cross, so we walked for two hours until we found a safe place to cross.

Day three
We made better progress today. We climbed about halfway up the mountain. By evening, we reached a ⁵ _____ . It was snowing, so we dug a snow ⁶ _____ and tried to get warm and sleep. Tomorrow we want to reach the ⁷ _____ of the mountain.

Listening a walk through the Amazon rainforest

2 🔊 **1.24** Listen to an interview with Daniel Fanning, the leader of an expedition through the Amazon rainforest. Which of the topics (1–6) does he talk about?

1. how to survive in the rainforest
2. how to prepare for the rainforest
3. what personal qualities you need
4. what you need to carry
5. dangerous animals in the rainforest
6. the physical and mental sides of walking long distances

3 🔊 **1.24** Listen again. Answer the questions.

1. What was Daniel's job on the expedition?
2. Why did he need to test the equipment and tents?
3. Why didn't he carry much clothing?
4. What are the most important things to carry?
5. How many kilos did he lose?
6. What personal quality does he think you need on this kind of expedition?

Vocabulary *in*, *on* or *at*

4 Complete the sentences with *in*, *on*, *at* or Ø (no preposition).

1. _____ May 1953, Edmund Hilary and Tenzing Norgay became the first men to reach the summit of Mount Everest.
2. _____ the evenings, we cooked dinner over a fire and watched the stars.
3. There's another train _____ five minutes. We can catch that one.
4. The two women reached the summit _____ exactly three o'clock that afternoon.
5. The expedition leaves _____ Monday.
6. The rescue team arrived _____ three days later.
7. Roald Amundsen was the first explorer to reach both the North and South Poles, but he died in a plane crash _____ June 18, 1928.
8. The two climbers returned safe and well _____ yesterday.
9. The group of explorers arrived home _____ New Year's Eve.

124

Unit 4 Adventure

4d Telling stories

Listening a true story

1 🔊 **1.25** Listen to a true story about Yossi Ghinsberg's journey through the jungle of Bolivia. Number the events (a–f) in the correct order (1–6).

a The men got lost.
b Yossi was lost in the jungle for three weeks.
c Yossi travelled on a raft down the river with Kevin.
d Yossi fell off the raft.
e Four men travelled into the jungle of Bolivia.
f Local people found Kevin.

Glossary
raft (n) /rɑːft/   a simple flat boat made with long pieces of wood

2 Dictation Yossi Ghinsberg

🔊 **1.25** Listen again and write the missing words in the story.

¹ _____, Yossi Ghinsberg started a journey with three other men. They were travelling through the jungle of Bolivia but, ² _____, they were lost. ³ _____, two of the group, Yossi and Kevin, built a raft so they could travel down the river and find help.

⁴ _____ they travelled down the river, but ⁵ _____ they hit a rock. Yossi fell off the raft and swam to the shore.

⁶ _____ Yossi was lost in the jungle, his friend Kevin was luckier. He stayed on the raft and ⁷ _____ some local men found him. ⁸ _____ they searched for Yossi and, ⁹ _____, ¹⁰ _____ they found him alive. ¹¹ _____, the other two men never returned.

Real life telling a story

3 Look at the words and phrases (1–11) you wrote in the text in Exercise 2. Match them with the headings (a–e) for telling a story.

a refers to days and period of time: _____, _____, _____, _____,
b sequences parts of the story: _____, _____,
c introduces new and surprising information: _____, _____,
d introduces good news: _____
e introduces bad news: _____

4 Pronunciation intonation for responding

a 🔊 **1.26** Listen to people saying these phrases. They either sound interested and surprised or they don't sound interested. Tick the phrases with interested or surprised intonation.

1 Why was that?
2 That was a good idea!
3 Oh no!
4 That was lucky!
5 Wow!

b 🔊 **1.27** Listen to the sentences again. This time the speakers all sound interested or surprised. Repeat, copying the intonation.

5 Listen and respond responding to good and bad news

🔊 **1.28** Listen to someone telling you a story. Respond to the good or bad news with a response from the box. Then compare your response each time with the model answer that follows.

| Why?   That was a good idea! |
| Oh no!   Wow!   That was lucky! |

I had a terrible journey into work this morning.   *Why?*

125

4e A story of survival

1 Writing skill *-ly* adverbs

a Add *-ly* to the word in the sentences where necessary.

1 We swam quick *ly* across the river.
2 We climbed the mountain fast ✓ .
3 The rain stopped and the sun shone bright____ .
4 The car sudden____ stopped.
5 There was a sudden____ movement in the trees.
6 The view from the summit was beautiful____ .
7 Amazing____, we survived at sea for ten days.
8 The whole experience was amazing____ .

b Complete the story from a blog for people with interesting survival stories. Use these adverbs.

| eventually | fortunately | hardly |
| incredibly | unfortunately | |

I was going on a trip though the Sycamore Wilderness Canyon in Arizona. In the USA, only the Grand Canyon is bigger and it has lots of visitors. ¹_____, the Sycamore Wilderness Canyon is over 20,000 hectares, with no roads, and you don't see another person for days.

Also, you won't see any water for most of the year so you have to carry your own. I was only carrying water for three days because I planned for that length of time. ²_____ on Day 1 I lost the trail. I spent hours looking for it again but it was getting dark so I put up my tent.

The next day I walked in high temperatures, but I still couldn't find the trail. I ³_____ had any water left and my mouth was dry. I camped again and got up early before the sun became too hot. I was badly dehydrated and desperate, but just as I came to the edge of a cliff, I looked down and ⁴_____ there was the Verde River.

It took two hours to climb down the side of the cliff, but ⁵_____ I reached the river and drank the water. The next day I followed the river for miles and then I found a trail. I arrived home a day later and I knew I was very lucky to be alive.

Glossary
hectare (n) /ˈhekteə/ an area of land, 1 hectare = 10,000 m²

2 Grammar extra adverbs without *-ly*

a Not all adverbs end in *-ly*. Find these adverbs in the story in Exercise 2 and notice their position.

| also | only | again | still | just | then |

b Write the adverb in the correct position in the sentences.

1 We walked for three hours, and we sat and enjoyed the view. (then)
2 I arrived home as the sun went down. (just)
3 The explorers tried to leave their camp, but the weather was still too bad. (again)
4 After three hours we were lost. (still)
5 We were three days from anywhere, but we had food and water for one more day. (only)
6 The jungle is hot. There are many dangerous animals. (also)

Writing a short story

3 Write a short story (100 words) which begins with the words: 'We only had food and water for one more day …' In your story, use six or more adverbs.

Wordbuilding negative prefixes (*in-*, *im-*, *un-*)

▶ **WORDBUILDING negative prefixes**

A prefix is a group of letters added in front of a word to change its meaning. Some prefixes have a negative meaning so you can make some adjectives have the opposite meaning. For example, we often use the negative prefixes *in-* (*incomplete*), *im-* (*impolite*) and *un-* (*unhappy*).

1 Look at the wordbuilding box. Then complete the words in the sentences with *in-*, *im-* or *un-*. Use a dictionary to help you.

1 It's _____ possible to climb the mountain today. The weather is so bad.
2 You spend too much time in front of the TV. I think it's very _____ healthy. Get some exercise!
3 Don't be _____ kind to your friends. You never know when you'll need their help.
4 Why are you so _____ helpful? I only want you to carry something for me.
5 Your idea is completely _____ practical. It can't work.
6 Your answer was _____ accurate. The correct answer was three hundred and sixty point five.

2 Complete these sentences with the correct form of the word with a negative prefix.

1 Why are you so *unambitious* (ambition)? You should do more challenging things with your life.
2 Don't be so _____ (patience)! Learn to wait.
3 Your daughter isn't _____ (intelligent) but she isn't very clever either.
4 I don't want to go in your car. It's totally _____ (rely). Let's take mine.
5 Good leaders mustn't be _____. (decide)

Learning skills planning your study time

3 Many people learn English with a class of other people. Having regular lessons at a certain time helps you learn but it's also important to study outside the classroom. Think about how you can plan your time for studying on your own. Choose the correct options to make these statements true for you.

> **HOW I STUDY**
>
> 1 My favourite time of day for studying is *in the morning / in the afternoon / in the evening*.
> 2 I think I can spend *about an hour / between two and three hours / more than three hours* a week studying on my own.
> 3 The best days in my week to study on are *Monday / Tuesday / Wednesday / Thursday / Friday / Saturday / Sunday*.
> 4 The best place for me to study is *in a particular place in my house / outside my house / in a room at the language school / other*.

4 Now think about these other suggestions for studying. Answer the questions for you.

> 5 This workbook is an important part of studying. How much of this workbook can you complete every week?
> 6 It is useful to read through the Student's Book and your notes after each lesson. When will you be able to do this?
> 7 Most people agree that it is better to study every day for ten or fifteen minutes than once a week for an hour or two. Is it possible for you to work this way? When could you spend a few minutes studying every day (e.g. on the bus to work or during your lunch break)?

Check!

5 Can you remember? You can find the answers in Unit 4 of the Student's Book.

1 Which adventurer or survivor in Unit 4 of the Student's Book was in these places?

> Denver airport   Hawaii   Atafu
> Siula Grande, Peru   Canary Islands

2 What happened to the person or people in these places?
3 How did they survive?

Unit 5 The environment

5a Recycling begins at home

Vocabulary household items

cling film

1 Look at these notes from a student's vocabulary notebook. Add similar information to the other words.

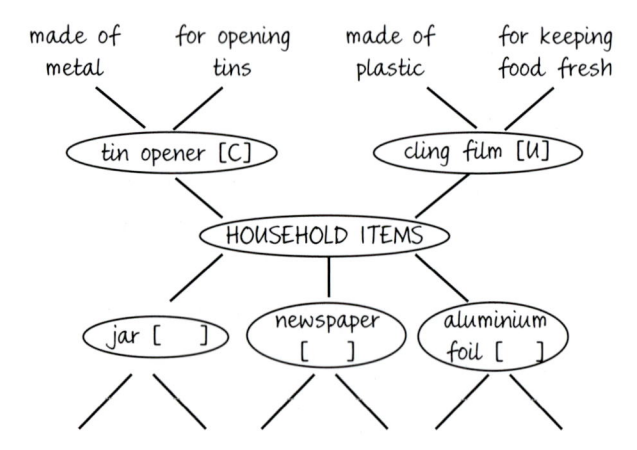

made of metal — for opening tins — tin opener [C]

made of plastic — for keeping food fresh — cling film [U]

HOUSEHOLD ITEMS: jar [ ], newspaper [ ], aluminium foil [ ]

Grammar countable and uncountable nouns

2 Complete the phrases with *a/an* for countable nouns and *some* for uncountable nouns.

1 _____ banana
2 _____ juice
3 _____ box
4 _____ can
5 _____ compost
6 _____ egg
7 _____ milk
8 _____ coffee
9 _____ carton

> ▶ SPELL CHECK plural countable nouns
> - With countable nouns, you usually add -s: egg → eggs
> - Add -es to nouns ending in -ch, -s, -ss, -sh and -x: sandwich → sandwiches
> - Change nouns ending in -y (after a consonant) to -i and add -es: city → cities
> - Don't change the -y to -i after a vowel: key → keys
> - Some nouns are irregular: man → men

3 Look at the spell check box. Then write the plural form of the countable nouns. Use your dictionary if necessary.

1 jar
2 bus
3 country
4 holiday
5 woman
6 can
7 box
8 child
9 phone
10 class
11 story
12 cartridge

Reading reusing household items

4 Read the article on page 129. Match the missing headings (a–e) with the gaps (1–5).

a Items made of paper
b Items to put things in
c Plastic bags
d House cleaning
e Clothing

5 Read the article again. Answer these questions.

1 What is better than recycling household items?

2 What can you use for cleaning instead of paper towels?

3 What types of storage items are good for reusing?

4 What three uses does the writer suggest for old newspapers?

5 How can you keep your plants warm in the winter?

6 What can you use instead of a plastic bag when you go shopping?

128

Recycling

Reusing household items is better for the environment than throwing them away or recycling them. Reusing needs less energy than collecting household rubbish or taking it to the recycling centre. Here are some ideas for reusing common items in your house.

1. The next time you don't have any paper towels for cleaning, don't go to the shop. Make your own from old cotton shirts, old socks and old towels. You can clean your car with them, wash the kitchen floor and dust the furniture. And they're cheap!

2. Wash your glass jars and reuse them to keep small items. In the kitchen, you can store beans, tea and spices in them. You can also wash yoghurt pots and other plastic containers and reuse them for food in the fridge.

3. Use your magazines and newspaper for wrapping presents or protecting fragile objects. Before you throw away the paper from your desk, ask yourself: *Can I write on the other side first?* And if you shred paper and use newspaper, it makes good compost.

4. Obviously, when your child's old shirt and trousers are too small, you can pass them on to smaller kids. Most countries also have second-hand shops so you can take your shoes and jumpers there. But you can also wrap old clothing around the plants in your garden in a cold winter.

5. We all use too many of these every day and they are hard to recycle, so reuse them for carrying your shopping. When you travel, you can put your liquids in them in case they open.

Grammar quantifiers

6 Complete the pairs of sentences with these words.

1. some / any
   a. There are _____ cakes on the table.
   b. There isn't _____ sugar left.

2. some / much
   a. There isn't *much* milk left.
   b. Don't worry, there's *some* more in the fridge.

3. any / many
   a. I don't have _____ eggs but I can give you one.
   b. I don't have _____ eggs. We'll have to buy some.

4. a lot of / much
   a. We've got _____ old aluminium foil we should recycle.
   b. We don't use _____ aluminium foil because cling film is better.

5. a few / a little
   a. There are _____ ink cartridges in that box.
   b. There's only _____ ink in this pen.

6. a few / many
   a. I don't get _____ days off for holidays.
   b. I have _____ days every year for holidays.

7. a little / much
   a. I only get _____ exercise at the gym each week.
   b. Do you get _____ exercise?

7 Complete the sentences with these words. Are the sentences true for you?

| any | few | lot | many | ~~some~~ |

1. There are *some* recycling bins in each office.
2. There aren't _____ plastic cups. Everyone has to bring in their own coffee cup.
3. There are a _____ signs in the offices to remind people to switch off anything electrical at the end of the day.
4. Some people drive to work but there aren't _____ places to park. Most people travel by bus or they cycle to work.
5. We try to reuse a _____ of our paper as well as recycling it.

5b What we consume

Listening everyday costs

1 🔊 **1.29** A researcher is interviewing different people in a shopping centre about their everyday costs. Match each interview (1–4) with the category (a–d).

a housing
b food
c transport
d other goods

2 🔊 **1.29** Listen again. Answer the questions.

Interview 1
1 What is in the shopper's bag?

2 Who is it for?

Interview 2
3 What does the person's internet package include?

4 How much does the package cost approximately?

Interview 3
5 Why did the customer ring the water company?

6 How much does she normally pay?

Interview 4
7 What is at the end of the person's road?

8 Why does he buy petrol there?

Vocabulary results and figures

3 Look at the pie and bar charts. Complete the phrases with these words.

| exactly | just over | nearly | well over |

1 .... half   2 .... 50%

3 .... the same   4 .... double

4 Read the phrases and shade the pie charts.

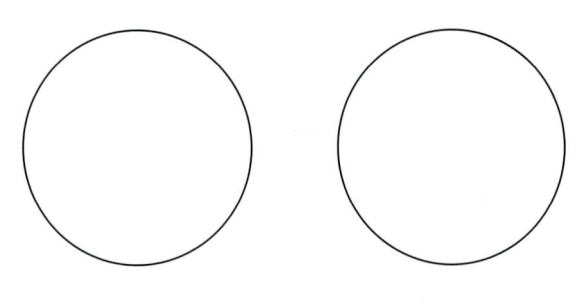

1 exactly half   2 Just over 75%

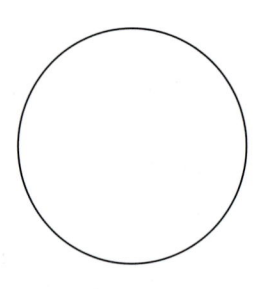

3 nearly 50%   4 well over 90%

Unit 5 The environment

Reading understanding a chart

5 Look at the chart from the 2009 Greendex Report. It compares how often people in different countries recycled their household materials in 2008 and 2009. Complete the statements (1–8) with the correct nationality.

Frequency of Recycling Materials

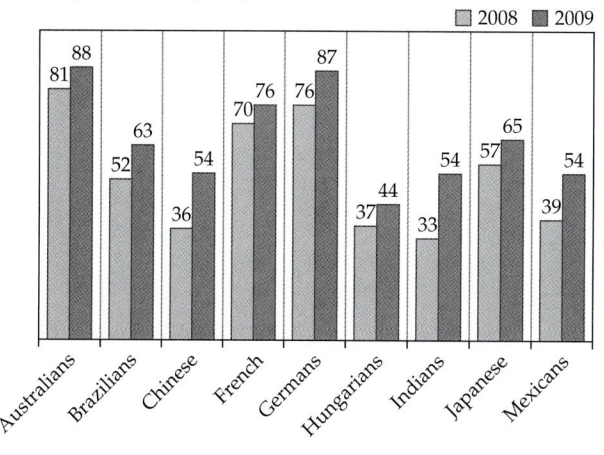

	2008	2009
Australians	81	88
Brazilians	52	63
Chinese	36	54
French	70	76
Germans	76	87
Hungarians	37	44
Indians	33	54
Japanese	57	65
Mexicans	39	54

1 In both years, the *Australians* recycled over eighty per cent of the time.
2 The _____ increased their recycling to over three quarters of the time.
3 In 2008, the _____ recycled exactly a third of the time. In 2009, they recycled just over fifty per cent of the time.
4 In 2009, the _____, the _____ and the _____ all recycled at the same frequency.
5 In 2008, the _____ and the _____ recycled over fifty per cent of the time and over sixty a year later.
6 The _____ increased their rate of recycling by exactly fifty per cent.
7 The _____ recycled just over seventy five per cent of the time in 2008 and then well over eighty per cent in 2009.
8 The _____ recycled just over a third of the time in 2008 and over forty per cent in 2009.

Grammar definite article (*the*) or no article

6 Complete the sentences with *the* or Ø (no article).

1 I love _____ pizzas!
2 One day I'd love to visit _____ Amazon rainforest.
3 _____ New Zealand is a country with every type of natural feature.
4 _____ Maldives are a group of islands in the Indian Ocean.
5 My favourite Hollywood actor is staying at _____ Astoria Hotel in London.
6 I don't like driving at _____ night.
7 One of _____ best holidays I had was staying at home for a week!
8 Do you also speak _____ English at home with your family?
9 What are you doing at _____ weekend? Would you like to go to the beach?
10 A: There's a strange car outside our house!
   B: It's _____ same one I told you about earlier.

7 Pronunciation /ðə/ or /ði:/

🔊 **1.30** Listen to the sentences in Exercise 6 with *the* in them. Do you hear the pronunciation /ðə/ or /ði:/?

/ðə/ Sentences: _____
/ði:/ Sentences: _____

8 Read this article. A definite article (*the*) is missing in seven places. Write it in.

Over three million people live in ∧*the* United States of America. It is world's most multi-cultural country. It was part of United Kingdom but it became a new country in 1776. Washington DC became capital city and the President still lives in White House today. However, it isn't biggest city. New York is. New York is also popular with tourists. In particular, they come to see Statue of Liberty.

5c Rubbish we produce

Word focus *take*

1 Replace *take* in the sentences with the correct form of one of these verbs or phrases.

| be careful | carry | drink | go by |
| go for | have | last | slow down |

1 Let's **take** a taxi. It's much faster.   *go by*
2 Would you like to **take** a walk?
3 The journey will **take** about three hours.
4 **Take your time!** There's no hurry.
5 It's time for you all to **take** a break.
6 You need to **take care** in the jungle. There are many dangerous animals.
7 You need to **take** 10 ml of this medicine twice a day for two weeks.
8 This boat can **take** up to 30 people.

2 Complete the sentences with your own words.

1 I usually take .... when I go to work.
2 The journey to my work takes ....
3 I normally take a break ....
4 It's important to take your time when you ....
5 It's important to take care when you ....

Listening one household's rubbish

3 🔊 1.31 Listen to a news report. Answer these questions.

1 What type of news is it about?
2 Which country is it about?
3 What examples of electronic devices does it mention?
4 Does the reporter think recycling electronic devices could have a big effect?
5 What kind of recycling has become successful in this country?

4 🔊 1.31 Listen again. Complete the facts with numbers.

	Average households
1	Total amount of rubbish produced = ... billion kilos
2	Amount recycled or composted = ... billion kilos
	Electronic devices
3	The average household owns .... electronic devices.
4	Households with three or more people own as many as .... devices.
5	Smaller households own about .... devices.
6	One million mobile phones could produce .... kilos of gold.
	Paper recycling
7	Average amount of paper recycled was .... kilos per person or .... kilos per household.
8	.... % of households can recycle paper.

By Karyn Maier, Demand Media

Glossary
trash (n) /træʃ/ (AmEng) rubbish

5d Ordering by phone

Listening an order by phone

1 1.32 Listen to a customer ordering a garden composter by phone. Complete the order form.

Item number: ¹ _____
Name of item: Garden Composter
Price: ² _____ (including delivery)
Surname of customer: ³ _____
Address: ⁴ _____ Windmill Avenue, Oxford
Type of credit card: ⁵ _____
Card number: ⁶ _____
Email: ⁷ _____

Real life making an order

2 1.32 Complete the conversation from Exercise 1 with the questions (a–i). Then listen again and check your answers.

a Can I take your surname?
b Does that include delivery?
c Do you have the item number?
d Can I help you?
e Would you like confirmation by email?
f Is that the garden composter?
g Which credit card would you like to pay with?
h Can I put you on hold for a moment?
i Is there anything else I can help you with today?

A = Sales assistant, C = Customer
S: Good morning. ¹ _____ ?
C: Hi, I'm calling about a product on your website. I'd like to order it but the website won't let me.
S: One moment … ² _____ ?
C: Yes, it's 7786-P
S: So, that's 7786-P. OK. ³ _____ ?
C: Yes, that's right.
S: Well, I can take your order by phone.
C: OK, but how much does it cost?
S: Hmm. ⁴ _____ ?
C: Sure.

[music]
S: Hello?
C: Yes, hello.
S: Hi, it's £22.
C: ⁵ _____ ?
S: Yes, it does.
C: OK. I'll order it.
S: Right. I'll need to take some details. ⁶ _____ ?
C: It's Bruce. B-R-U-C-E.
S: And the address?
C: 31 Windmill Avenue. And that's in Oxford.
S: ⁷ _____ ?
C: VISA and the number is 4456 8938 9604 9500.
S: Sorry, is that 9500 at the end?
C: Yes, that's right.
S: ⁸ _____ ?
C: Yes, please. My email is bob dot bruce fifty-one at email dot com.
S: Let me check. bob dot bruce fifty-one at email dot com.
C: That's right.
S: ⁹ _____ ?
C: No, thanks. That's everything.
S: OK. Goodbye.
C: Bye.

3 Listen and respond making an order

1.33 You are ordering an item by phone. Listen and respond to the sales person using the information below and your own details. Remember to spell your surname and email address.

Name of item: Laptop
Item number: GR897-01
Type of credit card: Mastercard
Card number: 7558 6799 3647 1023

4 Pronunciation sounding friendly

1.34 Listen to the sales person in the previous exercise again. Listen and repeat the expressions with similar intonation so that you sound polite and friendly.

1 Can I help you?
2 Do you have the item number?
3 Can I take your surname?
4 Which credit card would you like to pay with?
5 Can I take the card number?
6 Would you like confirmation by email?
7 Can I have your email address?
8 Is there anything else I can help you with today?

5e Correspondence

1 Writing skill formal language

Write the sentences (a–h) in the correct order in the correct email. One email is more formal than the other.

a   Please email this as soon as possible.
b   I'm happy to send you the running shoes.
c   But you didn't give me the item no. ☹
d   Thanks for placing another order with us!
e   We are grateful for your order dated 30th August.
f   Please send asap.
g   We would be delighted to send you the dress immediately.
h   However, we require the correct order number.

Hi Hans!

1 ....

2 ....

3 ....

4 ....

All the best
Malcolm

Dear Ms Powell

5 ....

6 ....

7 ....

8 ....

Malcolm Douglas
Customer Care Dept.

---

2 Replace the words in bold in the sentences with these more formal words.

apologise	'd be delighted	assistance	inform
provide	receive	refund	request
require	~~would like~~		

1   I **want** to **tell** you about your order. _would like_,
    ....
2   I'**m happy** to deliver it today. ....
3   We didn't **get** our order. ....
4   I'm writing to **ask for** a replacement. ....
5   We'**re sorry** for any delay. ....
6   Please **give** your email address. ....
7   When will you **give back** the money?
    ....
8   Do you **need** any **help**? ....,

Writing emails

3 Write three different emails between a customer and an online DVD supplier. Use the prompts for each sentence.

Email 1

(1 Request information about a DVD)

(2 Ask about the price)

(3 Request information asap)

Email 2

(4 Thank customer for enquiry)

(5 Say the price is $10)

(6 Add that delivery is included in price)

Email 3

(7 Thank the other person for replying)

(8 Confirm you want to order it)

(9 Ask for information on how to pay)

Wordbuilding hyphenated words

> **▶ WORDBUILDING hyphenated words**
>
> We sometimes use a hyphen to join two or more words. It's always useful to check in your dictionary but here are some examples of when we use a hyphen:
> - two or more words as a noun, e.g. *take-off*, *brother-in-law*
> - two or more words as an adjective, e.g. *eco-friendly*, *out-of-date*, *second-hand*
> - with a capitalised word, e.g. *anti-English*, *pro-American*
> - with numbers, fractions and measurements, e.g. *twenty-one*, *two-thirds*, *three-litre plastic bottle*, *five-star hotel*

1 Look at the wordbuilding box. Then write the missing hyphens in the sentences.

1. Please board the plane as we are ready for take off.
2. The chicken in this package is out of date.
3. A lot of people are pro European.
4. Nearly one half of the population regularly recycles glass.
5. I only use eco friendly washing detergent.
6. All the software on this computer is up to date.
7. My birthday is on the thirty first of January.
8. My wife's mother is my mother in law.
9. A marathon is a twenty six mile run. That's forty two kilometres.
10. All our products use state of the art technology.

2 Look at an English text (for example in a newspaper, on the internet or in the Student's Book) and circle more examples of hyphenated words.

Learning skills using a dictionary (2)

3 Find out more about using a dictionary by completing these exercises.

1. Look at the noun in this dictionary. Is it countable or uncountable? How do you know from the dictionary?

   > **information** /ˌɪnfəˈmeɪʃən/ noun [U]
   > knowledge or facts about a person or thing

2. Find these four nouns in your dictionary. Are they countable, uncountable or both?

   > foot   information   luggage   time   tooth

3. These words all have two or more parts. Find them in your dictionary. Which part of the word or phrase did you look for first?

   > out-of-date   eco-friendly   recycling bin
   > tin opener   user-friendly

4. Find the verb *take* in your dictionary. Answer the questions.
   a. How many different meanings does the word *take* have: fewer than 10? between 10 and 20? more than 20?
   b. Find a new collocation or expression with the word *take*.

5. Look up the word *reuse* in your dictionary. From the definition, guess the meaning of the prefix *re-*. Then check your answer by looking up the definition of *re-* in your dictionary.

Check!

4 What is the connection between these pairs of words from Unit 5 of the Student's Book? Check your ideas by looking back through the unit.

1. Accra ⟷ Ghana

2. computers ⟷ copper

3. a few ⟷ a little

4. tell ⟷ inform

5. Germans ⟷ $\frac{2}{3}$

6. Plastiki ⟷ plastic bottles

7. Pacific Ocean ⟷ Garbage Patch

8. toxic ⟷ poisonous

9. Argentina ⟷ beef

Unit 6 Stages in life

6a A new life in paradise

1 Vocabulary extra life events

Match the words in A with the phrases in B. Then complete the sentences.

A	become	get	go	leave	start	take

B	an adult a career break a family
	my driving licence home to university

1 I'll _____ when I'm eighteen. I want to study physics.
2 Young people in my country usually _____ and share a flat with friends as soon as they finish school.
3 At what age does a teenager _____? At eighteen?
4 If I _____, my parents are going to buy me a car!
5 I'm going to _____ in a few years' time and travel round the world.
6 We decided to _____, once we'd bought a house. Our first child was a girl.

Reading building a dream house

2 Read the article. Match the headings (A–D) with the paragraphs (1–4).

A Preparations before building
B The dream begins
C With help from their friends
D The obvious choice

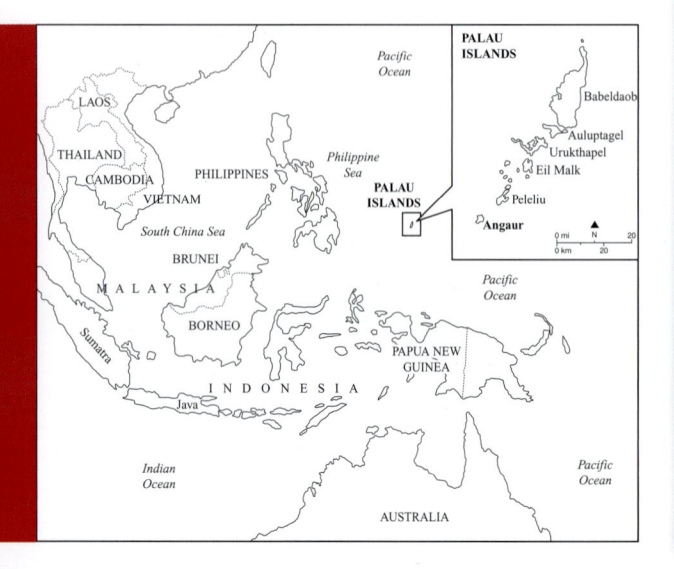

A new life in paradise

1 Alex Sheshunoff is a writer and Sarah Kalish is a lawyer. They both had good jobs and an apartment in Iowa city. However, one day they decided to build a new home for themselves. Most people would probably look locally, perhaps in the nicer neighbourhoods. But actually, they planned to find a place in paradise to create their home.

2 For Alex, it was fairly easy to choose an island with everything he wanted. As a keen scuba diver, Alex first visited the Palau group of islands years ago because of the beautiful ocean. He continued to go back there from time to time so this seemed like a good choice for paradise. The islands are about 7,500 kilometres west of Hawaii so they are difficult to reach. However, they have green forests with interesting wildlife and they are surrounded by a blue ocean full of colourful fish. In the end, Alex and Sarah chose one island in particular – Angaur.

3 Angaur is only thirteen kilometres around with a population of about 150 people. Before they could start to work on the house, they had to get permission from the head of the island – an 83-year-old woman. She was worried they intended to develop the area for other tourists but Alex said, 'We would like to build a simple house.' They agreed on the rent of $100 a month for twenty years. The head of the island was happy. She said, 'Angaur welcomes you.'

4 Then the real work began. Alex and Sarah didn't want to pay for a construction company, so they taught themselves a lot about building. They also had a lot of friends in Iowa. They came out to help and in return got a free holiday by the beach. The local people of Anguar also worked for the couple and after many months of hard work and a final visit from the head of the island, their dream house was ready.

3 Read the article again. Answer the questions.
1 Where does the writer think most people would plan to build a new house?
2 Why was it easy for Alex to choose a location?
3 How far are the islands from Hawaii?
4 What natural features do they have?
5 How many people live on Angaur?
6 Who gave them permission to build the house?
7 How much was their rent per month?
8 What did their friends get in return for helping?
9 Who visited the house when it was built?

Grammar verb patterns with *to* + infinitive

4 Underline examples of *to* + infinitive in the article in Exercise 2.

5 Match the sentence beginnings (1–8) with the endings (a–h).
1 Turn the key
2 Type in your password
3 Save your money
4 Use a dictionary
5 Go to Egypt
6 Look in the back of this book
7 Go to university
8 Take a taxi

a to find the translation.
b to access your files.
c to find the audioscripts.
d to unlock the door.
e to see the Sphinx.
f to have enough for a holiday.
g to arrive quickly.
h to get a degree.

6 Complete the conversation with these pairs of words as adjective + *to* + infinitive.

| afraid / move | difficult / keep | easy / make |
| great / live | nice / see | sad / see |

A: Hi. It's ¹ *nice to see* you again after all these years. It's been such a long time.
B: Yes, it has. But it's really ² _____ in contact with everyone.
A: Yes, it is. And we were so ³ _____ you leave. Remind me. Where did you move to?
B: Australia. We moved there five years ago.
A: Really? Five years ago! I'd be
⁴ _____ such a long way from my friends and family.
B: In fact, it was ⁵ _____ new friends. We're very happy there. And it's
⁶ _____ in a hot country with beaches and a beautiful coast.

7 Pronunciation sentence stress

🔊 1.35 Listen to these sentences. Then practise saying them. Stress the underlined words.
1 Pleased to meet you.
2 Nice to see you.
3 It's lovely to be here.

8 Complete these sentences with your own words.
1 I'm always happy to _____ .
2 It's hard to _____ .
3 I think people are crazy to _____ .

137

6b Special occasions

Vocabulary celebrations

1 Complete the text about different festivals with these words.

| bands | candles | costumes | fireworks |
| floats | masks | parades | |

Festivals around the world

St Patrick's Day

On 17th March, Ireland celebrates Saint Patrick's Day. There are [1] _____ down the streets and people ride on [2] _____ .

Maskarra Festival

Every October in Bacolod City in the Philippines, thousands of people go to the Maskarra festival wearing [3] _____ and [4] _____ .

Bonfire Night

On 5th November in the United Kingdom, people light fires and let off lots of [5] _____ into the night sky.

Santa Lucia Day

On 13th December, Swedish people celebrate the festival of Santa Lucia. Traditionally, girls wear white dresses and a crowns with [6] _____ . In the past they lit them, but nowadays they don't.

Teuila Festival

This festival in Western Samoa lasts two weeks. There are colourful decorations hanging in the streets and [7] _____ playing music everywhere you go.

Listening planning a celebration

2 🔊 **1.36** Listen to a group of people planning a party. Answer the questions. Choose the correct option (a–c).

1 What is the reason for the party?
 a a birthday
 b an anniversary
 c a retirement

2 Where do they decide to celebrate the party?
 a in the office
 b at a restaurant
 c at Rosemary's home

3 Who do they plan to invite?
 a only work colleagues
 b family and friends
 c They can't decide.

4 What present are they going to buy her?
 a a book on gardening
 b a cake
 c a plant

3 🔊 **1.36** Listen again. Answer the questions.

1 Why is the meeting secret?

2 Why does one person not want to have the party in the office?

3 Why do they choose Zeno's?

4 What is on the menu there?

5 How many people do they need to book the restaurant for?

6 What time is the party?

7 Why can't one person be there at five o'clock?

8 Why do they choose a particular present for Rosemary?

9 Why do they stop the meeting?

138

Grammar future forms: *going to*, *will* and present continuous

4 Choose the correct form to complete part of the conversation from Exercise 2.

C: What time ¹ *will everyone meet / is everyone going to meet* there?
A: Straight after work. At five.
B: But ² *I'll work / I'm working* late on Friday.
A: Well, between five and six then. We also need to get her a present.
C: Oh yes! What ³ *are we giving / are we going to give* her? I know she loves plants and I think ⁴ *she's going to spend / she's spending* a lot of time gardening when she retires.
A: Good idea. A plant.
C: And I think we should have a special cake as well.
A: ⁵ *Is the restaurant going to make / Will the restaurant make* us one?
C: Erm, I'm not sure. ⁶ *I'm going to / I'll ask* them.

5 Grammar extra (1) *will* or *going to*?

Choose the correct response (a or b) for the sentences (1–5).

1 Oh no! I've forgotten my wallet!
   a Don't worry. I'll pay.
   b Don't worry. I'm going to pay.

2 Can you help me later?
   a Sorry, I'll help Max later.
   b Sorry, I'm going to help Max later.

3 Are you in the parade this afternoon?
   a No, I'm not, but I'll watch it at three.
   b No, I'm not, but I'm going to watch it at three.

4 Why don't you want to come to the disco with me?
   a That's not true. I'll come.
   b That's not true. I am going to come.

5 Let's go to the cinema tonight.
   a Good idea. I'll see what's on.
   b Good idea. I'm going to see what's on.

6 Pronunciation contracted forms

🔊 1.37 Listen. Tick the sentences (a or b) you hear.

1 a Don't worry. I'll pay.
  b Don't worry. I will pay.
2 a I'm going to help Max later.
  b I am going to help Max later.
3 a Shelley's coming too.
  b Shelley is coming too.
4 a He'll be eighteen years old tomorrow.
  b He will be eighteen years old tomorrow.
5 a They're going to travel round the world.
  b They are going to travel round the world.
6 a Why aren't you watching the parade?
  b Why are you not watching the parade?

7 Grammar extra (2) *going to* or present continuous?

> ▶ **GOING TO or PRESENT CONTINUOUS**
>
> You can often use either form to talk about plans and arrangements in the future, e.g. *We're meeting in the café at five.* = *We're going to meet in the café at five.*
>
> When you use the present continuous to talk about the future, you normally need a future time reference, e.g. *We're meeting in the café **at five**.*
>
> When you don't use a future time expression, the present continuous often refers to the present time, e.g. *We're meeting in the café (now).*

Look at the grammar box. Then tick the sentences where you can replace *going to* with the present continuous without changing the future meaning.

1 We're going to meet my friends later today. ✓
  (We're meeting my friends later today.)

2 We're going to call you back. ✗
  (We're calling you back.)

3 Is the teacher going to tell us the answer?

4 Are you going to go to the festival tomorrow?

5 They're going to decorate the float.

6 The parade is going to pass my house this afternoon.

7 I'm going to tell you something I've never told anyone before.

8 Why is everyone going to wear a mask?

Unit 6 Stages in life

139

6c A rite of passage

Listening an ancient ritual

1 1.38 Listen to a documentary about a ritual for the Apache Indians. Number the pictures (1–5) in the order the speaker describes them.

a

b

c

d

e

2 1.38 Listen again. Complete the summary of the ancient ritual.

An ancient ritual

The Indian tribe called the Mescalero Apaches have a special ceremony every year. It starts on the
¹ _____ and lasts for four days. It is a ceremony for the young Apache ² _____.

At the beginning, each family makes food for many guests and the men build a special tepee. The girls will live in this for ³ _____ days. On the first day the girls run towards the ⁴ _____ and round a basket of food four times.

Each time represents the four stages of their life: infant, ⁵ _____, teenager and adult woman. On the last night, they have to dance for over ⁶ _____ hours. In the morning, the girls come out of the tent with white clay on their ⁷ _____. They run and wipe the clay off their faces. The tepee falls to the ground. The girls receive a new name and celebrate their new status – as ⁸ _____.

Word focus *get*

3 Complete the phrases with *get* in the sentences with these words.

| back | married | pension | plane | presents |
| ready | ~~up~~ | | | |

1 What time do you normally get *up* in the morning?
2 What time do you get _____ from work?
3 Hurry up and get _____. It's nearly time to leave.
4 Which gate do we need to get the _____ from?
5 What _____ did you get from everyone for your birthday?
6 In my country you get your _____ when you are 65.
7 We plan to get _____ when we both finish university but it won't be a big wedding.

140

6d An invitation

Real life inviting, accepting and declining

1 🔊 **1.39** Listen to two telephone conversations. Answer these questions.

Conversation 1

1 Where has Sonia been recently?

2 When does she want to meet Mihaela?

3 Where are they going to meet?

4 Who does Mihaela want to bring?

Conversation 2

5 What is Philippe going to do?

6 Why does Phillipe decline Mihaela's invitation?

7 What does Mihaela suggest?

8 Does Phillipe accept the invitation in the end?

2 🔊 **1.39** Complete the extracts from the conversations in Exercise 1 with these expressions. Then listen again and check your answers.

| Do you want   How about   I'd like   I'd love to |
| It sounds   That would   It's very nice |
| Why don't you   Yes, OK |

Conversation 1

Sonia: I'm at work so I can't talk long.
         ¹_____ to meet after work?
Mihaela: ²_____. Do you mean tonight?
Sonia: Yes. ³_____ meeting outside my office? We could go to that new Lebanese restaurant on the corner of Main Street.
Mihaela: ⁴_____ great. Oh, I've just remembered. I have a friend from France staying. He's doing a language course at the college near me.
Sonia: That's OK. ⁵_____ invite him as well?
Mihaela: ⁶_____ be great. I'll do that.
Sonia: OK. See you later.

Conversation 2

Mihaela: I'm meeting a close friend of mine tonight and ⁷_____ to take you to meet her.
Philippe: ⁸_____ of you to ask, but I'm busy tonight. I have an exam tomorrow so I need to revise at home.
Mihaela: Are you sure? We're going to eat at a new restaurant. We could get home early or you could study first and come out later.
Philippe: Honestly, ⁹_____ but I'm afraid this exam is really important.
Mihaela: I completely understand. But if you change your mind, give me a call. OK?

3 Listen and respond responding to an invitation

🔊 **1.40** Listen and respond to two different invitations. For each one, first decline the invitation, and give a reason, then accept it. Compare your responses with the model answer that follows.

> Do you want to go to the cinema tonight?

> Sorry, I can't because I'm going to a football match tonight.

4 Pronunciation emphasising words

a 🔊 **1.41** Listen to these sentences. You will hear a speaker saying the sentence in two ways. Which speaker has the most natural sentence stress? Write *1* or *2*.

1 I'm really sorry but I can't.   *1*
2 That'd be great.
3 It's so nice of you to ask.
4 I'd love to.
5 It sounds nice.

b Practise saying the sentences.

Unit 6 Stages in life

141

6e An annual festival

1 Writing skill descriptive adjectives

a Replace the words in bold in the sentences with these more descriptive adjectives.

| colourful | dull | exciting | massive |
| miserable | tasty | | |

1 I sat down with the fishermen to eat a **nice** meal of fresh fish from the sea. ....
2 The women were wearing **red, yellow and blue** dresses for the party. ....
3 The parade through the streets was long and a bit **boring** after a while. ....
4 The mountains outside our hotel were **big** and had snow on the top. ....
5 The children didn't seem **unhappy** even though they had very little food. ....
6 The bus journey from my hotel to the centre wasn't very **interesting**. ....

b Match the topics (a–f) in the table with the sentences in Exercise 1a.

a clothes	b food
c people	d transport and towns
e festivals	f nature and geographic features

c Imagine you are writing a description which includes the six topics (a–f) in Exercise 1b. Which of these adjectives would be useful for each topic? Write them in the table in Exercise 1b. You can use some adjectives for more than one topic. Use a dictionary to help you.

amazing	attractive	beautiful	delicious
dull	enormous	friendly	fun	miserable
polluted	pretty	smart	speedy
uncomfortable	unhealthy		

d Add one more of your own adjectives to each topic in Exercise 1b.

Writing a description

2 A student has prepared this plan for a description of the annual festival in her town. Use the notes in the plan and write the description. Write one paragraph.

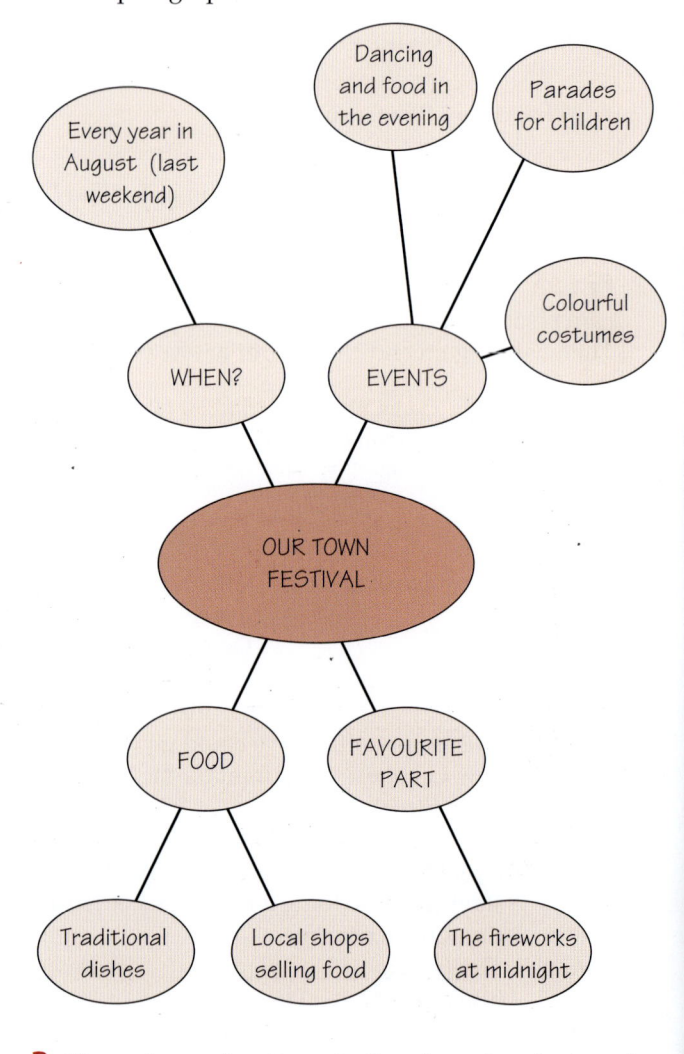

- OUR TOWN FESTIVAL
  - WHEN?
    - Every year in August (last weekend)
  - EVENTS
    - Dancing and food in the evening
    - Parades for children
    - Colourful costumes
  - FOOD
    - Traditional dishes
    - Local shops selling food
  - FAVOURITE PART
    - The fireworks at midnight

3 Now plan and write a similar short description of an event that happens in your town once a year.

Unit 6 **Stages in life**

Wordbuilding synonyms

1 Cross out the word in each group which isn't a synonym. Use a dictionary to help you.

1 sorry   apologetic   ~~afraid~~
2 fast   warm   speedy
3 scary   awful   frightening
4 good-looking   strong   handsome
5 tall   thin   skinny
6 well-dressed   polite   smart
7 hide   find   discover
8 see   notice   touch
9 needy   important   essential
10 relaxed   happy   cheerful

Learning skills assessing your own progress

2 You are now halfway through this course. Think about your progress so far. Answer the questions on the self-assessment questionnaire on the right. After each answer, write a comment to explain your answers.

Check!

3 Look at these words from Unit 6 of the Student's Book. Answer the questions.

| candle | feijoda | firework | infant | Masai |
| middle-aged | osingira | pensioners | Tremé |

1 Which words are not English words but names of things in different languages?
2 Put the words into the five categories below.

A place	
A type of dish or something you can eat	
Something that gives light	
A stage of life	
A group of people	

Assess your progress

1 How would describe your progress in English on the course so far?

Excellent ☐   Good ☐
Satisfactory ☐   Not very good ☐

Comment on your answer:
_____
_____

2 Which areas would you like to work on most for the rest of the course?

Speaking ☐   Grammar ☐
Listening ☐   Writing ☐
Pronunciation ☐   Vocabulary ☐
Reading ☐

Comment on your answer:
_____
_____

3 Which types of activities in class do you think are most useful for you?
_____
_____

4 What's one thing you would like more of on this course?
_____
_____

5 What's one thing you would like less of?
_____
_____

6 What question do you have for your teacher about the rest of the course? Write it here and ask your teacher to reply.
_____
_____

143

Audioscripts

Unit 1

1.2
A: Hey, there's a quiz here to test your stress levels. You said you were stressed all the time, so let's find out.
B: Er, OK. I don't really have time. I have to get this report finished.
A: That's just my point. You need to take a break at lunchtimes.
B: OK, then. Ask me.
A: Do you often worry about money?
B: Er no, not really. I don't have time!
A: OK. So we'll say once a month. Two. Do you have problems sleeping? Never, sometimes or always?
B: Well, it depends. At the moment, no, but sometimes I stay awake thinking about work and things.
A: OK, so that's … sometimes. Three. Do you find it difficult to concentrate?
B: Well, at work I do because people interrupt me all the time with things like quizzes!
A: I think you're fine so I'll tick 'rarely'. And the last one. Describe your lunchtimes. Do you do work while you're eating your lunch?
B: Always. It's the only time I do things like answer all my emails.
A: OK, I'll tick 'a'. But you know, you should leave the office and go for a walk.
B: Well, that's great in theory but …

1.3
a I'm driving to the city.
b You are not coming.
c She's leaving now.
d It isn't raining.
e Why are they running?
f We aren't stopping anywhere.

1.4
I usually get up at about seven o'clock and go running for half an hour. Then I feel ready for the day. I leave the house at about eight thirty and arrive at the hospital by nine. Currently, I'm seeing lots of children with flu. After work, I often walk home. Sometimes friends come round for dinner, but I need eight hours of sleep a night, so I'm always in bed by eleven o'clock.

1.5
I = Interviewer, D = Dunn
I: What makes you feel happy? Is it food that tastes delicious? A painting that looks beautiful? Or maybe just going to a café and having a coffee with friends. To tell us what makes us happy, I'm talking to psychologist Elizabeth Dunn. So Elizabeth, I know that you do a lot of research into happiness and in particular into money and happiness. So tell us, how much money do you need to make you happy?
D: It's a complicated question. Some people think money is the most important thing in the world for happiness. That's definitely not true. Some people think that money doesn't make you feel happier. That's also not true.
I: So, perhaps the question isn't about money but how people spend it.
D: Yes, to find out we did an experiment with some students. We gave them twenty dollars in the morning, and one group spent it on themselves and the other group spent it on someone else. By the end of the day, the people who spent it on others were happier.
I: So, we need to think about the way we use money.
D: Yes, this is something a lot of people find. Often it's the experiences that you have. Like visiting a new country or going to a concert to listen to your favourite musician.

1.6
1 bad, said, head, bed
2 sore, ear, or, saw
3 of, off, cough, soft
4 ate, wait, late, eat
5 here, ear, see, near
6 try, why, play, fly

1.7
D = Doctor, P = Patient
D: How do you feel today?
P: Not very well. I've got a terrible sore throat.
D: I see. Let me have a look. Open wide. Yes, it's very red in there.
P: I've also got a bad cough.
D: Do you feel sick at all?
P: No, not really.
D: Have you got a temperature?
P: I don't think so. I don't feel hot.
D: Let me check it … Yes, it's a bit high. Do you have anything for it?
P: I bought some pills at the pharmacy, but they didn't do any good.
D: Well, take this prescription to the pharmacy. You need to take some different pills. They are good for your throat. Take one every four hours. You need to go to bed for a couple of days, and try drinking lots of water.
P: OK. Thanks.
D: If you still feel ill in a few days, come back and see me, but I think it's flu. Everyone has it at the moment.

1.8
F = Friend, MA = Model answer
F: I've got a headache.
MA: You need to take some pills.
F: I've got a sore throat.
MA: Try drinking some hot water with lemon and honey.
F: I've got a bad back.
MA: Go to bed for a couple of days.
F: I feel sick.
MA: You need to see a doctor.
F: I've got a high temperature.
MA: Take this medicine. It's good for flu.

Unit 2

1.10
Kristi Leskinen is a famous skier. She loves skiing all over the world but her favourite place is Mammoth Mountain in the USA. She's good at other sports such as kayaking but she doesn't like running or going to the gym. Recently she was in a TV show called *The Superstars*. In the show, famous sports people compete in different sports that they don't normally do. Kristi won the competition. But soon it's winter again so she needs to go back to the mountains and start training again. This year she'd like to win a lot more medals.

144

1.11
1. You mustn't play.
2. They don't have to win.
3. He can lose the match.
4. The team must score another goal.
5. A player can't hit the ball twice.

1.12
Freediving is the general word for any type of underwater sport without any kind of breathing equipment. So you have to take a deep breath before you go underwater. One of the most competitive types of freediving is when a diver goes deep under the water. A Swedish woman called Annelie Pompe has the world record in freediving. She went down 126 metres into the Red Sea with no air.

Annelie loves being in the sea and she likes swimming without lots of equipment. She spends every weekend training in the sea, and before a competition, she trains for about twenty hours a week. However, she also has time for other sports and these help her prepare for freediving. For example, she does yoga in the morning because it helps her to relax. She also goes running, does some weightlifting and goes cycling.

Annelie also likes mountain climbing and next year she would like to climb Mount Everest. If she climbs Everest, she'll have another world record, as the woman who went higher and deeper than any other woman.

1.13
A: Hey, this looks interesting.
B: What?
A: This leaflet for fitness classes at the gym. Are you interested in doing something like that?
B: Maybe. But I'm not very good at sport.
A: But this isn't competitive. It's for getting fit. This one sounds good. Boot Camp. What about joining that?
B: What is Boot Camp?
A: It's like the army. You have someone who tells you what to do. I think we should do it.
B: When is it?
A: At six.
B: Great. So, we can go after work.
A: No, it's six in the morning.
B: What?! You must be joking. I hate getting up early. What about doing something later?
A: Well, there's one at lunchtime. It's called Zumba. It's a kind of dance, I think.
B: I don't like dancing.
A: Go on. It looks fun.
B: What about something after work?
A: There's a Pilates class. It doesn't say an exact time but it says it's after work.
B: Well, I'd prefer that to Boot Camp or dancing.
A: Yes, it looks good.

1.14
F = Friend, MA = Model answer
F: Are you interested in Boot Camp?
MA: No, I wouldn't like to do it.
F: Go on. You'd enjoy it. It's before work at six in the morning.
MA: I hate getting up early.
F: What about joining the Zumba class? It's a kind of dancing.
MA: I'm not very good at dancing.
F: Pilates sounds good. You should do it with me.
MA: Yes, I'd prefer that to Boot Camp or Zumba.

Unit 3

1.18
Last year in India, people bought around 1.5 million new cars. This will probably go up to three million a year in the next few years. That's how the Indian economy is changing. Many Indians in the big cities are richer than ever and they want to spend money on new products. However, most of the money is still in the big cities. There is still a lot of poverty in the villages and countryside.

Now the government hopes a new road in India can help to change India's economy. The Golden Quadrilateral road or GQ connects the country's four biggest cities: Delhi, Mumbai, Chennai and Kolkata. Hopefully, the road will carry business from the giant cities to the smaller and poorer villages and the other half of India's population.

The GQ is nearly 6,000 kilometres long and the most hi-tech highway in the world. At the administration headquarters in Delhi, you can watch thousands of vehicles moving around the country on a computer screen. If there is a problem anywhere with the road, electronic sensors tell the headquarters and engineers instantly drive there.

When you drive on the highway, there is every kind of transport. There are animals pulling carts, motorcycles, lines of old trucks and fast-moving modern cars. Sometimes the road goes right through the middle of a city, so there are often traffic jams and pedestrians trying to cross the six lanes. Industry is also growing along the new highway. When a large company opens a factory, lots of other smaller factories and offices also open. Trucks then drive and deliver all over India along the new highway. For India, all this is a symbol of the country's future.

1.20
Conversation 1
A: Hi. Do you go to the centre?
B: Which part?
A: Near the cinema.
B: Yes, we stop outside it.
A: Great. Can I have a return ticket, please?

Conversation 2
A: I'd like a first-class ticket, please.
B: That's twenty euros fifty.
A: Here you are. Which platform is it?
B: It's at five fifteen from platform twelve.

Conversation 3
A: How many bags are you checking in?
B: Two. And I've got a carry-on.
A: I'm afraid your ticket only includes one bag. You'll have to pay an extra ten pounds for that one.
B: Oh, OK. Can I pay by credit card?
A: Sure.

Conversation 4
A: It's just up here on the right. You can drop me off over there.

B: I can't stop there. It's a bus stop. But here's OK.
A: OK. How much is that?
B: That's thirteen dollars thirty cents. Have you got the right change?

1.21
Message 1
Get on the number 68 bus from the bus stop outside your house. Take it to the underground station. Catch the first train and get off at Oxford Road station. Then call me. I'll come and get you.

Message 2
My flight is late and I'm still in Berlin. Don't wait for me at the airport. I'll catch the bus to the city centre and walk to your house. See you later.

Message 3
Chris wants to meet us tonight, so please can you call him and tell him where to meet us. And send me the address of the restaurant as well. What time do you want to meet?

Unit 4

1.24
I = Interviewer, D= Daniel
I: Could you walk through the jungle and survive? One man who knows all about this is rainforest conservationist Doctor Daniel Fanning. Daniel led a team through the Amazonian rainforest. Together they walked for six months. Daniel is here today to explain how he prepares for this kind of expedition.
D: Well, I think preparation is probably the most important part of any expedition. I spent about three months getting ready for this trip. I tested equipment for the walk. For example, I needed to know if the tents could survive the difficult conditions in the rainforests.
I: So, how much did you have to carry in the end? For example, how much clothing did you take?
D: Humans don't really need clothes in the rainforest. It's hot so I recommend shorts and a good raincoat.
I: But don't you need good walking boots?
D: The problem is that you get lots of sand, mud and water inside the boot – especially when it rains which is nearly all the time. So a pair of sandals is fine. Food and water are the most important things to carry.
I: I was wondering about that. What did you eat?
D: Food like rice is good, but you lose a lot of weight when you walk. I lost about twenty kilos.
I: And one final question. We've talked about the physical side of walking in the jungle, but what about the mental side?
D: Well, you're with other people, but yes you're on your own for long periods of time. But that's good for you I think. It's like a kind of meditation. I also think a journey like this is about determination. I knew that nothing would stop me from reaching the end. So the mind is as important as the body on an expedition.

1.25
One day, Yossi Ghinsberg started a journey with three other men. They were travelling through the jungle of Bolivia but, after a few days, they were lost. In the end, two of the group, Yossi and Kevin, built a raft so they could travel down the river and find help.

For some time they travelled down the river, but suddenly they hit a rock. Yossi fell off the raft and swam to the shore.

While Yossi was lost in the jungle, his friend Kevin was luckier. He stayed on the raft and luckily some local men found him. Then they searched for Yossi and, amazingly, after three weeks, they found him alive. Sadly, the other two men never returned.

1.28
F = Friend, MA = Model answer
F: I had a terrible journey into work this morning.
MA: Why?
F: My car broke down on the motorway.
MA: Oh no!
F: Anyway I called the police immediately.
MA: That was a good idea!
F: Luckily, while I was calling, a police car drove past and stopped to help me.
MA: That was lucky!
F: Anyway, they called the garage to get my car and then they brought me to work!
MA: Wow!

Unit 5

1.29
I = Interviewer, C = Consumer
Interview 1
I: Hello, I work for a market research company and today we're interviewing shoppers about their everyday costs. Do you have a spare moment?
C: Err, well what kind of questions?
I: For example, I can see you've got a bottle of water in your shopping bag. Do you normally buy bottled water?
C: Actually, no, I don't. The bottle is for my sister. She only drinks bottled water.

Interview 2
I: How much do you think you spend on the internet?
C: Erm, I'm not sure because it's all part of a package. It includes my mobile phone and the TV.
I: Maybe a hundred a month?
C: Yes, I suppose about that.

Interview 3
I: OK. So next, can I ask about your monthly bills. For example, how much is your water?
C: Oh, it costs a fortune! In fact, I rang the company last week to complain about the price! They sent me a bill for three hundred pounds. Normally I only pay a hundred for my water ...

Interview 4
I: And do you buy your fuel at a local petrol station?
C: Yes, I like to buy things locally so I go to the supermarket at the end of my road. They also sell petrol and it's the cheapest in the area.

1.31
Now, on to environmental news. A new report has some interesting facts and figures on how much rubbish a house in America produces. Together, American households produce 243 billion kilos of trash. About 82 billion kilos of this – that's about a third – was made into compost or it was recycled. For individual households, that means about 0.7 kilogrammes was recycled out of nearly two kilos.

As for electronics, the average American household owns 24 electronic devices. These are mostly mobile phones, music players, laptops and computers, and digital cameras.

Audioscripts

Households with three or more people often own as many as 32 devices, while smaller households own around 17 devices. Recycling more of these items could have a big effect. For example, recycling one million mobile phones can produce 3,500 kilos of gold. Recycling one million computers helps to stop greenhouse gases. It's about the same as taking 16,000 cars off the road.

In 2009, the amount of paper recovered for recycling averaged 150 kilos per person in the United States or about 380 kilos for each household. Paper recycling has become successful in the US because about 268 million people, or about 87 per cent of American households now have paper recycling projects nearby.

1.32
R = Customer Care Representative, C = Customer
R: Good morning. Can I help you?
C: Hi, I'm calling about a product on your website. I'd like to order it but the website won't let me.
R: One moment ... Do you have the item number?
C: Yes it's 7786–P.
R: So that 7786–P. OK. Is that the garden composter.
C: Yes, that's right.
R: Well, I can take your order by phone.
C: OK, but how much does it cost?
R: Hmm. Can I put you on hold for a moment?
C: Sure. …
R: Hello?
C: Yes, hello.
R: Hi, it's twenty-two pounds.
C: Does that include delivery?
R: Yes, it does.
C: OK. I'll order it.
R: Right. I'll need to take some details. Can I take your surname?
C: It's Bruce. B–R–U–C–E.
R: And the address?
C: 31 Windmill Avenue. And that's in Oxford.
R: Which credit card would you like to pay with?
C: VISA, and the number is 4456 8938 9604 9500.
R: Sorry, is that 9500 at the end?
C: Yes, that's right.
R: Would you like confirmation by email?
C: Yes, please. My email is bob dot bruce fifty one at email dot com
R: Let me check. bob dot bruce fifty one at email dot com
C: That's right.
R: Is there anything else I can help you with today?
C: No, thanks. That's everything.
R: OK. Goodbye.
C: Bye.

1.33
Hello. Can I help you?
Do you have the item number?
Can I take your surname?
Which credit card would you like to pay with?
Can I take the card number?
Would you like confirmation by email?
Can I have your email address?
Is there anything else I can help you with today?
Good bye.

Unit 6

1.36
A = Boss, B = Colleague 1, C = Colleague 2
A: OK everyone. Thanks for coming. The reason I wanted to keep the meeting secret was because, as you know, Rosemary is retiring from the company on Friday and so we're going to have a small leaving party for her.
B: Sorry, but where are we going to have a party? The offices are big but they aren't a very good place to … well, to have fun.
C: That new restaurant next door is good. It's called Zeno's. They serve pizzas and Italian food.
B: Oh, yes. I went there last week.
A: Sounds good. There are going to be about twenty of us. Can someone call the restaurant and find out?
C: I'll do it! I'll call them this afternoon and see what they say.
A: Great.
B: So, who are we going to invite? Just staff? What about wives, husbands, boyfriends, girlfriends as well?
A: Oh no. Only the people she works with.
C: What time is everyone going to meet there?
A: Straight after work. At five.
B: But I'm working late on Friday.
A: Well, between five and six then. We also need to get her a present.
C: Oh yes! What are we going to give her? Oh, I know, she loves plants and I think she's going to spend a lot of time gardening when she retires.
A: Good idea. A plant.
C: And I think we should have a special cake as well.
A: Will the restaurant make us one?
C: Erm, I'm not sure. I'll ask them.
A: Great. Anything else?
B: Look out! She's coming back from her lunch.

1.37
1 Don't worry. I'll pay.
2 I am going to help Max later.
3 Shelley is coming too.
4 He'll be eighteen years old tomorrow.
5 They are going to travel round the world.
6 Why aren't you watching the parade?

1.38
In New Mexico, the Indian tribe of Mescalero Apaches prepares for a special ceremony every year. Beginning on the 4th July, a group of young Apache girls will spend four days taking part in an ancient ritual which tests their strength and character. By the end of the ritual, they will be women. Preparations begin with each family of the girls making food for many guests and members of the local tribe.

Nearby the men start to build a special tepee. The girls will live in this for the four days.

The ritual begins on the first day at sunrise. The girls run towards the morning sun and then they run round a basket of food four times. Each time represents the four stages of their life: infant, child, teenager and adult woman.

Then they live in the tepee, where they don't have much food. This is part of their test of strength and they must not show any emotions during this period. On the last night, they start to dance. This dance lasts over ten hours through the night and they cannot stop.

On the final morning, the girls come out of the tepee for the last time. They have white clay on their faces, which they slowly wipe off. The tepee falls to the ground and they are now women. The girls receive a new name and their family and friends come to the girls and they celebrate their new status, as women.

🎧 1.39
Conversation 1
S = Sonia, M = Mihaela
S: Hi Mihaela. It's me. Sonia.
M: Hi Sonia. How are you? How was your holiday?
S: Great thanks. But I'm at work so I can't talk long. Do you want to meet after work?
M: Yes, OK. Do you mean tonight?
S: Yes. How about meeting outside my office? We could go to that new Lebanese restaurant on the corner of Main Street.
M: It sounds great. Oh, I've just remembered. I have a friend from France staying. He's doing a language course at the college near me.
S: That's OK. Why don't you invite him as well?
M: That would be great. I'll do that.
S: OK. See you later.
M: Bye.

Conversation 2
P = Phillipe, M = Mihaela
P: Hello?
M: Phillipe. It's Mihaela.
P: Oh hi, Mihaela.
M: Where are you at the moment?
P: I'm about to go into my lesson.
M: Oh. OK. I'll be quick. I'm meeting a close friend of mine tonight and I'd like to take you to meet her.
P: It's very nice of you to ask, but I'm busy tonight. I have an exam tomorrow so I need to revise at home.
M: Are you sure? We're going to eat at a new restaurant. We could get home early or you could study first and come out later.
P: Honestly, I'd love to but I'm afraid this exam is really important.
M: I completely understand. But if you change your mind, give me a call. OK?
P: OK. And thanks for asking me.
M: See you later.

🎧 1.40
F = Friend, MA = Model answer
Invitation 1
F: Do you want to go to the cinema tonight?
MA: Sorry, I can't because I'm going to a football match tonight.
F: How about going to the cinema tomorrow night instead?
MA: OK. That'd be great.

Invitation 2
F: Would you like to come to a friend's wedding party?
MA: It's very nice of you to ask, but isn't it only for your friend's family and close friends?
F: But I'd like to take you. You'd enjoy it.
MA: OK. I'd like that very much. Thank you.

Answer key

Unit 1

1a (pages 96 and 97)

1
1 works   2 specialises   3 goes   4 studies   5 wants
6 spends   7 don't stay   8 travel   9 visit   10 don't realise   11 helps   12 don't have

2
1 starts   2 watches   3 flies   4 passes   5 lives
6 studies   7 finishes   8 relaxes

3
/s/   helps, visits, wants
/z/   has, is, spends, stays, studies, travels
/ɪz/   realises, specialises

4
1 Where does Nathan work?
2 Where does he often go?
3 What does he find and study?
4 Where does he spend a lot of time?
5 Why do new viruses travel more easily?
6 What does he need for his work?
7 Do many people have electricity and running water?
8 How does Nathan communicate?

5
1 c   2 b   3 a   4 a

6
1 I always do exercise in the evening.
2 It is always colder in the winter.
3 I take this medicine twice a day.
4 They don't often go on holiday.
5 We are sometimes busy at weekends.
6 She rarely eats out during the week.
7 You are never on time for work.
8 Do you always check your emails at lunchtime?

1b (pages 98 and 99)

1
1 b   2 c   3 b   4 b   5 c   6 c   7 b   8 a

2
1 patient   2 mothers-to-be   3 hospital   4 nutrition
5 vaccinations   6 shortage   7 preventative   8 advice
9 intensive training   10 ongoing

3
Today they <u>are visiting</u> their first patient.
Sarubai <u>is checking</u> Rani …
While they <u>are checking</u> the baby …
… and the number <u>is growing</u>.

4
1 I'm driving
2 has
3 do you come
4 is flying
5 I never cycle
6 is standing
7 Do you understand
8 it's getting
9 aren't staying
10 Are you working; are you taking

5
a 5   b 4   c 3   d 3   e 4   f 4

6
1 living   2 dropping   3 letting   4 swimming   5 having
6 lying   7 taking   8 travelling   9 getting   10 jogging

7
I usually get up at about seven o'clock and go running for half an hour. Then I feel ready for the day. I leave the house at about eight thirty and arrive at the hospital by nine. Currently, I'm seeing lots of children with flu. After work I often walk home. Sometimes friends come round for dinner, but I need eight hours of sleep a night so I'm always in bed by eleven o'clock.

1c (page 100)

1
1 happy   2 money   3 students   4 concert

2
1 c   2 b   3 b   4 c   5 a   6 a

3
1 f   2 c   3 b   4 a   5 d   6 e

4
1 e   2 d   3 a   4 c   5 b

5
Possible answers:
How do you feel?
Do you feel like a coffee?
Do you feel like doing something?
How do you feel about pizza for dinner?
Do you feel OK?
What do you feel like doing?
How does the weather feel?
What's the weather like?

1d (page 101)

1
1 nose   2 ear   3 tooth   4 head   5 throat   6 back
7 mouth   8 stomach

2
1 bad   2 ear   3 off   4 eat   5 see   6 play

3
Tick the following for 1–3:
1 sore throat, cough   2 high   3 pills
4 Advice: Go to bed for two days. Drink lots of water. Come back if you still feel ill.

4
1 How do you feel
2 Let me have a
3 Do you feel
4 Have you got
5 Let me check
6 take this prescription
7 You need to
8 They are good
9 try drinking
10 If you still feel ill

149

5
Model answers:
You need to take some pills.
Try taking some hot water with lemon and honey.
Go to bed for a couple of days.
You need to see a doctor.
Take this medicine. It's good for flu.

1e (page 102)

1
1 Food   2 Career   3 Computer   4 Town   5 Love

2
1 Do you have any advice?
2 What can I do?
3 Can anyone help?
4 Does anyone have any good advice?
5 What should I do?

3
Students' own answers.

4
1 You should take these pills twice a day.
2 You shouldn't smoke.
3 You should do some exercise.
4 You should work eight hours a day.
5 You shouldn't drink caffeine in the evenings.

5
1 If you want to lose weight, you could start running or you could go cycling.
2 Take some of this medicine and take two of these pills.
3 I do sports such as tennis or golf but I don't like team sports.
4 Drink lots of water because your body needs about two litres per day.
5 Your body needs about two litres per day so drink lots of water.

6
Students' own answers.

Wordbuilding / Learning skills (page 103)

1
1 run a marathon
2 go hiking
3 play the piano
4 read books
5 do exercise
6 take public transport
7 check … emails
8 have a coffee

2, 3, 4 and 5
Students' own answers.

6
Across: 3 Sardinia   6 gardening   7 temperature   8 centenarian   10 happiness
Down: 1 advice   2 medicine   4 forum   5 Okinawa   9 nap

Unit 2

2a (pages 104 and 105)

1a
a love   b really like   c enjoy   d don't mind   e don't like   f hate, can't stand

1b
Students' own answers.

2
1 Playing   2 Competing   3 cycling   4 Learning
5 losing   6 Sitting   7 being   8 flying

3
1 bat   2 track   3 goggles   4 net   5 glove   6 pitch
7 pool   8 club

4
1 S   2 D   3 S   4 S   5 S   6 D

5
1 I'd like to play
2 They'd like to play
3 likes finishing
4 would like
5 I like parachuting
6 would like to become
7 don't like playing
8 would you like to do

6
1 c   2 e   3 b   4 d   5 a   6 f

7
1 loves skiing all over the world
2 She's good at other sports
3 doesn't like running or going to the gym
4 sports people compete in different sports
5 they don't normally do
6 the competition
7 she'd like to win

2b (pages 106 and 107)

1
1 T   2 F   3 T   4 T   5 T   6 F   7 F   8 T

2
1 surfing   2 rowing   3 kneel   4 oars   5 waves
6 athletic

3
1 have to   2 can   3 mustn't   4 have to   5 don't always have to   6 must

4
1 mustn't   2 don't   3 can   4 must   5 can't

5
1 Basketball: Each team has to / must have five players on the court.
2 Football: Players can get a red card.
3 Boxing: The fighters can't / mustn't leave the ring during the fight.
4 Running: You don't have to use any special equipment.
5 Tennis: The ball has to / must go over the net.

6
1 trophy   2 beat   3 score   4 fans   5 referee   6 judge(s)
7 prize   8 spectators

2c (page 108)

1
1 b   2 c   3 d   4 a

2
1 c   2 b   3 c   4 a   5 c

Answer key

3
1 e 2 f 3 c 4 d 5 g 6 a 7 b

4
1 'd like to play tennis later / feel like playing tennis later
2 look like someone
3 'd like to play
4 'd like some ice cream
5 isn't like

2d (page 109)

1
1 A 2 A 3 B 4 C 5 C 6 A 7 A

2
1 Boot Camp 2 Zumba 3 Pilates

3
1 interested in 2 not very 3 sounds good
4 we should 5 What about 6 Go on 7 I'd prefer
8 it looks

4
Model answers:
No, I wouldn't like to do it.
I hate getting up early.
I'm not very good at dancing.
Yes, I'd prefer that to Boot Camp or Zumba.

2e (page 110)

1
Possible answer:

> **COME JOIN THE FUN AFTER WORK THIS WEEK!**
> - **Where?** In the park
> - **What?** A barbecue with a 'fun' football match afterwards
> - **When?** Friday at six
> - **Why?** It's a great chance to meet some of your colleagues out of the office and really get to know each other.
>
> Please confirm by emailing me on r_shaw@shaw.com

2
1 capital letter 2 full stop, exclamation mark 3 comma
4 apostrophe

3
1 I (capital letter) 2 ✓ 3 gaming, cycling (comma)
4 It's (apostrophe) 5 ✓ 6 Canada (capital letter)
7 Saturday (capital letter) 8 ✓ 9 month. We (full stop) 10 win. (full stop) / win! (exclamation mark)

Wordbuilding / Learning skills (page 111)

1
1 competitive 2 competition 3 photograph
4 advertisement 5 interested 6 professional

2
com<u>pete</u>, com<u>pet</u>itive, compe<u>ti</u>tion, com<u>pet</u>itor
<u>pho</u>tograph, photo<u>graph</u>ic, <u>pho</u>tograph, pho<u>tog</u>rapher
<u>ad</u>vertise, ad<u>ver</u>tisement, <u>ad</u>vertiser
<u>in</u>terested, <u>in</u>terest
pro<u>fes</u>sional, pro<u>fes</u>sion, pro<u>fes</u>sional

3
1 pronunciation 2 verb 3 present participle
4 past participle 5 definition 6 noun 7 plural form
8 first meaning 9 second meaning 10 main stress
11 adjective 12 example sentence

4
1 92 2 1972 3 60 4 1500 5 4 6 5 7 2 8 42

Unit 3

3a (pages 112 and 113)

1
a

2
1 T 2 F 3 F 4 T 5 F

3
1 rush hour 2 traffic jam 3 road works 4 petrol station 5 speed limit

4
more interesting, better, slower, the greenest, the most rewarding, longer, much cheaper, more detailed, greener than

5
1 cheaper, cheapest 2 angrier, angriest 3 larger, largest
4 bigger, biggest 5 safer, safest 6 funnier, funniest
7 thinner, thinnest 8 lower, lowest 9 easier, easiest
10 greener, greenest 11 fitter, fittest 12 faster, fastest

6
Possible answers:
1 travelling by bus is more relaxing than travelling by car
2 cake is tastier than bread
3 email is faster than letters
4 teachers work harder than politicians
5 aeroplanes are less bad for the environment than trains

7
1 tallest 2 smallest 3 fastest 4 longest 5 most dangerous
6 largest

8
1 <u>Your car</u> is <u>faster</u> than <u>mine</u>.
2 <u>Bicycles</u> are the <u>greenest</u> <u>transport</u>.
3 <u>Walking</u> is <u>slower</u> than <u>cycling</u>.
4 <u>Trains</u> are <u>cheaper</u> than <u>planes</u>.
5 <u>Hybrid</u> transport is the <u>most efficient</u>.

3b (pages 114 and 115)

1
1 Horses are as good as modern transport in the forest.
2 The weather is always as hot as this in my country.
3 Silver isn't as expensive as gold.
4 New cars aren't as stylish as cars from the sixties.
5 Bicycles are as fast as cars in the city centre.
6 I'm not as young as I used to be.

3a
1 giraffe 2 owl 3 bird 4 bee 5 horse 6 lion 7 bat
8 mouse

3b
1 bat 2 horse 3 giraffe 4 bee 5 owl 6 mouse
7 lion 8 bird

151

4
1 d 2 b 3 a 4 c

5
1 as there was a traffic jam 2 You look as 3 (the speed of) a bicycle is as 4 as we were driving home

6
1 b 2 a 3 a 4 a 5 c 6 b 7 c

7
1 Because they can walk further across deserts than any other kind of animal.
2 Carrying heavy loads, producing milk and meat.
3 No. People at the competition from countries like Oman, Saudi Arabia and Qatar think they are beautiful.
4 Ten days.
5 Around 24,000.
6 Rice, meat and the hump of the camel.

3c (page 116)

1
1 d 2 b 3 c 4 a

2
1 c 2 b 3 b 4 c 5 a 6 b

3
1 pick up 2 catch 3 go by 4 miss 5 go in 6 go

4
/æ/ catch, jam, plan, rank, taxi
/eɪ/ change, day, gate, plane, take, train

3d (page 117)

1
1 fare 2 rank 3 a receipt 4 gate 5 book 6 passport 7 an aisle 8 first

2
1 bus 2 train 3 plane 4 taxi

3
1 Outside the cinema. 2 A return ticket. 3 €20.50
4 At five fifteen. 5 Platform twelve. 6 Two bags.
7 £10 8 Yes. 9 Because it can't stop at a bus stop.
10 $13.30

4
1 Do you go 2 Can I have 3 I'd like a
4 Which platform 5 How many 6 Can I pay
7 How much 8 Have you got

3e (page 118)

1
Message one: Get on the number 68 bus from the bus stop outside your house. Take it to the underground station. Catch the first train and get off at Oxford Road station. Then call me. I'll come and get you.

Message two: My flight is late and I'm still in Berlin. Don't wait for me at the airport. I'll catch the bus to the city centre and walk to your house. See you later.

Message three: Chris wants to meet us tonight, so please can you call him and tell him where to meet us? And send me the address of the restaurant as well. What time do you want to meet?

2
Possible answers:
Message one: Get on 68 bus from bus stop to underground. Catch train to Oxford Road station. Call. I'll get you.

Message two: Flight late. Still in Berlin. Don't wait. Will catch bus to yours.
Message three: Chris meeting us too. Tell him and me restaurant address and meeting time.

Wordbuilding / Learning skills (page 119)

1
1 credit 2 time 3 centre 4 transport 5 snow
6 driver 7 town 8 seat

2
1 alarm clock 2 bank account 3 boxing gloves
4 football pitch 5 letter box 6 mobile phone
7 tennis court 8 town centre

3 and 4
Students' own answers.

5
1 sledge 2 Kolkata 3 Iditarod 4 aisle 5 elephant
6 adjective

Unit 4

4a (pages 120 and 121)

1
1 take risks 2 adventure 3 dangerous 4 my biggest achievement 5 a big challenge 6 ambition 7 crazy

2
1 visited 2 arrived 3 dried 4 stayed 5 jogged 6 lived
7 studied 8 moved

3
1 was born 2 studied 3 became 4 went 5 started
6 survived 7 grew up 8 played 9 learned 10 joined

4
1 F (Eskil was born in Norway.)
2 F (Brady did but Eskil didn't.)
3 T
4 F (Eskil joined a circus.)
5 T
6 F (A python attacked Brady on his TV show.)
7 F (Eskil started performing on his own after he left the circus.)
8 T

5
1 When were you
2 did you grow up
3 did you study at university
4 did you learn
5 When did you join
6 When did you start

6a
1 bit 2 bought 3 hit 4 did 5 said 6 went
7 fought 8 brought 9 met

6b
/e/ said, went, met
/ɪ/ bit, hit, did
/ɔː/ bought, fought, brought

4b (pages 122 and 123)

1
1 determination 2 ambition 3 careful 4 decision
5 experienced 6 intelligent 7 patience 8 reliable

2
<u>determ</u>ined, determ<u>i</u>nation, am<u>bi</u>tious, am<u>bi</u>tion, <u>care</u>ful, care, de<u>ci</u>sive, de<u>ci</u>sion, ex<u>pe</u>rienced,

Answer key

ex<u>pe</u>rience, int<u>e</u>lligent, int<u>e</u>lligence, <u>pa</u>tient, <u>pa</u>tience, rel<u>i</u>able, rel<u>i</u>ability

3
1 careful   2 determined   3 intelligent   4 ambitious
5 patient   6 experienced   7 reliable   8 decisive

4
1 E   2 B   3 D   4 A   5 C, E   6 B, E   7 B   8 B, E

5
was changing, was flying, were climbing, was sailing

6
1 The sun was shining and people were sunbathing on the beach.
2 The phone was ringing, but I was leaving the house so I didn't answer it.
3 We weren't studying when the teacher walked in.
4 We were walking past the building when the fire started.
5 She wasn't thinking about her exam results when the envelope arrived.
6 It wasn't raining, so we went for a picnic.

7
1 Did you see   2 were following   3 saw   4 didn't hear
5 was listening   6 Did you have   7 didn't arrive
8 Were you waiting

8
a 3, 5   b 1   c 2, 4

9
1 was, wasn't   2 were   3 wasn't, was   4 weren't
5 weren't, was

4c (page 124)

1
1 lake   2 face   3 glacier   4 crevasse   5 ridge   6 cave
7 summit

2
Topics 2, 3, 4, 6

3
1 He led the team.
2 To find out if the tents could survive the difficult conditions in the rainforests.
3 Humans don't really need clothes in the rain forest.
4 Food and water.
5 He lost about twenty kilos.
6 Determination.

4
1 On   2 In   3 in   4 at   5 on   6 Ø   7 on   8 Ø   9 on

4d (page 125)

1
1 e   2 a   3 c   4 d   5 f   6 b

2
1 One day   2 after a few days   3 In the end
4 For some time   5 suddenly   6 While   7 luckily
8 Then   9 amazingly   10 after three weeks   11 Sadly

3
a One day, after a few days, after three weeks, For some time
b While, Then, In the end
c suddenly, amazingly
d luckily
e Sadly

4
Speakers 1, 3 and 5

5
Model answers:
Why?
Oh no!
That was a good idea!
That was lucky!
Wow!

4e (page 126)

1a
1 quickly   2 ✓   3 brightly   4 suddenly   5 ✓   6 ✓
7 Amazingly   8 ✓

1b
1 Incredibly   2 Unfortunately   3 hardly   4 fortunately
5 eventually

2b
1 We walked for three hours, and **then** we sat and enjoyed the view.
2 I arrived home **just** as the sun went down.
3 The explorers tried to leave their camp **again,** but the weather was still too bad.
4 After three hours we were **still** lost.
5 We were three days from anywhere, but we **only** had food and water for one more day.
6 The jungle is hot. **Also,** there are many dangerous animals.

3
Students' own answers.

Wordbuilding / Learning skills (page 127)

1
1 im   2 un   3 un   4 un   5 im   6 in

2
1 unambitious   2 impatient   3 unintelligent
4 unreliable   5 indecisive

3 and 4
Students' own answers.

5
Denver airport:
1 Maria Garza
2 A fire on the plane
3 She climbed out of the window.

Hawaii:
1 Bethany Hamilton
2 A shark attacked her.
3 By swimming back to the beach with one arm.

Atafu:
1 Three teenage boys
2 Lost at sea in a small boat
3 A fishing boat pulled them from the sea.

Siula Grande, Peru:
1 Joe Simpson and Simon Yates
2 Joe fell down a crevasse.
3 He crawled back.

Canary Islands:
1 Steven and Rachel Carlson
2 Their boat sank.
3 No answer

Unit 5

5a (pages 128 and 129)

1
Possible answers:
jar [C] – made of glass – for storing food
newspaper [C] – made of paper – for reading
aluminium foil [U] – made of metal – for wrapping food

2
1 a 2 some 3 a 4 a 5 some 6 an 7 some 8 some
(also *a coffee* as in *a cup of coffee*) 9 a carton

3
1 jars 2 buses 3 countries 4 holidays 5 women
6 cans 7 boxes 8 children 9 phones 10 classes
11 stories 12 cartridges

4
1 d 2 b 3 a 4 e 5 c

5
1 Reusing them.
2 Old cotton shirts, old socks and old towels.
3 Glass jars, yoghurt pots and plastic containers.
4 Wrapping presents, protecting fragile objects and compost.
5 Wrap old clothing around them.
6 A cloth bag.

6
1 a some, b any 2 a much, b some 3 a many, b any
4 a a lot of, b much 5 a a few, b a little 6 a many, b a few
7 a a little, b much

7
1 some 2 any 3 few 4 many 5 lot

5b (pages 130 and 131)

1
1 b 2 d 3 a 4 c

2
1 A bottle of water 2 Her sister 3 Mobile phone and TV 4 One hundred a month 5 To complain about the price 6 One hundred 7 A supermarket 8 It's the cheapest in the area.

3
1 just over 2 well over 3 exactly 4 nearly

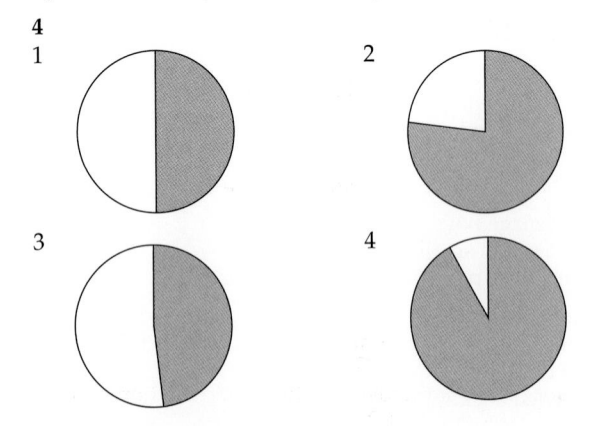

4

5
1 Australians 2 French 3 Indians
4 Chinese, Indians, Mexicans 5 Brazilians, Japanese
6 Chinese 7 Germans 8 Hungarians

6
1 Ø 2 the 3 Ø 4 The 5 the 6 Ø 7 the 8 Ø
9 the 10 the

7
/ðə/ Sentences 4, 7, 9 and 10
/ðiː/ Sentences 2, 5

8
Over three million people live in **the** United States of America. It is **the** world's most multi-cultural country. It was part of **the** United Kingdom but it became a new country in 1776. Washington DC became **the** capital city and the President still lives in **the** White House today. However, it isn't **the** biggest city. New York is. New York is also popular with tourists. In particular, they come to see **the** Statue of Liberty.

5c (page 132)

1
1 go by 2 go for 3 last 4 Slow down! 5 have
6 be careful 7 drink 8 carry

2
Students' own answers.

3
1 Environmental news
2 The USA
3 mobile phones, laptops, computers, digital cameras
4 Yes
5 Paper recycling

4
1 243 2 82 3 24 4 32 5 17 6 3,500 7 150, 380 8 87

5d (page 133)

1
1 7786-P 2 £22 3 Bruce 4 31 5 Visa
6 4456 8938 9604 9500 7 bob.bruce51@gmail.com

2
1 d 2 c 3 f 4 h 5 d 6 a 7 g 8 e 9 i

5e (page 134)

1
1 d 2 b 3 c 4 f 5 e 6 g 7 h 8 a

2
1 would like … inform 2 'd be delighted 3 receive
4 request 5 apologise 6 provide 7 refund
8 require … assistance

3
Possible answers:
1 Could you send me information about a DVD called 'Casablanca'?
2 I'd like to know the price.
3 Please send me details asap.
4 Thank you for your interest in our products.
5 The price of this DVD is $10.
6 This includes cost of delivery.
7 Thank you for your immediate reply.
8 I would like to order the DVD.
9 Please send me information on how to pay.

Wordbuilding / Learning skills (page 135)

1
1 Please board the plane as we are ready for take-off.
2 The chicken in this package is out-of-date.
3 A lot of people are pro-European.
4 Nearly one-half of the population regularly recycles glass.
5 I only use eco-friendly washing detergent.
6 All the software on this computer is up-to-date.
7 My birthday is on the thirty-first of January.
8 My wife's mother is my mother-in-law.

Answer key

9 A marathon is a twenty-six mile run. That's forty-two kilometres.
10 All our products use state-of-the-art technology.

2
Students' own answers.

3
Students' own answers.

4
1 Accra is the capital of Ghana.
2 Computers use copper inside them.
3 They have the same meaning but use *a few* with countable nouns and *a little* with uncountable nouns.
4 They have the same meaning but 'tell' is less formal and more commonly used than the word 'inform'.
5 Just over two-thirds of Germans drink a bottle of water a day.
6 The Plastiki was made with plastic bottles.
7 The Pacific Ocean has an area called the Great Garbage Patch.
8 Something that is toxic is poisonous.
9 90% of people in Argentina eat beef nearly every day.

Unit 6

6a (pages 136 and 137)

1
1 go to university   2 leave home   3 become an adult
4 get my driving licence   5 take a career break
6 start a family

2
1 B   2 D   3 A   4 C

3
1 Locally – perhaps in the nicer neighbourhoods.
2 He had visited the islands many times.
3 About 7,500 kilometres west of Hawaii.
4 Green forests and a blue ocean.
5 150
6 The head of the island.
7 $100
8 A free holiday by the beach.
9 The head of the island.

4
However, one day they decided <u>to build</u> a new home for themselves.

But actually, they planned <u>to find</u> a place in paradise to create their home.

For Alex, it was fairly easy <u>to choose</u> an island with everything he wanted.

He continued <u>to go</u> back there from time to time, so this seemed like a good choice for paradise.

The islands are about 7,500 kilometres west of Hawaii so they are difficult <u>to reach</u>.

Before they started <u>to work</u> on the house, they had <u>to get</u> permission from the head of island – an 83-year-old woman.

She was worried they intended <u>to develop</u> the area for other tourists, but Alex said, 'We would like <u>to build</u> a simple house.'

Alex and Sarah didn't want <u>to pay</u> for a construction company, so they taught themselves a lot about building.

They came out <u>to help</u> and in return got a free holiday by the beach.

5
1 d   2 b   3 f   4 a   5 e   6 c   7 h   8 g

6
1 nice to see   2 difficult to keep   3 sad to see
4 afraid to move   5 easy to make   6 great to live

8
Students' own answers.

6b (pages 138 and 139)

1
1 parades   2 floats   3 masks / costumes
4 masks / costumes   5 fireworks   6 candles   7 bands

2
1 c   2 b   3 a   4 c

3
1 Because Rosemary is retiring from the company on Friday, and so we're going to have a small leaving party for her.
2 Because they aren't a good place to have fun.
3 It's next door and good.
4 Pizzas and Italian food.
5 About 20.
6 Between five and six.
7 The person is working late.
8 She loves plants and is going to do lots of gardening when she retires.
9 Because Rosemary is coming back from lunch.

4
1 is everyone going to meet
2 I'm working late on Friday
3 are we going to give
4 she's going to spend
5 Will the restaurant make
6 I'll ask

5
1 a   2 b   3 b   4 b   5 a

6
1 a   2 b   3 b   4 a   5 b   6 a

7
1 ✓   2 ✗   3 ✗   4 ✓   5 ✗   6 ✓   7 ✗   8 ✗

6c (page 140)

1
1 d   2 c   3 b   4 a   5 e

2
1 4th July   2 girls   3 four   4 sun   5 child   6 ten
7 faces   8 women

3
1 up   2 back   3 ready   4 plane   5 presents   6 pension
7 married

6d (page 141)

1
1 On holiday.   2 After work.   3 Outside Sonia's office.
4 A friend from France.   5 Go into his lesson.
6 He has an exam tomorrow.   7 They could get home early or he could study first.   8 No.

2
1 Do you want   2 Yes, OK   3 How about   4 It sounds
5 Why don't you   6 That would   7 I'd like
8 It's very nice   9 I'd love to

155

3
Model answers:
Invitation 1
Sorry, I can't because I'm going to a football match tonight.
OK. That'd be great.

Invitation 2
It's very nice of you to ask, but isn't it only for your friend's family and close friends?
OK. I'd like that very much. Thank you.

4a
1 Speaker 1   2 Speaker 1   3 Speaker 2   4 Speaker 2
5 Speaker 1

6e (page 142)

1a
1 tasty   2 colourful   3 dull   4 massive   5 miserable
6 exciting

1b
1 b   2 a   3 e   4 f   5 c   6 d

1c
Possible answers:
a amazing, beautiful, dull, enormous, fun, pretty, smart, uncomfortable
b amazing, delicious, dull, unhealthy, enormous
c fun, amazing, attractive, smart, dull, unhealthy, enormous, miserable, friendly, beautiful
d amazing, polluted, speedy
e fun, amazing, enormous, friendly, beautiful
f amazing, enormous, beautiful

1d
Possible answers:
a scruffy clothes   b huge meals   c energetic people
d busy transport and towns   e international festivals
f stunning nature and geographic features

2
Model answer:
Our town festival is once a year at the end of August. It's always great fun because there are lots of different events. For example there are parades for children with colourful costumes. Then in the evening there is a big party with dancing and food. The food is always delicious. Lots of local shops sell food and you can try some of our traditional dishes. But my favourite part of the whole event is at midnight when there are lots of fireworks. They light the whole night sky up, and then it's time to go home.

3
Students' own answers.

Wordbuilding / Learning skills (page 143)

1
1 afraid   2 warm   3 awful   4 strong   5 tall   6 polite
7 hide   8 touch   9 needy   10 relaxed

2
Students' own answers.

3
A place: Osingira, Tremé
Type of dish or something you can eat: Feijoda
Something that gives light: firework, candle
Stage of life: infant, middle-aged
A group of people: Masai, pensioners

CREDITS

Although every effort has been made to contact copyright holders prior to publication, this has not always been possible. If notified, the publisher will undertake to rectify any errors or omissions at the earliest opportunity.

Text:
The publisher would like to thank the following sources for permission to reproduce their copyright protected text:

National Geographic for extracts adapted from "Quiz: Need more sleep?", http://ngm.nationalgeographic.com/; "Longevity, The Secret to Long Life", http://ngm.nationalgeographic.com/; "The Big Idea", 15 October 2009, http://ngm.nationalgeographic.com/; Elizabeth W. Dunn PhD for a mock interview based on 'The Best Things in Life Aren't Things' 28 October 2010, http://blogs.nationalgeographic.com. Used with kind permission; Demand Media Studios for extracts from 'Green transport: How to Green Your Transportation Choices' by Jeannette Belliveau, Demand Media, http://greenliving.nationalgeographic.com/green-transportation-choices-2478.html, and 'Household rubbish: How Much Does One Household Produce in Recyclables?' by Karyn Maier, Demand Media, http://greenliving.nationalgeographic.com/much-one-household-produce-recyclables-2575.html, copyright © Demand Media; Guardian News & Media for material based on 'The 10 best survival stories' by Ed Douglas, *The Guardian*, 17 October 2010, copyright © Guardian News & Media Ltd 2010; GlobeScan Incorporated for the 'Greendex bar chart 'Frequency of Recycling Materials' from Greendex 2009: Consumer Choice and the Environment-A Worldwide Tracking Survey, p.246, copyright © GlobeScan Incorporated, www.GlobeScan.com

In some instances we have been unable to trace the owners of copyright material and we would appreciate any information that would enable us to do so.

Photos:
The publisher would like to thank the following sources for permission to reproduce their copyright protected photos:

Cover: Michael Melford/National Geographic Image Collection

Inside: 6 t Kristin Piljay/Alamy, 6 b Danita Delimont/Alamy, 7 t John Woodworth/Alamy, 7 b Chris Rainier/Jeremy Fahringer, 7 cb Nadia Isakova/Alamy, 7 ct dbimages/Alamy, 8 tl Brendan McCarthy/The Bendigo Advertiser, 8 tc Patrick Mcfeeley/National Geographic Society/Corbis UK Ltd, 8tr Amy Johansson, 8 bl Zoltan Takacs/Zoltan Takacs, 8 bc Barcroft/Fame Pictures, 8 br Christian Ziegler/National Geographic Image Collection, 8 cbl Michael S. Yamashita/National Geographic Image Collection, 8 cbc NASA, 8 cbr Cary Wolinsky/National Geographic Image Collection, 8 ctl Stephen Alvarez/National Geographic Image Collection, 8 ctc Peter Essick/National Geographic Image Collection, 8 ctr Bill Ellzey/National Geographic Image Collection, 9 Brendan McCarthy/The Bendigo Advertiser, 11 Shutterstock, 12 David McLain/National Geographic Image Collection, 13 Corbis UK Ltd, 15 Pete McBride/National Geographic Image Collection, 17 tr Steve Cukrov/Alamy, 17 t Shutterstock, 17 b Steve Cukrov/Alamy, 17 Frank Tschakert/Alamy, 17 cb Steve Cukrov/Alamy, 17 ct Steve Cukrov/Alamy, 18 Peter Horree/Alamy, 20 Cesare Naldi, 21 Patrick Mcfeeley/National Geographic Society/Corbis UK Ltd, 22 Bettmann/Corbis UK Ltd, 24 t Ric Thayer/Reuters/Corbis UK Ltd, 24 c Jim Cole/AP/Press Association Images, 24 b All Canada Photos/Superstock Inc., 25 Ross McDermott, 26 Ivan Kashinsky/National Geographic Image Collection, 27 t Ivan Kashinsky/National Geographic Image Collection, 27 b Ivan Kashinsky/National Geographic Image Collection, 28 t Shutterstock, 29 blickwinkel/Alamy, 30 Peter Macdiarmid News/Getty Images, 32 Ross McDermott/Ross McDermott, 33 Amy Johansson, 36 l Patricio Robles Gil/Sierra Ma/Corbis UK Ltd, 36 r Joe Petersburger/National Geographic Image Collection, 37 Alison Wright/National Geographic Image Collection, 39 Ami Vitale/Getty Images, 40 l Shutterstock, 40 r Shutterstock, 40 cl Shutterstock, 40 cr Shutterstock, 42 dbimages/Alamy, 44 Li Huang/ColorChinaPhoto/AP/Press Association Images, 45 Stephen alvarez/National Geographic Image Collection, 46 l AFP/Getty Images, 46 r Steve Bouey/The World By Road Collective, 47 Reza/National Geographic Image Collection, 48 Bryce Milton Photography, 50 tl AF archive/Alamy, 50 tr Jim McKnight/AP/Press Association Images, 51 Buz Groshong, 52 Robert Houser/Photolibrary Group, 53 l Shutterstock, 54 Kristin Piljay/Alamy, 56 l Pacific Stock/Photolibrary Group, 57 Peter Essick/National Geographic Image Collection, 59 t Peter Essick/National Geographic Image Collection, 59 b Peter Essick/National Geographic Image Collection, 62 Paul Miller/epa/Corbis UK Ltd, 63 Luca Babini/myoo, 64 l TEcoArt, LLC , 64 r TEcoArt, LLC , 65 jeremy sutton-hibbert/Alamy, 66 aberCPC/Alamy, 68 Shutterstock, 69 Bill Ellzey/National Geographic Image Collection, 70/71 Richard Ligato, 72 tl Nathan Benn/Alamy, 73 Krista Rossow/National Geographic Image Collection, 74 Louise Gubb Saba/Corbis UK Ltd, 75 Peter Adams/Getty Images, 76 Superstock/Photolibrary Group, 77 Shutterstock, 78 Sean Drakes/LatinContent/Getty Images, 80 Justin Kase z01z/Alamy, 96 Rebecca Hale/National Geographic Image Collection, 98 Lynn Johnson/National Geographic Image Collection, 99 Shutterstock, 100 Kris Krug, 103 l Cengage Learning (EMEA) Ltd, 103 r Cengage Learning (EMEA) Ltd, 105 Doug Pensinger/Getty Images, 106 Reuters/Lucy Pemoni/Reuters Media, 108 Sebastian Näslund/Scanpix/Press Association, 109 t Peter Chadwick/Gallo Images/Getty Images, 109 c PhotoAlto sas/Alamy, 109 b Richard Levine/Alamy, 112 Getty Images, 113 Shutterstock, 114 bbl Shutterstock, 114 bbr Shutterstock, 114 btl uwesMASAIMARA/Alamy, 114 btr Shutterstock, 114 tbl Shutterstock, 114 tbr Shutterstock, 114 ttl Shutterstock, 114 ttr Shutterstock, 115 t Shutterstock, 116 t Charles W. Berry/National Geographic Image Collection, 116 b Ed Kashi/National Geographic Image Collection, 117 Shutterstock, 120 Brady Barr/National Geographic Image Collection, 121 Barcroft Media/Getty Images, 122 Royal Geographical Society/Alamy, 124 Getty Images, 125 Yossi Ghinsberg, 128 t Foodcollection.com/Alamy, 129 Shutterstock, 130 b Detail Nottingham/Alamy, 131 b Shutterstock, 132 Shutterstock, 133 Shutterstock, 137 Shutterstock, 138 Thomas Cockrem/Alamy, 141 Art Directors & TRIP/Alamy

Illustrations by Beehive Illustration pp50 b, 58, 72 b; David Russell pp53 r, 60, 72 tr, 136; EMC Design p28 b; Kevin Hopgood Illustration pp23, 34, 56 r, 140 ; Matthew Hams pp10, 123; NB Illustration Ltd p34; Sylvie Poggio Agency p16